CBI SERIES IN MANAGEMENT COMMUNICATIONS

Developing Reading Skills for Business and Industry

CBI SERIES IN MANAGEMENT COMMUNICATIONS

William J. Gallagher, Series Editor
Arthur D. Little, Inc.

Developing Reading Skills for Business and Industry

Richard P. Santeusanio, Ed.D.

CBI

CBI PUBLISHING COMPANY, INC.
51 Sleeper Street
Boston, Massachusetts 02210

Production Editor: Becky Handler
Text Designer: Roy Howard Brown
Compositor: Modern Graphics
Cover Designer: Betsy Franklin

Library of Congress Cataloguing in Publication Data

Santeusanio, Richard P   1942-
   Developing reading skills for business and industry.

   (CBI series in management communications)
      1.   Business—Addresses, essays, lectures.
2.   Rapid reading—Addresses, essays, lectures.
3.   Reading comprehension—Addresses, essays, lectures.
I.   Title.   II.   Series.
HF5351.S33   428.4'3'024658   80-23463
ISBN 0-8436-0792-0

Printed in the United States of America

Printing (*last digit*): 9 8 7 6 5 4 3 2 1

To JOAN

whose patient encouragement
made this book a reality.

Contents

Copyright Acknowledgments

Editor's Foreword

Despite the magnitude and acceleration of change during the past two decades, the functions of management remain essentially the same: to make decisions, to plan, to organize, to get things done, and to measure the results. Before decisions can be made, however, information must be transferred. Before tasks can be accomplished, behavior may have to be modified. And communication is still the only means we have to reach these objectives.

The basic problem with communication stems from how we view the process. The first image the term evokes is usually of someone speaking or writing. Implicit in this image, of course, is that this activity is directed at someone else in the background. But the emphasis is on the transmitter rather than on the receiver. According to this perception, communication is always one-directional.

This perception assumes that to communicate, all we need to do is talk or write. The corollaries of this assumption are that the message intended is always conveyed and that logic and clarity are enough to guarantee persuasion. Consequently, a great deal of the training in oral and written communication has been oriented toward the speaker or writer. Guidelines for the listener or reader are usually ignored.

This text is one of a series based on the premise that no one merely communicates. Rather, he or she communicates something to someone. And that someone—the listener or reader—is very important. He or she is not, as many apparently believe, a passive element receiving information without coloring or response. On the contrary, the receiver is continually reacting to the expression of ideas in light of personal experience, interests, and values. Therefore, in any communication the receiver adds their own dimension to the meaning and then responds to what he or she has added. Communication is thus interactive, and being interactive, it requires the cooperation of sender and receiver.

Effective communication ensures cooperation by anticipation and adaptation. It considers the communication objective, the subject, and the audience. It recognizes the environment in which the communication is to take place, the external and internal factors that affect it, and the extent of the control needed by both sender and receiver to neutralize these factors. It recognizes that selecting the appropriate medium is as important as tailoring the presentation.

This communication series was prepared in recognition of the fact that the receiver is the most important element in communication, for he or she is not only the reason for the communcation but the measure by which its success is evaluated. In the texts designed to help the sender, the guidelines are aimed at improving skills by anticipating problems posed by the receiver. In the texts designed for the receiver, the guidelines are aimed at improving the ability to assimilate information by cooperating with the sender.

The authors of the CBI Series in Management Communications have a distinctive combination of skills as practitioners and teachers. Each is employed by an organization that places heavy emphasis on communication. Each has also spent many years in teaching communication through formal academic courses and through seminars sponsored by government and industry. Collectively, they possess diverse experience in industry, government, and education.

The texts therefore address the needs of business and government and the various circumstances in which these needs for communication skills are evident. Each of the authors is aware of these needs not only because of his position, but because of the numerous opportunities he has had to discuss them with others at various levels of management The guidelines presented, therefore, offer a realistic and practical approach to effective communication.

The texts can be used as guides for self-training or as the basis for formal group training in college classes or in seminars sponsored by government and industry. Although written independently with only broad guidelines and coordination by the editor, they have a unity of purpose and design. The books can therefore be used collectively by those interested in the broad spectrum of communication or individually by those with selected interests.

Since all of the authors are realists, we do not offer guidelines as magic potions guaranteeing instantaneous success. Principles and techniques do not ensure success. Motivation and a great deal of effort are also required. Our objective is to show you the way; the goal is yours to attain.

William J. Gallagher, Editor
CBI Series in Management Communications

Preface

The purpose of this book is to provide people in the business world with practical techniques for becoming more efficient readers. The book's premise is that when individuals approach the reading task with a specific purpose and recognize a writer's techniques of communication, they will read faster and understand and retain more of what they read. The skills developed in this book are based on a definition of reading that stresses the interaction of the reader and writer.

The writer begins with ideas. He then puts these ideas into writing or, stated differently, translates them to the written medium. The task of the reader is to translate the written medium back to thoughts or ideas. Thus, the reader and writer are involved in an interaction whereby the reader tries to think with and like the writer.

When you were a student in the primary grades, you were taught how to read words. In all probability, your teachers taught you beginning reading by using the phonics method, the sight or whole word method, or, most likely, a combination of the sight and phonics approaches. As you matured and moved on to the intermediate and secondary grades, you reached a level of what reading expert Dr. S. J. Samuels calls "automaticity"; that is, you read the words on the page instantaneously without consciously thinking about the process. The mere fact that you are probably reading this preface fluently indicates that you have reached the level of "automaticity." However, you probably feel that you would like to become a more efficient reader. That is the ultimate goal of this book—to help you to comprehend quickly and accurately the ideas of a writer.

Learning to become a better reader is hard work. There are no short cuts or simple gimmicks that will instantly help you to double your reading rate without a loss in comprehension. You will find no exercises on unorthodox eye-hand movement techniques in this book. Nor are the articles contained in the chapters reproduced on filmstrips and flashed on a screen by a reading machine. Reading is a thinking process, and gimmicky activities do not enhance that process.

Having taught reading to hundreds of children and adults for a number of years, I am convinced that the best way to help individuals to improve their reading efficiency is to approach reading as a thinking process. Therefore, reading as a thinking process, rather than reading as a mechanical process, is the approach used in this book.

The organization of most chapters follows a similar pattern. First, a brief introduction tells you what you will learn, why you should learn it, and how to learn it. Articles of interest from publications such as the *Wall Street Journal, Administrative Management,* and the *Harvard Business Review* are provided to give you an opportunity to practice the skill. All the chapters on organizational patterns include an explanation of the pattern, a guided analysis of an article that exemplifies the pattern, and an opportunity to complete rapid reading and skimming exercises. The book also includes pre- and posttests that will enable you to evaluate your progress. When necessary, you may write your answers to certain Comprehension Checks on the Notes pages in the back of the book.

It is my hope that you will find this book useful and absorbing and that your improved reading skills will lead to greater personal and professional rewards.

I wish to acknowledge the many individuals who assisted in the development of this book. Although many authors and professors contributed to my understanding of teaching reading to adults, I have been most influenced by the concepts and approach developed by Allan Sack and Jack Yourman. Their ideas have been expanded and modified as a result of criticisms of my students and colleagues.

Special recognition should be given to Thomas F. McLaughlin, Jr., Educational Director of the Boston Chapter of the American Institute of Banking, for providing me with the opportunity to teach reading improvement courses to hundreds of men and women in business.

Appreciation must also be extended to: Richard Sordillo for suggesting several articles that ultimately were included in the book; Romeo and Louise Santeusanio, Kathy Keohane and Dr. Richard Cooper for their assistance in the preparation of the reading rate charts; William Gallagher and Margaret T. Richter for reading the entire manuscript and for offering suggestions for improvement; Norman A. Stanton, for providing guidance throughout the writing of the text; and Judy Kuell for her typing assistance. Finally, I am greatly indebted to my wife and children for their love, encouragement, time, and patience.

R.P.S.

1
Reading Rate and Comprehension: Pretests

INTRODUCTION

You are reading this book because you want to improve your reading skills. After you complete the book, the one question you will want answered is, "How much did I improve?" This question can be answered for you if you complete the pretests contained in this chapter and the posttests contained in chapter 9.

People in the business world who have read the articles and completed the exercises contained in this book have been encouraged by the improvement in their reading skills. The method for determining your degree of improvement is outlined in chapter 9. But our main concern now is to determine your current level of reading performance. Therefore, you will take two pretests, which will provide you with a benchmark for ascertaining the improvement you make after completing the exercises in this book. Directions for scoring the tests appear on pages 11-12. To get an accurate measure of your current reading performance, be sure to read the articles for the two pretests the way you normally read.

INSTRUCTIONS FOR PRETEST 1: "The Theme of the Park is Safety"

Read the following selection in your usual manner. You must also time yourself. Use either a stopwatch (preferred) or a regular watch with a second hand. As soon as you finish reading the selection, record your reading time in minutes and seconds or in total seconds in the space provided at the end of the selection. Then answer the comprehension questions in Pretest 1 based on the selection. Directions for determining your reading rate and for correcting your answers to the questions follow the two pretests. Check your answers with the Answer Key.   1

Pretest 1

The Theme of the Park is Safety
Virginia Reinhart

Nothing so quickly ruins a happy outing as a serious accident.

And nobody knows that better than amusement park operators, who, to keep their customers happy (or to keep them at all), must keep them safe in a variety of unusual circumstances: screaming through roller-coasters, touring make-believe nations by boat, gliding high above ground in gondola cars, wandering among exotic animals, simply sharing the same strange habitat with tens of thousands of other visitors.

Since the birth of Disneyland in California 20 years ago, amusement parks, particularly the "theme parks," have grown into a vast business, with variations on the theme springing up all around the country: Disney World in Florida, wild game preserves seemingly beside every major highway, Six Flags Over half-a-dozen states. Even the Grand Ole Opry has sprouted a park.

All are different, but all share the same kinds of safety problems. Their employees, like those of any other business, fall under the protection of the Occupational Safety and Health Act. Although the parks tend to think first of their customers, they find that visitor safety cannot be divorced from employee safety. Failure in either could be enormously expensive, not only in potential liability suits but in lost good will, morale, and customers.

WHERE SAFETY STARTS

In an amusement park, as in any industry, the finest safety engineering can't prevent accidents if the workers don't use it properly. At "The Old Country," the newest of the half dozen "Busch Gardens," in Williamsburg, Virginia, safety begins with the selection of the workers.

"We pick them more for their heads than for their hands," says Tom Heilman, general services manager and safety director. "We want caring people, who like other people, who will remember that older folks do not move as quickly and that children get excited and don't always watch what they are doing."

Each employee spent more than 40 hours in training sessions before opening day; retraining courses are held throughout the season.

The year-round employees tend to be highly skilled experts. The steam engine engineer, for example, has more than 20 years' experience. Often, year-round employees, totalling about 100, include mechanics, maintenance people, and the like, who handle repairs and installation of new attractions in the closed season, November to May.

But 10 times that many workers are seasonal. They do everything from sweeping the streets to acting in the bird show. And many are students. "Since they represent the park to the public, we take a great deal of interest in their being trained properly," said spokesman Randall Foskey.

Training includes reviews of what to do in case of storms or accidents. "We close down the rides in an electrical storm," Foskey points out, and there are emergency plans for closing down individual rides in case of trouble. Each attendant knows what he must do, whether pushing a powerless monorail car back along the track to the station or putting up stanchions and ropes to warn away would-be riders.

In cold fact, employees are costly; and management knows it well from experience with five other parks in the Busch chain. Training, costuming, and salaries are costly—and any accident unnecessarily runs up the tab.

So The Old Country constantly works on safety angles, whether it's special engineering of costumes or notice to workers that guests who need extra care—such as the crippled or aged—will be arriving.

One way to keep employees safe is to rotate them on job stations to break the monotony. Workers on the bobsled ride, for example, shift positions every hour. This cuts boredom and insures that they are alert and ready to protect themselves and customers.

Not all jobs can be rotated, of course. Cashiers do not change places with cooks at the food stands. But the cashiers do benefit from another safety device: Because a lot of money comes to them in a day's work, they conceivably could be robbed, a particularly unattractive job hazard. So the management installed a pneumatic system to carry off the money by tube to a central office, leaving only small sums in any ticket booth at any time.

A large crew starts work only after the park closes at 10 P.M. These workers lubricate and maintain all the machinery. The rides, in particular, have operated for 12 straight hours and need nightly attention. Before any ride opens in the morning, it must bear a tag showing the maintenance crew has checked it out and found it ready.

The morning crew runs the empty ride through its full cycle four or five times as a warm-up. Then the staff takes a test run as a final check before the customers are allowed to board.

When 22,000 persons may be using a walkway on a given day, a few popsicle sticks or bits of slick paper become a large hazard. Here spotless equals safe, so a large clean-up crew works all day. Even employees whose jobs have nothing to do with maintenance have caught the clean-park fever and often pick up litter as they head for their jobs.

LONG BEFORE THEY OPEN

Like many of the better parks, The Old Country is engineered for safety from the ground up. And safety for rides, walkways, and amusements means safety for employees—because as part of their jobs they, too, use the rides and other attractions as they accompany visitors. Opened only this summer, the park reflects safety planning—from the non-slip concrete on the walkways to the double-locked safety bars that hold visitors in their seats on the Sky Ride that courses, in places, 120 feet above ground.

Safety director Heilman recalls the discovery, long before the park's May opening, that at one Sky Ride station a long-armed man who draped his elbow outside the gondola (against all warnings) might bang it into part of the ride's steel framework. "So we got out the torches and revised the framework."

Meanwhile, at ground level, steep grades were being converted to shallow ramps, almost totally eliminating stairs. "We want the park to be for everyone," says one official, "including the young, the old, and the handicapped. By cutting out stairs, even folks in wheelchairs can go everywhere in the park."

There is one exception—the Rhine River Cruise that takes place on a lake, surrounded by steeply sloped shores. Here, customers in wheelchairs are not permitted on the boats, which take a visitor from "France" to "Germany."

But there's an alternative route—the Sky Ride.

At the waterfront, a vistor boards a boat designed to hold 65 persons. But the park allows only 45 aboard, both as a safety measure and to increase the passengers' comfort.

On rides such as The Catapult, there's a double-check to see that customers are locked into their seats. Safety bars audibly snap into place, then an attendant checks to be sure. And with those rides that pass through darkened buildings, an attendant must signal that all safety bars are in place before the lights go out.

When push comes to shove, it shouldn't be in an amusement park. One of the most popular rides is an automobile racing course. To accommodate 1,200 passengers each hour, separate platforms were built for loading and unloading. This eliminates pushing and confusion, two natural enemies of safety. The cars, although they move only six miles an hour on their pre-set courses, have safety belts; and attendants enforce their use.

The Sky Ride has an additional safety factor. Two separate keys lock and unlock the safety bar for each car. Because of the ride's height, the engineers felt it vital to keep all attendants alert, so the two keys are not interchangeable.

On the monorail, each segment of the 7,000-foot track has its own switches so two trains, theoretically, can never meet. Like spacecraft, the monorail cars feature redundant systems: Each has two motors; if one should fail, the second takes over. Two thousand passengers can ride each hour; they get on and off at opposite sides of the train, again to minimize confusion and crush.

Safety features also extend outside the park, with a gently curving driveway long enough to keep 400 cars safely off the highway while they wait to enter. Inside,

the parking lots are designed with separate sections for buses and campers, and are laid out so that vehicles can pull in, park, and leave again without backing up.

The designers agree with the farmer in Robert Frost's poem that "good fences make good neighbors."

"We've built fences to keep the deer, elk, mallard ducks, and our other animals away from the people," said Foskey. The fences are hidden by shrubs and vines, but they prevent any tot from rushing into the lake after a swan. (They also protect the "wild" animals from thoughtless humans.)

"We had a different kind of problem with the trained bears," said safety director Heilman. "We want the audience to have an unrestricted view of their tricks, but we don't want anybody to accidentally join the show. So we installed a plexiglass barrier around the moat."

Before the park opened, a team of safety professionals from the Anheuser-Busch headquarters in St. Louis examined it with as cold an eye as any compliance officer's.

Like Heilman himself, they checked out the rides for danger points, examined the grounds, and gave orders. They decided, for example, that a toddler might somehow slide through the railing of one footbridge and fall into the water. Fencing was installed.

In safety planning, the engineers thought not only of staff and public, but also of the public's pets. Near the entrance is a pet check building, where dogs and cats are kept until the owners return from their day in the park. "We think it's safer and cleaner not to have pets in the park, and we believe the animals will have a better time away from the crowds, in a shady, open space," says Foskey.

Centrally located in the park is the first aid and lost parent station. Presided over by registered nurses with a doctor on hand on busiest days and one on call at any time, the station is prepared for troubles ranging from blisters to heart attacks.

"We have set up procedures to be followed in all foreseeable emergencies and have established a liaison with the local hospital and ambulance units," Foskey notes

The park had intended to set up its own ambulance service, but the local rescue squad proved it could be on hand within minutes after a call.

Non-medical employees, who cannot be expected to tell the difference between a faint and a coronary, are under strict instructions to leave the fallen alone, except to cover them with blankets, while phoning for trained help.

As this article was going to press (just 12 days after the park had opened), the first-aid station had seen little it couldn't handle with a bandaid and a kind word.

One of the worst cases was a 76-year-old woman who had tripped and fallen. As the nurse tried to examine her, Foskey remembers, "She almost tore the place apart, screaming that she was O.K., and hollering to be let go. We finally got the idea: She was angry because we were keeping her from having any fun in the park.

"All our problems should be so difficult."

Finishing time:_____

PRETEST 1: "The Theme of the Park is Safety"

1. Most theme parks have similar:

   a. _____ rides.

   b. _____ safety problems.

   c. _____ employees.

2. The Old Country is owned by:

   a. _____ Anheuser-Busch.

   b. _____ Disney.

   c. _____ Great Adventurer.

3. Old Country's service and safety director characterizes his employees as:

   a. _____ brilliant.

   b. _____ mechanically inclined.

   c. _____ caring.

4. What is the ratio of seasonal workers to full-time workers at Old Country?

   a. _____ Ten to one.

   b. _____ Fifteen to one.

   c. _____ Twenty to one.

5. Employee boredom is reduced at Old Country because employees:

   a. _____ stay busy talking to the customers.

   b. _____ rotate from job station to job station.

   c. _____ are allowed to take free rides.

6. The concrete walkways at Old Country are:

   a. _____ extra wide.

   b. _____ well landscaped.

   c. _____ nonslip.

7. At Old Country, you'll find no:

a. _____ stairs.

b. _____ hills.

c. _____ mosquitoes.

8. Robert Frost was quoted as supporting the notion that:

a. _____ fences are needed to protect both children and animals.

b. _____ Old Country supports the fine arts.

c. _____ he favored theme parks.

9. Once you park your car at Old Country, you will not have to:

a. _____ move it.

b. _____ lock it.

c. _____ back it up.

10. The seventy-six-year-old woman screamed because:

a. _____ she was tired of waiting in line for a ride.

b. _____ she was badly hurt.

c. _____ she wanted to get back to the rides.

Check your answers with the Answer Key.

INSTRUCTIONS FOR PRETEST 2: "To Whom Should You Extend Credit—Nonfinancial Analysis"

Read the following selection in your usual manner. As soon as you finish reading the selection, record your reading time in minutes and seconds or in total seconds in the space provided at the end of the selection. Then answer the comprehension questions in Pretest 2 based on the selection. Check your answers with the Answer Key.

Pretest 2

To Whom Should You Extend Credit—Nonfinancial Analysis

Rick Stephan Hayes

The job of a credit agent is to know whether a customer or a prospective customer will pay the bills. When you are right about the customer, your company makes money, you save a lot of time and energy, and you look good to management. When you are wrong, you and your company lose. Your company loses money to bad debts and ties up working capital, and you lose prestige. The better your judgment, the better off everyone is.

There are two ways to judge an account: on a nonfinancial analysis basis and on an in-depth financial basis. Nonfinancial analysis is less expensive in time and money, but it is not as accurate as financial analysis in predicting success of the credit. In most cases, fortunately, nonfinancial analysis is all that is required to make a good judgment.

Nonfinancial judgments are based on account credit information, payment performance and antecedents, owners' and managers' experience and background, business age and growth, impressions of company employees, financing and adequacy of capital, business trends, and other factors including attitude of the customer.

AGENCY REPORT INFORMATION

A typical agency report indicates when a business started, when the present owners took over, and when and if it was incorporated. The report also gives you a brief biography of the principals.

By reading the reports you will find that Hero Manufacturing, for example, started ten years ago, came under its present management control two years ago, and was incorporated in California last year. John Hero, the president, is forty-eight and married. Before he became president of Hero, he worked in the aerospace industry making space-age hamburger containers. Before that he had two more enterprises that were sold to large conglomerates. Hero has a MBA from University of Southern California. The report also tells about the comptroller, vice president, and other executives.

If there was any derogatory information about anyone in the firm such as convictions for fraud, it would be reflected in this report. Any bankruptcy in the past would also be listed in the report. Reports also tell you the location, appearance of buildings, and legal composition of the company.

In short, industry and agency reports briefly cover management and the age of the company. The reports identify, but do not reveal, the growth trend, the extent of expansion, the potential for

success, and the ability of the employees.

If the company you are investigating is very large with good credit, you probably do not need any more than what the agency reports will tell you. But consider this: the Dun and Bradstreet Reference Book lists over three million businesses in the United States, and well over half of them are worth less than $50,000. Only 5 percent of the businesses they list are worth over $500,000. So the majority of companies you will be dealing with are small businesses. Accordingly, there is a lot more involved with evaluating a small business than a brief history. The main characteristic of a small business is there is one individual, usually not a professional manager, who is running the show.

PAYMENT PERFORMANCE AND ANTECEDENTS

All credit persons know how important it is to know the history of potential customers. There is no better indicator of the future than an analysis of the past. If the owners have been hardworking, prompt, and ambitious in the past, there is little reason to believe that this will change in the future. We are told by psychologists that a child has his moral pattern set for life by the time he is nine years old. Surely the way people handle themselves morally when they start their very first business is an indicator of their future business behavior. Since businesses do not run themselves, the most important indicator of business behavior is the behavior of the owners.

Payment Performance

Probably the best indicator of a business's payment ability in the future is a review of its historical payment ability and past payment record. If you have information about the business's payment performance with other companies, it is a good idea to review this information. You may also discover any special financial arrangements a company may have, and, most important, where a company buys. Historical payment performance is available in agency reports.

It is important to gather a representative sampling from other suppliers when you are evaluating the payment performance of a business. A company's payment record may vary widely with different suppliers. Even though a company may be in trouble, it may maintain a few prompt accounts for reference purposes. It is also possible that a customer could be prompt with others but slow with you.

A careful look at suppliers will also indicate a pattern of taking discounts, paying on a geographical basis, and sometimes a pattern of no patterns. The amount of high credit that is extended to a customer is something to consider as well as the amount currently owing. It is okay for a customer to have a high percentage owing during seasonally busy times when the credit limit is high and a low percentage during the seasonal lulls. Any deviation from this pattern, however, should provoke your investigation.

Past due accounts should always concern you. Be aware, though, that the slowness might be temporary. You know the reasons for slowness and the inability to repay: financial or legal problems, management turmoil, the owner drawing too much money, overbuying, disasters, etc. Sometimes, however, the slowness is just temporary due to misunderstandings between shipper and buyer on terms, amounts shipped, etc., and slowness due to inadequate accounts payable to personnel. If the customer is slow, it is a good idea to find out why.

In summary, usually a supplier will report that an account either takes discounts, anticipates (pays in advance of the discount period), is slow or is prompt. The report that concerns you the most is that the account is slow. If you get this in a report, try to find out for how long, and, if possible, why.

Antecedents

Before undertaking an evaluation of a business's antecedents, verify if the business has activities conducted under other names, any gaps in the owner's history, and owner's previous employment.

When you boil down nonfinancial credit analysis to the most important factor, that factor is *character*—the character of the owners. Good character is a pretty undefinable quality, but most people can tell you what bad character is. These factors of character do not usually appear on agency reports, but you can find them out fast enough by talking to other suppliers and the company employees.

Any history of business failure should be of particular concern to you as a credit manager. Business failures include bankruptcies, general compromises and extensions, and informal discontinuances. An informal discontinuance is when an owner gives (or sells for $1) the business to someone else to take over, thereby removing himself from the situation entirely. It is important to determine the type of failure, the cause of failure, and the settlement with creditors. Whether the bankruptcy was voluntary or involuntary may expose a great deal about the owners. A voluntary bankruptcy is a bankruptcy requested by the owners of the business. An involuntary bankruptcy is a bankruptcy initiated by creditors selling goods to the business. Knowing how much the creditors received and how willing management was to meet most of their obligations is important. If the cause of the bankruptcy was bad management (94 percent of all manufacturing bankruptcies are), how has management improved since then?

If there has ever been a fire, investigate the facts involving this fire. Even the most innocent fires cause delays in collections and can often result in credit losses because fire insurance policies, even though they do cover the damage, do not always result in 100 percent coverage of loss. There is usually a time delay before compensation is made, fixed expenses continue, and business activities are disrupted. The loss of business momentum alone will cut a company's sales and profits. Many times business records are lost and the company has to request duplicate invoices. Unfortunately, sometimes fires and losses are suffered because a desperate person turns to arson to solve a company's problems. For these reasons it is important that you find out if a business has had a fire before, or worse yet, several fires. You should determine the date of the fire, insurance recovery, cause of the fire, assets damaged, whether it was a partial or total loss, and if the business continued operations or temporarily suspended operations after the fire.

A history of civil and criminal proceedings against the business, its officers, or its employees should receive further investigation. A civil proceeding is a law suit in which one party claims that he has been damaged by the company, its employees, its officers, or its products or services. The fact that a suit has been filed in the courts does not mean that the defendants are liable for anything. A pattern of suits brought against or brought by a customer, however, can be a good indication that payment problems might be encountered. To guard yourself against any unwanted legal problems, you must ask: Has payment of a judgment caused an impairment in the financial condition of the company?

Criminal proceedings against officers or employees can have an effect on the business for several reasons including excessive financial drain and time away from the business. If the customer is judged innocent or pardoned, but has a pattern of criminal charges, the credit risk can still be considered high. A person continually defending himself does not have the time and energy to run a business properly.

Finishing time:_____

PRETEST 2: "To Whom Should You Extend Credit—Nonfinancial Analysis"

1. Compared to financial analysis, nonfinancial analysis is:

    a. _____ more accurate.

    b. _____ about as accurate.

    c. _____ less accurate.

2. The Hero Manufacturing example was used to illustrate a:

    a. _____ typical agency report.

    b. _____ payment performance.

    c. _____ civil and criminal proceedings report.

3. Compared to large businesses, small businesses are:

    a. _____ more difficult to evaluate.

    b. _____ equally difficult to evaluate.

    c. _____ less difficult to evaluate.

4. Which of the following statements is generally true regarding payment performance?

   a. _____ It is acceptable for the customer to have a high percentage owing during the slow season.

   b. _____ It is acceptable for the customer to be prompt with some accounts and slow with others.

   c. _____ It is acceptable for the customer to have a high percentage owing during the busy season.

5. The most important factor in a non-financial credit analysis is the owner's:

   a. _____ financial background.

   b. _____ character.

   c. _____ family background.

6. The greatest cause of bankruptcy is:

   a. _____ poor location.

   b. _____ bad management.

   c. _____ inflationary times.

7. Customers who have a pattern of criminal charges against them might be considered a credit risk because they are probably:

   a. _____ dishonest.

   b. _____ unstable.

   c. _____ losing the time and energy needed to run the business correctly.

8. The author referred to the behavior of children to illustrate his point regarding an owner's:

   a. _____ future business behavior.

   b. _____ attitude toward people in general.

   c. _____ religious and moral code.

9. Which of the following topics would *not* be included in an agency report?

   a. _____ Appearance of buildings.

   b. _____ When a business started.

   c. _____ Interpretation of financial statements.

10. The most important aspect of a report from a supplier is the customer's:

   a. _____ pattern of taking discounts.

   b. _____ promptness in paying.

   c. _____ payment on a geographical basis.

Check your answers with the Answer Key.

HOW TO SCORE AND INTERPRET YOUR PRETESTS

Reading Rate

Refer to the Words Per Minute: Rapid Reading Chart on page 247 to determine your reading rate for each pretest. First, find the column marked *Pretest 1* along the top of the chart. Next, use either the *Minutes and Seconds* column on the far left of the chart or the *Seconds* column on the far right. To find your reading rate for any selection, look across the top of the page until you locate the name of the selection you have read. Then look down either the *Minutes and Seconds* column or the *Seconds* column until you come to the figure closest to your actual reading time (your finishing time) for that selection. In the columns under each selection title, find the words-per-minute rate that corresponds to your reading time.

For example, if you finished Pretest 1 in six minutes and thirty seconds, or a total of 390 seconds, your reading rate for that selection would be 292 words per minute.

On page 12 you will find the Pretest Reading Efficiency chart. In the blank located between the words *Pretest Rate 1* and *WPM* (words per minute), write in your reading rate score. Do the same for Pretest 2.

Comprehension

The answers to the comprehension questions for the two pretests appear in the Answer Key that precedes the charts. Credit yourself with ten points for each question you answered correctly. When you have determined your pretest scores, enter them on your Pretest Reading Efficiency chart. Place your comprehension scores in the blanks between *WPM* and *% Comprehension.*

Averages

To determine your average reading rate score, add your reading rate scores for the two pretests and divide by two. Determine your average comprehension score by adding your comprehension scores for the two pretests and dividing by two. Enter these average scores on the pretest chart.

Reading Efficiency

You can now compute your current Reading Efficiency by taking your average rate (WPM) and multiplying it by your average percent of comprehension.

$$\frac{\rule{3cm}{0.4pt}}{\text{Average Rate}} \times \frac{\rule{4cm}{0.4pt}}{\text{Average \% Comprehension}} = \frac{\rule{3cm}{0.4pt}}{\text{Reading Efficiency}}$$

Enter this score on your chart.

Rate Flexibility Score

A flexibility score is included to make you aware that efficient readers do not have a single reading rate; they adjust their rate according to: 1) the difficulty of the material (the complexity of vocabulary and sentence length); 2) their purpose for reading the selection (either to get a general idea or to read for detail and retention); and 3) their familiarity with the material (if readers are familiar with the topic, a fast rate is called for; if not, a slower rate is called for). Since it is impossible to determine the latter two conditions for every reader, the flexibility score is based on the reading difficulty of the material. The concept of flexibility of reading speed is further developed in chapter 2.

You can determine your rate flexibility score by subtracting your Pretest 2 Reading Rate score (line 2) from your Pretest 1 Reading Rate score (line 1). Write this number in the space next to *Rate Flexibility Score* located on your Pretest Reading Efficiency chart. If your reading rate for Pretest 2 was higher than it was for Pretest 1, then write a zero next to the flexibility score.

A completed hypothetical Pretest Reading Efficiency chart appears below.

Pretest Reading Efficiency

Pretest Rate 1	316	WPM	.80	% Comprehension
Pretest Rate 2	236	WPM	.70	% Comprehension
Rate Flexibility Score	80			
Average	275	WPM	.75	% Comprehension
Reading Efficiency	206	(275 × .75 = 206.25)		

Analyze Your Scores

The reading level of the two articles you read differed. The first selection is considered easy; its readability level is grade 10. The second selection is considered difficult; its readability level is college. How did you do?

A score of 70 percent or higher on comprehension is considered acceptable, and a score below 70 percent is considered unacceptable. An average reading rate for the first pretest selection is 250 words per minute; for the second selection, it is 205 words per minute. The average flexibility score (the reading difference between Pretests 1 and 2) is 45. The average reading efficiency score is 159.

HOW MUCH WILL I IMPROVE?

If you complete the exercises in this book, your reading efficiency probably will improve between 40 percent and 200 percent. After you complete the posttests, you then can determine exactly how much you have improved. Instructions for calculating the percentage of your improvement are included in the directions (chapter 9) for scoring your posttests.

2
Skimming

INTRODUCTION

Chapter 1 discussed the concept of flexibility of reading rate. Efficient readers adjust their reading rate according to the difficulty of the material, their familiarity with the topic discussed in the material, and their purpose for reading the material. When readers wish to get only some main ideas and a few supporting details, they should read at a very rapid rate, which is called *skimming*.

People who skim lower their level of comprehension consciously. Generally, they read quickly only to fulfill their purpose (which may simply be to get a general idea of the article) and they deliberately skip much that is in the article or book.

Because readers skim for a specific purpose, there are no mechanical rules for skimming. If you have a specific question or questions in mind, you know what to look for and thus you search the information to find the answer(s) to your question(s). Skimming, then, is not a simple mechanical process of turning pages, moving your fingers, flexing your eyes, or reading every other line on the page.

Every business or business-related article you contemplate reading should first be skimmed. There are several reasons for this. Skimming gives you the overall framework of an article—a few main ideas and some details. It provides you with some essential information and tells you how writers have organized their information and how they will develop their topic. You get a good idea of what to expect and where the authors are heading with their ideas.

Once you have this background information, you can decide either to read the article more thoroughly or to skim further for a different purpose. Should you decide to read the article in more depth you will be prepared to adjust your reading rate to:

1. *Your personal purpose.* (Do I want to use the information in a report? Do I simply want this information for myself? Do I want to discuss this information at a meeting?)
2. *Your own background.* (How much do I already know about this?)
3. *The difficulty of the material.* (Are the ideas complex? Easy? How has the writer organized the ideas?)

Here are some general guidelines you can follow to improve your ability to skim.

1. Read the title.
2. If a beginning *summary* appears, read it completely. (For example, the front page of the *Wall Street Journal* includes summaries of some of its articles, and each article published in the *Harvard Business Review* is summarized at the beginning.)
3. Quickly read the first few opening paragraphs to get a good introduction to the article and a sense of the writer's style and organization.
4. Read all bold-face subtitles. They give you summarized ideas and more hints about the writer's organizational pattern.
5. "Float" over the material quickly to pick up "images" of what is involved. While you consciously skip much material, try to pick out phrases that might answer some important questions about the article:

   Who the article is about.

   What the article is about.

   When certain events have taken place.

   Where the events have taken place.

   Why certain events have taken place.

   How the article is organized.
6. Read quickly all of the final paragraphs or the sections labeled *Summary* or *Conclusions.* They add more detail to what you learned from reading the beginning summary (step 2).

The following section presents one way in which you might skim an article. This method, which was developed by Dr. Edward B. Fry of Rutgers University, reviews the points made above and provides a few more tips on skimming.

HOW YOU MIGHT SKIM AN ARTICLE

Usually the first paragraph will be read at average speed all the way through. It often contains an introduction or overview of what will be talked about.

Sometimes, however, the second paragraph contains the introduction or overview. In the first paragraph the author might just be "warming up" or saying something clever to attract attention.

Reading a third paragraph completely might be unnecessary but ... ...
... ...
... ...
... ...
... ...
the main idea is usually contained in the opening sentence
... ...
... ... topic sentence ... ...
... ...
... ...
... ...
... ...

Besides the first sentence the reader should get some but not all the detail from the rest of the paragraph ... ...
... ...
... ...
... ...
... ...
... ...
... ...
... ...
... ... names ...
... ...
... ... dates ... ...
... ...
... ...

This tells you nothing ... ...
... ...
... ...
... ...
hence sometimes the main idea is in the middle or at the end of the paragraph.

Some paragraphs merely repeat ideas ... ...
... ...
... ...
... ...

Occasionally the main idea can't be found in the opening sentence. The whole paragraph must then be read.

Then leave out a lot of the next paragraph ... ...
... ...
... ...
... ...
... ... to make up time.
... ...
... ...
... ...

Remember to keep up a very fast rate ... ...
... ...
... ...
... ... 800 w.p.m.
... ...
... ...

Don't be afraid to leave out half or more of each paragraph
... ...
... ...
... ...
... ...

Don't get interested and start to read everything ... ...
... ...
... ...
... ...
... ...

... ...
skimming is work ... ...
... ...
... ...
... ...
... ...
... ...
Lowered comprehension is expected ... ...
... ... 50% ... ...
... ...
... ...
... ... not too low
... ...
... ...
Skimming practice makes it easier ... ...
... ...
... ...
... ...
... gain confidence ...
... ...
Perhaps you won't get anything at all from a few paragraphs
... ...
... ...
... ...
... ... don't worry
... ...
... ...
Skimming has many uses ...
... ...
... ... reports ...
... ... newspapers ...
... ... supplementary
... ... text ... ...
The ending paragraphs might be read more fully as often they contain a summary.

Remember that the importance of skimming is to get only the author's main ideas at a very fast speed.

Practice the skill of skimming on the following six purposeful skimming articles. Remember, you are reading at your most rapid rate, skipping much of the material as you seek the answers to specific questions that have been raised. For each reading, it is suggested that you finish skimming the article within a specified amount of time. This is done so that you will skim at a rate of no less than 800 words per minute. Because the length of each article varies, the maximum skimming time suggested varies. But in all cases, the time indicated is designed to force you to skim at a rate of no less than 800 words per minute.

INSTRUCTIONS FOR PURPOSEFUL SKIMMING: " 'Sexism' and Modern Business Communications"

Skim this article in order to identify five ways in which sexism can be avoided in business communications. Allow yourself no more than 90 seconds to skim the article. After skimming the article, write down your answers to the test that follows.

Purposeful Skimming

"Sexism" and Modern Business Communications
Robert J. Motley

Today much emphasis is being placed on women's rights and equal treatment of the sexes in business. Attention has been given to such areas as hiring practices, salaries, and promotions, but another aspect that needs attention is oral and written communications in business. Communications, particularly written communications, are loaded with sexist overtones and worn-out expressions.

BUSINESS LETTER SALUTATIONS

Traditionally, we have been taught that the proper salutation for a letter addressed to a company is *Gentlemen.* Why should we assume this? Are all companies comprised only of men? Isn't it true that most companies today are made up of both men and women? Let's solve this problem by eliminating the salutation completely. After all, does a salutation such as *Gentlemen* or *Dear Ms. Jones* really mean anything or are they just formalities carried over from a bygone era that is being perpetuated because we are too bound by tradition to make a change? A letter addressed to a company name needs no salutation. Unless there is some reason for not divulging the subject of your letter in the opening, such as in a bad news letter, substitute a subject line in place of the salutation as recommended by the AMS simplified letter style. The subject line has meaning and adds to the communication qualities of the letter, while the salutation *Gentlemen* or *Ladies* is only a formality and really means little. If it is not appropriate to use a subject line in the letter, simply double or triple space after the inside address and begin the first paragraph.

Instead of using a salutation such as

Dear Ms. Jones for a letter addressed to an individual, why not just double or triple space after the inside address and personalize the opening line of the first paragraph—"Thank you, *Ms. Jones, for* your letter of March 5." Isn't this much more natural and conversational than *Dear Ms. Jones?*

TITLES IN BUSINESS LETTERS

Why do we complicate matters by making a distinction between a married woman and an unmarried woman by using the title *Mrs.* and *Miss* in the inside address and body of a business letter? Should the marital status of a woman be of any significance in business? The title *Ms.,* which does not designate any marital status, has been in existence for years. Why don't we use it exclusively for all woman?

Generally, it is not necessary or desirable for a woman to place the title *Miss* or *Mrs.* before her name in a letter signature line to designate marital status. The only time a title is necessary before a name in the signature is for clarity when the name itself does not designate gender. For instance, if a man has a first name such as *Ruby* or *Opal,* he should type his signature as *Mr. Ruby L. Smith.* Likewise, a woman with a first name such as *Kendall* should use the typewritten signature *Ms. Kendall A. Snouffer.* This, of course, will avoid the possibility of someone mistakenly using the wrong title when answering the letter. Preferably, a person should adopt an official signature that reveals gender. For instance *A. Leon Grimes* or *Anne L. Grimes* would be preferred over *A. L. Grimes.*

GENDER PRONOUNS

Gender pronouns are particularly troublesome since the English language has no singular pronoun meaning *he* or *she.*

Traditionally, it has been considered correct to always use the masculine *he* when the gender is not known or clear, or if both men and women are included. If we are conscious of this problem, we can do a great deal to minimize it. For instance, instead of saying *"One* can usually improve if *he* really tries," we can reword and use the plural form—*"People* can usually improve if *they* really try." Of course, it is also possible to use both pronouns— *"One* can usually improve if *he* or *she* really tries"; however, this becomes very awkward if repeated frequently and should be avoided. An alternative might be to alternate *he* and *she* in examples such as "You have often heard managers say '*He* really has initiative' or '*She* has a great sense of responsibility,'" rather than using the masculine *he* for all examples.

SUBSERVIENT EXPRESSIONS

Many subservient expressions are used in written and oral business communications, often without consciousness of them or awareness of how they really sound. Many times a male executive or supervisor will use an expression such as "My *girl* will handle that problem" or "The *girls* will be in charge of planning the program." On the other hand, he seldom would refer to a male subordinate as my *boy.* When referring to adult females, use *women* rather than *girls* or *ladies.* If referring to one female employee, use the appropriate title or name— *my secretary* or *Ms. Smith*—rather than *my girl.* Don't use unequal terms when referring to males and females such as *man and wife* or the *men and the girls.* Instead, use parallel expressions such as *husband and wife* or *men and women.*

Avoid using examples or making comparisons that insinuate women are less capable than men—"She drives the delivery truck as well as any man," or "Even though she is a woman, she manages the department very well."

OCCUPATIONAL EXPRESSIONS

Be careful with the use of occupational terms ending in *man* such as *foreman, businessman, congressman, salesman, mailman, insurance man,* and *chairman.* Preferred expressions are *supervisor; business manager or executive; member of congress* or *representative; sales representative, sales person,* or *sales clerk; mail carrier; insurance agent;* and *moderator, presiding officer, leader, head,* or *coordinator.*

Do not use gender modifiers to emphasize stereotyped roles of either men or women—*male nurse, male secretary, lady lawyer,* and *woman vice-president.* Really, gender should be of no significance in such occupations. However, if you feel identification is necessary, by all means do it properly. Use *woman* or *female* rather than *lady* as a modifier. Gender may also be identified by the choice of pronouns—"The vice-president of sales gave *her* recommendation" or "The secretary is at *his* desk."

In summary, we can get our business communications in tune with the times by implementing the following ideas: (1) Avoid using the salutation Gentlemen *for a letter addressed to a company name; substitute a subject line instead. (2) Rather than using salutations such as* Dear Ms. Jones *or* Dear Mr. Smith, *substitute a subject line and personalize in the opening sentence. (3) Use the title* Ms. *for all women. (4) Place a title before the name in the signature line only when necessary to designate gender. (5) Avoid overusing the gender pronoun* he *when referring to individuals in general. (6) Avoid the use of subservient expressions such as* my girl *when referring to subordinates. (7) Use parallel expressions when referring to people—*men and women *rather than* men and girls. *(8) Avoid occupational terms ending in* man, *and do not use gender modifiers to emphasize stereotyped roles of men and women such as* male secretary *and* woman vice-president.

PURPOSEFUL SKIMMING COMPREHENSION CHECK:
" 'Sexism' and Modern Business Communications"

List five ways you can avoid sexism in your business communications.

1.   4.

2.   5.

3.

Check your answers with the Answer Key.

INSTRUCTIONS FOR PURPOSEFUL SKIMMING: "Secretarial Survival Sills"

Skim this article to identify at least six survival skills secretaries need. Allow yourself no more than 110 seconds to skim the article. After skimming, write down your answers to the test that follows.

Purposeful Skimming

Secretarial Survival Skills

Jane M. Banks, CPS

The U.S. Department of Labor projects approximately 295,000 annual job openings for secretaries through 1985. Shorthand, typewriting, and English skills will undoubtedly continue to be important to the secretarial graduate in obtaining the position of his/her choice. They will not, however, ensure the success—or even the survival—of the new secretary in that choice position.

What are some needed secretarial survival skills? And how could secretarial teachers help students develop these skills? The author's recent secretarial experiences as an office temporary in a large metropolitan city, conversations with practicing secretaries, and observations of secretarial "situations" suggest three broad areas of survival skills: communication, organization, and decision making.

COMMUNICATION

The telephone is literally the lifeline of business. Many clients, customers, and business associates have only a telephone contact with a company's representative, and the secretary's handling of telephone calls is critical to the success of the company.

The new secretary may be faced with: a 30-button call director with no listing of names corresponding with extensions, a telephone with intercom connections, a telephone with WATS line(s), a telephone with receiver switch that can directly transfer outside calls to other extensions. Students should have the actual experience of using a variety of telephones so that buttons, lights, multiple extensions, and various call-placing, -receiving, -holding, and -transferring operations become familiar.

Students should learn to ask questions. What is the name of each person on each extension? Does anyone answer his/her calls personally? What extensions are connected by the intercom? How is the intercom connection made? How are calls transferred?

Students should learn to listen. Smith, Brown, Jones may be the names listed most frequently in the telephone directory, but they are not the names most frequently heard on the telephone! Listen to the caller as he/she identifies him/herself; write the name on a scratch pad; repeat the caller's name during the conversation; ask the caller to spell the name. Several names have multiple spellings; the executive wants the correct one.

Students should learn to record information. Listen carefully to the caller's conversation, message, question—but don't trust the information to memory. Interruption can play havoc with even the best memory. Write as much as possible on a scratch pad, and condense the message later on the telephone message pad. Inexperienced secretaries can't listen, condense, and write a "finished" message simultaneously. Be certain the telephone number as well as the message is accurate; repeat the information to the caller before concluding the conversation.

ORGANIZATION

Lucky is the new secretary who has the opportunity to work with the "retiring" secretary before his/her departure. In many instances, however, the newcomer will be afforded little or no assistance, and learning who's who or who's where can be a confusing experience.

Students should learn to locate information. After becoming familiar with the operation of the telephone and identifying the various individuals and extensions, the secretary should locate telephone directories, name/address files, the company directory—invaluable aids to survival. The organization of the name/address file should be noted, because the former secretary may not have filed cards in an alphabetic sequence but rather in a subject sequence (i.e., banks, restaurants, suppliers). When the new secretary is asked to locate a telephone number, he/she may have to question the executive about the subject or category under which the name may be filed. If sources of information are not available to the secretary, he/she must begin to develop a directory as soon as possible.

Students should learn to develop chronological files. The new secretary may find it useful to prepare a chronological file copy of *everything* that is typed, including materials that need not be placed in the alphabetic/subject files. Copy that is given to the executive for distribution at a meeting or for his personal use may be misplaced by the executive; the executive may take the copy with him to a meeting in a distant office, and the secretary may need to refer to the copy during his absence.

Students should learn to follow directions. "Time is money," and busy executives cannot afford to waste either time or money. Consider the plight of the executive who spent 10 minutes giving directions to his secretary regarding telephone calls to be placed, project follow-up to be completed, messenger service to be arranged, and a VIP luncheon to be organized. When he completed his directions, he remarked that he hadn't seen her write down any of his directions—would she remember all of them? The secretary assured him

she would; but, when she began her work later that morning, she interrupted the executive innumerable times to ask for repeated directions—and missed the messenger service pick-up deadline for an important letter that was to be hand-delivered to a VIP that afternoon.

Directions/instructions must be written accurately, in their entirety, and must be followed to the letter. The new secretary encounters much confusion regarding tasks and procedures and should welcome directions/instructions from the executive.

Students should learn to "track" the executive. Executives make telephone calls, schedule appointments, and leave the office—without informing the secretary, who may unwittingly be placed in an embarrassing situation. The secretary should check the employer's calendar each morning and note any discrepancies that may appear between the executive's and secretary's calendars. When the executive leaves the office, the secretary should tactfully inquire about the destination and expected time of return to the office. Emergencies such as the following do occur, and the secretary must be able to contact the executive in such situations.

Executive A left the office, stating he was attending a meeting at the XYZ office across town; 15 minutes after A's departure the out-of-town Executive B (whom A was planning to meet at the XYZ office) called to say that B would be late in arriving at A's *office* for the meeting. (Executive A had not informed B where the meeting was to be held; he had not recorded the meeting info on his calendar nor had he told his secretary that B was expected to attend the meeting.) The secretary graciously apologized for the mix-up, assured B she would verify the meeting info, and said she would call B back within a few minutes. Fortunately, the secretary had jotted down the place of A's meeting when he gave her the info. She called the XYZ office to confirm A's arrival and to inform A that B would be late. She then called B at his hotel, confirming his expected attendance.

DECISION MAKING

Secretaries are required to use initiative and good judgment and to make decisions within the scope of assigned authority. Decision making is a secretarial activity that begins the moment the secretary opens the office at 9 A.M. and continues until he/she closes the office at 5 P.M. "My secretary will handle that"; and the secretary must decide: Who should be notified? What follow-up is necessary? What communication service should be used? How should multiple copies be produced? What format should be used?

Students should learn to make decisions. No employer asks the secretary to produce communications from textbook-style typewritten copy with a word count; rather, handwritten copy (sometimes illegible) with paste-ups, corrections, misspellings, errors in grammar and punctuation is the norm, not the exception, in business. The employer rarely suggests that the secretary locate needed data for communications from specified pages of specific sources; secretaries are expected to be able to determine the sources and the location of the required information. No employer details the decision-making steps to be followed in problem solving; secretaries are expected to have developed expertise in problem solving during their secretarial training.

Students should learn to work under pressure. Deadlines, interruptions, rush jobs, unfamiliar tasks—all contribute to the pressure under which secretaries work. Even the most well-organized secretary often finds "the best laid plans, etc." Realistic learning situations that require deadlines, provide interruptions, and include rush jobs and unfamiliar tasks should be encountered by secretarial students. Instruction that meets these requirements may, of course, permit the student to learn at his/her own pace, but the student's pace should be similar to the employer's—"I need it yesterday."

Shorthand, typewriting, and English skills will continue to permit secretarial graduates both horizontal and vertical mobility in their secretarial careers. However, secretarial survival skills must also be incorporated into the secretarial training program so that students will "survive" the first secretarial position to enjoy that mobility.

PURPOSEFUL SKIMMING COMPREHENSION CHECK:
"Secretarial Survival Skills"
List six survival skills for secretaries:

1.   4.

2.   5.

3.   6.

Check your answers with the Answer Key.

INSTRUCTIONS FOR PURPOSEFUL SKIMMING: "Real Estate"

Skim this article in order to determine three ways in which real estate people can create buyer hysteria among some senior citizens. Allow yourself no more than 85 seconds to skim the article. After skimming the article, write down your answers to the test that follows.

Purposeful Skimming

Real Estate

The Editors, Consumers Tribune

Certainly there are financially sound, carefully planned land developments, retirement homes and condominiums for senior citizens.

But senior citizens sometimes create problems for themselves by investing in distant retirement homes, condominiums or speculative land developments without first investigating.

They believe what they read in the pamphlet a promoter sends them—or if they happen to be on site, they believe the patter they hear from a glib salesman.

For instance, one retiree reported:

"We decided to buy a small place in a new land development in Pennsylvania. The developer's brochure was so inviting. It spoke of a recreation area, new beach house, a golf course, and eventually a whole new town. So we invested everything we had—$10,000—in a piece of land as a down payment on a house the developer was to build for us. What we got was a foundation, a dirt street, no sewers, no water or utility access, and a tax bill.

"The developer and the contractor went into bankruptcy. The county officials involved wouldn't allow septic tanks. They said the water was unfit to drink and they cancelled the building permits for the whole development.

"We lost everything."

In another instance, hundreds of Massachusetts retirees lost more than $6 million in a Canadian land speculation along the St. Lawrence Seaway. An oil refinery was supposed to be built on the site. The lots they bought sight unseen for as much as $2700 each turned out to be big enough for only a one-car garage. And when the Canadian authorities and the U.S. Securities and Exchange Commission moved in on the promoters, there was only $100,000 in their accounts.

Senior citizens who consider buying a site for a retirement home or investing in a land development are strongly advised:

• Base your decision on facts, not promises. In the case of a land development, its value depends on the developer fulfilling his end of the bargain.

• Determine what utilities will be available and who will pay for installing them.

• Find out the cost of any required municipal improvements such as sidewalks, sewer or water assessments, and the like.

• Explore the financing and insurance costs for the area. Is it really growing? If you build a home, what will the cost of fire, flood or other insurance be?

• Ask about the property tax. Are there any assessments for common services such as roads, sewers, water mains, and so on?

• If you plan to retire, find out whether

hospital and medical facilities are available. Who will clear the snow from the roads and sidewalks? Are the roads kept open by the city or county or the developer during the winter? If you are building in the South or along any shore, are there special beach assessments or permits?

- Find out about the drainage and water conditions. Are you building on a flood plain? Is the area prone to brush fires? If the site is in the desert, is water available?

- View the property yourself. Don't depend on the salesman's description. Is the property next to the town dump? Is there an airport landing or take-off zone overhead? Are the facilities promised in the brochure or by the salesman's pitch really there? Oral promises are worthless once you sign a carefully worded contract that most developers use.

- Have your attorney go over the contract before you sign it. If it is an installment contract, you receive nothing—no deed or title—until all payments are made. If you receive a deed with a mortgage, you are liable for all property taxes the minute you take title.

- If the contract includes a building contract and mortgage, make sure you know who the builder will be and who will be responsible if there are any problems. Never sign unless your attorney has reviewed the contract and the mortgage. If the developer objects to that, forget him.

Slick sales people create "buyer hysteria" among some senior citizens in several calculated ways.

For example:

- A salesman told a Cambridge, Mass., couple, "Florida land doubles in value every five years." Not if the land is under water much of the year, as it was in this case.

- To get prospective buyers viewing the property to sign a sales contract quickly, the salesman carries a walkie-talkie over which an accomplice tells him loudly, "Take lots 147 and 392 and 841 off your list. They've been sold. Also, deposits have already been made on the 200 series." That's intended to prod the prospective buyers into snapping up the property on the spot.

- The salesman says there's gold or silver or oil or gas in "them thar hills." If there were, why would they be selling the property?

- The "free" lot is another salesman's trick. "All you have to do to get this beautiful half-acre in this garden-spot development," he says, "is pay the deed transfer cost of $149." What they don't say is that the developer bought the land for $10 an acre, that the zoning law requires homes be built on one-acre lots, and the half-acre to go with the "free" half-acre will cost $2000. At the land office, incidentally, transfer fees are about $25.

Senior citizens buying a condominium should take all the steps they would take if they were buying a single home. They should check their share of all costs, and they should also remember that if a majority of owners in the condominium want to make improvements, they will have to go along and pay their fair share of the bill. In any case, before a condominium buyer signs papers, he should have an attorney examine every element of the transaction. In all cases, remember, "Investigate Before You Invest."

More and more senior citizens are buying mobile homes. Before they make that investment, they should find out:

- The total price of the home, not just the monthly payment on it.
- How much it will cost to buy or rent the land on which the home will stand.
- The zoning regulations of the community in which they intend to put the home.
- The regulations and the restrictions of the park, if that's where they intend to live.
- Regulations and procedures for moving the home.
- Names and addresses of other mobile home purchasers from the retailer they're dealing with, so they can get an assessment of his reliability and the services he provides after the sale.
- The satisfaction or dissatisfaction of residents in the park they're considering.
- Whether the park operator requires a commission on the sale of a home on his grounds—and whether he's entitled to it.

And, as always, when in doubt, ask the Better Business Bureau or state or local authorities before you buy.

PURPOSEFUL SKIMMING COMPREHENSION CHECK: "Real Estate"

List three ways in which sales people can create buyer hysteria among some senior citizens.

1.   3.

2.

Check your answers with the Answer Key.

INSTRUCTIONS FOR PURPOSEFUL SKIMMING: "The Office of the Future and Its Impact on Employees"

Skim this article in order to identify at least five characteristics of future offices and office employees. Allow yourself no more than 105 seconds to skim the article. After skimming the article, write down your answers to the test that follows.

Purposeful Skimming

The Office of the Future and Its Impact on Employees
Zane K. Quible

The office of the future is currently a much-discussed topic. Although no one can describe with certainty the office of the future, predictions are possible. One certainty, however, is that the office of the future will have an impact upon everyone who works in an office as well as everyone who comes in contact with an office.

Several phenomena are occurring in today's offices that will necessitate the office of the future. These conditions include:

1. *Rapidly increasing labor costs.* The

continuous increase in salary costs of office employees will require the efficient utilization of workers.

2. *Increasing costs of office space.* The cost of space is increasing at a constant rate. Since office space is not an "unlimited commodity," more work will have to be done in an ever-decreasing amount of space.

3. *Increasing costs of processing office work.* Approximately 40 percent of an organization's operating expenses can be attributed to administrative costs, resulting primarily from the processing of office work. By developing efficient procedures for processing office work, administrative costs can be stabilized or in some cases even reduced.

4. *Increasing volumes of business transactions and accompanying paper work.* As the number of business transactions increases, so does the amount of paper work that is needed to process these transactions. Increasing numbers of transactions will make the use of electronic technology desirable, if not necessary.

5. *Increasing numbers of technological developments.* Almost daily a new device for processing office work is introduced on the market. While some of it is totally new, other equipment is a refinement of already existing equipment. Much of the new equipment will be justifiable on a cost-efficiency basis.

6. *Increasing need for accurate, timely information for making decisions.* As the pace of life increases, so does the need for accurate, up-to-date information. Many of today's executives do not have the time lag their predecessors had for making decisions.

CHARACTERISTICS OF THE OFFICE OF THE FUTURE

A characteristic of the office of the future will be the use of a "total systems" approach in the administration and operation of the organization. No longer will an organization operate as isolated components, but rather it will be comprised of interrelated, integrated functions, encompassing such areas as accounting, sales, marketing, and administrative services.

Another characteristic of the office of the future will be the heavy dependence on electronic devices for processing data and information. In today's offices, much of the work is still processed manually or semielectronically. The increased use of electronic devices will cost less than the salaries of office employees whose function is to process the work that the equipment is capable of processing. This does not mean that vast numbers of employees will lose their jobs, but rather employees will be utilized in more efficient, productive ways. (The vast misplacement of humans by computers did not occur as many feared.) The fact that employees strike for higher wages, require fringe benefits, and have nonproductive days makes the use of electronic devices desirable whenever feasible.

Another reason for the widespread increase in the number and extent of electronic devices in the office of the future is that paper is likely to become less used as a medium for processing office work. (In fact, predictions are that offices will be virtually paperless by the 1990's.) The continued use of paper to process many business transactions will not only be inefficient but also unproductive.

Several of the electronic devices that are likely to be used extensively in the office of the future already exist. Examples are automatic keyboarding devices, facsimile devices, and telephonic-communication systems. The difference will be the applications of these electronic devices by interfacing one device with another.

Another characteristic of the office of the future will be the concern for energy conservation. At the present time, there are environmental systems that adjust the temperature and light levels in work areas according to whether or not people are present in the room. Another environmental system draws heat from human bodies in the summer and expels the heat from the premises in order to conserve on cooling costs. In the winter time, this same body heat is used as a supplement to the building's heating system.

Another dimension to energy conservation is the possibility that employees will not have to be physically present in the building to do work. Because of advanced technology, communication between two points will be almost as effective as if the persons were physically present.

The final characteristic of the future office to be discussed in this article (although there are others that can be identified) is the openness of the office layout. Large open areas are more efficient than small, compartmentalized areas, so instead of using permanent walls to design work areas, extensive use will be made of movable partitions and modular furniture. Not only are these new developments more flexible, but they also facilitate frequent changes in work processes.

DESCRIPTION OF THE OFFICE OF THE FUTURE

The office of the future will be largely electronic with a greatly reduced use of paper. Vast amounts of data and information will be processed and stored by means of electronic devices—without the use of paper.

Because the traditional role of office employees is paper-oriented, vast changes will take place in the way jobs are completed. Many of the individuals who perform secretarial and clerical work in today's offices will most likely become administrative assistants. Many employees—both executives and their administrative assistants—in the office of the future will be supplied with desktop electronic devices that incorporate a cathode ray tube screen and a keyboard. The device will provide access to information and to data stored in the computer. The keyboard will be used for data entry, while the screen will be used for data output.

For example, assume Executive A wishes to see the communication received from Systems Corporation on November 17 of last year. Using the proper codes, the keyboard will be used to access this communication, which is stored in the computer. In a fraction of a second, the information will be displayed on the executive's screen.

In another case, assume that an administrative assistant wishes to make an appointment to talk with a vice-president on July 18. The vice-president's appointments schedule will be stored in the computer. By means of the keyboard-screen device, the administrative assistant can determine when the vice-president will be available on that date and can then use the keyboard portion of the desk-top device to reserve the desired time.

A number of office operations that are electronic in nature already exist. Examples are electronic funds transfer (EFT) that eliminates checks in banking and "electronic mail" which transmits written communication between two points by means of facsimile devices. The signals are transmitted between the two points through telephone lines.

A new development in the word processing concept will probably be extensively used in future offices. This development provides word originators with a cathode ray tube screen. Rather than using rough-draft paper copies when reviewing, revising, or editing work, the material appears on the screen.

CHARACTERISTICS NEEDED BY FUTURE OFFICE EMPLOYEES

Because many current office operations will be different, the duties performed by office employees in the future will also change. They will not necessarily require characteristics unlike those needed by today's office workers, but future office employees will need certain higher level characteristics. Some of the more important characteristics needed of future office employees are as follows:

1. *Adaptability.* As new technology is developed, work processes will also change. Office employees of the future will need to be able to cope with these frequent changes and state of flux.

2. *Flexibility.* Employees in the future office will also need to be more flexible. The nature of many present office jobs is fairly routine, seldom requiring much deviation, but such will not be the case in the future.

3. *Decision-making skills.* With increased administrative responsibilities in the office of the future, employees will have need for higher level decision-making and judgmental skills.

4. *Technological orientation.* Since many operations in the office of the future will be more technologically oriented, employees will need an appreciation for and an understanding of these processes. Those not willing to develop such an appreciation and understanding will most likely find the office of the future a frustrating place of employment.

5. *Creativity.* The office of the future will provide many opportunities for employees to use their creativity and imagination. In fact, one of its more rewarding features will be the number of opportunities for employees to make use of their creative talents.

Working in the office of the future need not be looked upon with anxiety or skepticism. Many will find it a more rewarding and satisfying experience than working in today's office.

PURPOSEFUL SKIMMING COMPREHENSION CHECK:
"The Office of the Future and Its Impact on Employees"

List five characteristics of future offices and office employees.

1.   4.

2.   5.

3.

Check your answers with the Answer Key.

INSTRUCTIONS FOR PURPOSEFUL SKIMMING: "Essentials for Becoming a Top-Level Secretary"

Skim this article in order to identify the most important characteristic or ability that, according to the author, separates the "top" secretary from the "mediocre" secretary. Allow yourself no more than 95 seconds to find the answer. After skimming the article, write down your answer to the test that follows.

Purposeful Skimming

Essentials for Becoming a Top-Level Secretary

Eunice T. Smith

The titles "executive secretary," "administrative assistant," or similar descriptions are suggestive of an individual who can provide administrative support at the highest level. Many qualities are sought in the person who is to assume a top-level position in the secretarial career field. Typically, this competent, take-charge person is "made," not born.

Among the ingredients that go into the "making" of the top-level career secretary are the following essentials: (1) knowledges, (2) technical skills, (3) attitudes, (4) experience, and (5) a commitment to career development. However, it is in the area of decision making where the potential executive secretary or administrative assistant is separated from the mediocre secretary. Therefore, the secretarial training program should prepare the prospective career secretary to assume decision-making roles. Further, the future secretary should know how to plan a program of career development once on the job.

A better-than-average amount of knowledge, technical skills, and desirable personal qualities must be acquired and developed by the prospective top-level secretary. Curriculum requirements of postsecondary secretarial training programs usually include courses in content subjects such as business law, accounting, and office management.

Courses to develop technical skills (for example, typewriting, dictation and transcription, word processing, and office appliances) provide another important aspect of training. Considerable emphasis is also placed on the development of attitudes, office etiquette, and other behaviors that contribute to success on the job.

Using the Q-sort technique, Weber identified curriculum areas where business executives *and secretaries* placed considerably more emphasis than secretarial teachers. One important area was "a familiarity with the various functions of management and a knowledge of executive responsibilities."[1] The results of Weber's study indicate that courses which would provide this background should receive greater attention in the secretarial curriculum.

Few, if any, top-level jobs are given to beginning office workers. Consequently, experience is an important factor in the development of the executive secretary. Secretarial training programs are not so uniform in requiring or providing experience as in the requirements for the development of knowledges, technical skills, and attitudes. The types of experiences required vary from simulated offices and on- and off-campus super-

[1] Weber, Warren C. "Curriculum Priorities in Secretarial Education." *Delta Pi Epsilon Journal* 12:9; February 1970.

vised work experience to nonsupervised work experience. Much variation also exists between the nature and length of the experience required, if any. The real work situation, however, does afford the optimum proving ground for the integration of knowledges, skills, and attitudes.

The prospective top-level secretary, however, must add to the better-than-average acquisition of knowledges, technical skills, attitudes, and experience a strong personal commitment to the achievement of success as measured by reaching the top of the career field. A genuine liking for the nature of the work should exist. The ability to develop effective interpersonal relations is also important. Then, the career secretary should have a desire to take on the added responsibilities of the executive secretary or administrative assistant. This commitment to high performance and achievement in these aspects of the job will make the investment of time and effort to reach the top seem worthwhile. Obviously, the top-level jobs are not for the person who shuns responsibility, as more decision making is one of the characteristics of the job as one moves up the secretarial career ladder.

In this era of specialization, greater demands are being made of secretaries. Business executives are frequently out of town; and, according to Robert O. Snelling, Sr.:

. . . they need someone with administrative abilities who can keep the office running during their absence—someone who can think and make decisions. They need someone with initiative to supplement efficiency, someone with conceptual skills as well as mechanical skills—in other words, someone who can enact, not just react.[2]

To "enact," as Snelling suggests, the executive secretary or administrative

---

[2] Snelling, Robert O., Sr. "The Businessman Looks at Secretarial Education." *Effective Secretarial Education.* Twelfth Yearbook. Washington, D.C.: National Business Education Association, 1974. Chapter 1, p. 1.

assistant will need to draw on a background of knowledge and experience to make effective decisions. The future career secretary should not leave the acquisition of these essentials to chance.

Reading Professional and Trade Literature

Reading and study are basic tools for broadening one's knowledge. In addition to professional journals, company manuals and publications and trade journals in the employment field should be added to the list of required reading. By all means, the secretary should read in the area related to immediate job performance. However, the magazines and journals that the executive reads may provide the insight needed to be a more valuable assistant.

Continuing Education

The career secretary should take advantage of the numerous opportunities to continue one's education. If the company provides educational benefits in the form of tuition rebates, the secretary uses them! The career-oriented person attends classes, seminars, workshops, and the like, especially in areas that deal with the development of leadership abilities, human relations skills, communications skills, modern information systems, and others designed for career development.

Getting More Beneficial Experience

While in school, the future secretary should make the most of simulated office experiences, if available. Even if the curriculum does not require it, actual office experience should be acquired as early and as often as possible. Furthermore, the secretarial student should make office visitations and conduct informal surveys. Super secretaries should be observed at work, and if possible, the student should arrange to interview some of these individuals to determine their success formulas. Once out of school and employed, the secretary should grasp opportunities to take on added responsibilities. Initiative should show in the handling of routine tasks and in looking for ways of improving effectiveness and reducing office costs.

To accelerate the move up the career ladder, the secretary has to become more career-minded. It should be clear that the job is important, and if the secretary is a female, she must confront sex stereotypes.

To this point, the feminine gender has been purposely avoided. While there are some male secretaries and an increasing demand for more of them, the reality is that the secretarial field is dominated by women. Another cold fact is that sex stereotyping is found all too often in the business world as affirmed by a study of *Harvard Business Review* subscribers in management positions. Out of 5,000 forms mailed, 1,500 responses were obtained from representatives of major industries and job functions. Two general patterns of sex discrimination were found: (1) there is a greater organizational concern for the careers of men than there is for women, and (2) there is a degree of skepticism about women's abilities to balance work and family demands.[3]

---

[3] Rosen, Benson, and Jerdee, Thomas H. "Sex Stereotyping in the Executive Suite." *Harvard Business Review* 52:58; March-April 1974.

Yet, there is no conclusive evidence to suggest that females will not make good managers and supervisors and otherwise assume leadership roles, given the drive and the desire to attain such positions. Therefore, the career-minded secretary — and in most cases she is a woman! — must let it be known that "she" expects opportunities to grow and develop. She must be ready to seize and make the most of these opportunities, and she will be if she has at her command the knowledges, technical skills, attitudes, and experiences upon which to build a career.

Finally, like other professionals, the career-minded secretary will affiliate with professional organizations. She recognizes that striving for professional excellence is a worthwhile endeavor perhaps to the extent of becoming a Certified Professional Secretary.

Success in any field seldom "just happens." It is the result of planning and plain hard work. Those who aspire to reach the top of the secretarial field should know the demands and the requirements of high-level positions, and they should plan their career development accordingly. Women must work to overcome sex stereotypes and other forms of sex discrimination and thereby obtain opportunities for professional growth and development. They can start by sharpening their decision-making abilities and by having the courage and willingness to accept the responsibility for the decisions made.

PURPOSEFUL SKIMMING COMPREHENSION CHECK: "Essentials for Becoming a Top-Level Secretary"

Complete the statement: The characteristic that separates the top-level secretary from the average secretary is that the top-level secretary can

---

Check your answer with the Answer Key.

INSTRUCTIONS FOR PURPOSEFUL SKIMMING: "The Moral and Ethical Climate in Today's Business World"

Skim this article in order to determine the author's opinion on the moral and ethical climate in today's business world. Also, identify at least three ways his company has tried to ensure that its business is conducted "in a legal and ethical manner." Allow yourself no more than three minutes to skim the article. After skimming the article, write down your answers to the test that follows.

Purposeful Skimming

The Moral and Ethical Climate in Today's Business World

William M. Agee

Big business today is increasingly international in scope; even small businesses are affected by the interdependence of our economies. Now it is not only goods and services but what the economists call the factors of production—capital, technology, even labor—which move and flow from country to country. This mobility creates problems, of course, but it is a powerful and efficient mechanism for allocating global resources. Governments are constantly tinkering and interfering with it, far too much in my opinion, but no one seriously believes that the process can or should be halted.

So we live, increasingly, in an international economy. But this cannot obviate the fact that we all are rooted somewhere. We all live in Detroit, or East Lansing, or Tokyo, Rome, or Casablanca, and this means that as we move out into the business world we find ourselves dealing with people whose language, values, methods, and prejudices are quite different from our own.

Here, I think, we have one clue to the moral and ethical climate in today's business world. It is a troubled climate for a number of reasons, some of which have less to do with ethics than with politics and economics; but one obvious factor, surely, is that our international operations have brought us face to face with an old and very difficult moral problem. This is the problem of relativity. In the sixteenth century, the French philosopher Montaigne was struck by the fact that "what's right on this side of the Pyrenees," as a proverb put it, "is wrong over there"—meaning in Spain. And today, of course, we are dealing in societies which are considerably more distant from one another, morally and geographically, than France and Spain. We have to decide whether our principles of behavior are absolute and universal, or whether we obey the ancient maxim and do in Rome as the Romans do.

In normal times, if there are any such, this might have been no more than a subject for philosophical speculation, but these certainly are not normal times.

For some years the atmosphere in the business world has been roiled by reports of scandalous behavior. Week after week we have been assailed with a lurid series of revelations on payoffs, kickbacks, bribes, and illegal political contributions. These events have shaken foreign governments, embarrassed our foreign policy makers, and forced the chief executive officers of several of our largest corporations to resign. Investigations have been launched by the Securities and Exchange Commission and the Internal Revenue Service; inevitably, a half dozen bills have been introduced in Congress. All this, needless to say, came hard on the heels of scandals in Washington which had badly tarnished the executive and legislative branches of our government. Americans were left with the impression—and, according to the opinion polls, they have come to believe it is true—that their major institutions were hopelessly and irremediably corrupt.

So we have a problem. And the conventional wisdom would have us believe that it is a very grave problem, one which places the survival of our business system in question.

But does it? I know that it is always fashionable to take the direst possible view, but suddenly the proposition that our corporations are rotten and doomed to extinction because a few people were caught with their hands in the till strikes me as exaggerated, even wrong. In fact, the more I think of it the more incongruous it seems. There is a character in Shakespeare's *Twelfth Night* who is said to be "sick of self-love." Well, sometimes we seem to be sick of self-hatred—and for business people I cannot imagine a more pernicious kind of sickness, one that muddies the judgment and paralyzes the will.

Perhaps it is because we live in a media-dominated world, which consumes sensation at such a fearsome rate. Whatever it is, I suddenly find it impossible to believe that those opinion polls really mean what they appear to be saying, and I am stuck by the fact that, after all the furor of these past years of scandal and disgrace, after tons of newsprint, hundreds of study seminars,

and innumerable congressional hearings and speeches, the problem of improper payments seems slowly but unmistakably to be receding into the past.

Now, let me not be misunderstood. I am not suggesting that it was all a mirage, that these things did not happen, that they were not reprehensible or important. Of course they happened. Of course they were reprehensible. Of course they were important. But the fact remains: Not only are they receding into the past, but also they have become something of a bore. This is rather odd, but it *is* a fact. And it seems to me that it tells us something about ourselves and the way we work.

What it tells us, I think, is not that the problem of morality has been solved and put behind us—the Second Coming has not yet occurred. Nor would it be fair to say that it has simply been swept under the rug. The events of the past few years have amounted to a sort of trial by fire, a process of self-examination under pressure which, I submit, is characteristic of the American corporate system. In one way or another, just about every publicly held company in this country will have been through this process. And none will emerge unchanged, neither the relatively righteous—the overwhelming majority—nor the small number whose sins were uncovered and exposed to the public wrath.

My point is that the system, in the time-honored phrase, has worked. Our sins were uncovered noisily, as they always are, and with so much gusto that it was easy for the impressionable to believe that we were going to hell in a handbasket. Well, maybe we were. But somehow we have not. And now that the dust has begun to settle we can survey the scene, estimate the damage, and get on with the job.

To get on with the job, however, no

longer can mean merely that we have goods and services to produce and distribute, people to recruit and train, assets to preserve and enhance. These are practical tasks. We know how to get our hands—and our minds—on them. But this is not all. Faced with the enormous non sequiturs of public opinion, we also know that we must make an effort to explain what we are about. And this is a very different kind of task.

One of the effects of the crisis was to remind us—although we did not really need a reminder—that our large corporations have long since ceased to be private institutions, in any meaningful sense of the term. It has become commonplace to say that our companies today are accountable not only to their shareholders and their employees but also to what is amorphously called the public, which may mean anything from the Sierra Club to the Federal Trade Commission or a congressional committee. Business, as we say, has become everybody's business. And this means that the self-examination to which I have referred has been, and must continue to be, a very public affair.

The striking thing about our corporate system, in fact, is that it has become so open, so vulnerable to pressure, so tentative about its future, that it is scarcely a system in the ideological sense at all. Our managers continue to talk about private enterprise and the market economy and the entrepreneurial spirit, but they are aware that these concepts are changing and, indeed, that change has become the one great constant of corporate life.

Now this, it seems to me, is a specific case in point. The morality flap has been—among other things—a test of our ability to adapt. It was hardly a pleasant experience, but I think it fair to say that the results, for the vast majority of our companies, have been conclusive.

The key to the process, of course, was disclosure. We did not do it willingly or happily, but we did it. And many companies disclosed not only what they were legally required to disclose, as publicly held companies, but a great deal more. They were painfully aware that personal and professional damage would result, but they had come to understand that these were lesser evils compared to a cover-up and the festering infection it brings. And this, of course, helps to explain something that so puzzled our friends abroad—why, once we had become aware of the problem of improper payments, we indulged in what appeared to them a veritable orgy of self-flagellation.

The point is that there is no way, in a society such as ours, with the media, the regulatory agencies, and the congressional committees all competing for public attention, to ensure that disclosure will be measured, moderate, and in proper perspective. It tends to be a rough and tumble business under the best of circumstances, and in this case, of course, it had all the elements of a prime time spectacular—royalty, money, sex, and foreign intrigue.

That much is history. But disclosure, after all, was only the beginning of the process. While the media storms were raging and desks were being pounded on Capitol Hill, the real business of adaptation got under way. Corporate counsel began working their way through the stacks of questionnaires which arrived, inevitably, from the IRS and the SEC. Boards of directors met and set up procedures—such as audit committees—to measure the extent of their problem, if indeed they had a problem. Our business leaders made some responsible speeches. The Conference Board, the trade association, the public interest groups formed committees, organized meetings and seminars, issued publications. In short, corporate America agonized over the problem, analyzed it, determined that it was real, and methodically set to work.

For a professional manager, remember, a problem is manageable by definition, otherwise it ceases to exist. So it is not surprising that the philosophical aspects of the morality issue have been left, on the whole, to the academics, journalists, and other outside observers. Corporate people have concerned themselves with practical procedures. Somewhere out there, say, a harbormaster is holding up a shipment of perishable goods. He is demanding $5,000, failing which our shipment, which is worth twenty times as much, will be totally lost. What do we do? The harbormaster, of course, is the prime minister's brother-in-law, so there is no point in complaining to the police.

The answer, perhaps, is in Kant's categorical imperative or somewhere in Spinoza, but the American corporate response—lacking these resources—has been simply to review corporate policies to ensure that they were appropriate and effective in cases of this kind and then to see to it that these policies were understood and applied. Effective, of course, is a relative word, and every story could not have a happy ending; but the techniques were the familiar ones: definition, decision, communication, and control.

Now, obviously, there is far more to the problem of corrupt practices than is suggested in the example I have given. And, for that matter, there are many other issues which affect the moral and ethical climate in which we work—regulatory issues, for example, tax rules, industrial and community relations—and these are no less important for being, at the moment, less prominently in the public view. But the point I have been making is simply that we do have the resources to deal with them, which means to understand them, reduce them to size, and manage them, just as we are doing with the problem of improper payments abroad.

And this, perhaps, is enough to explain why this problem now seems to be receding into the past. We have folded it into our standard operating procedures. And in that sense it is under control.

Let me conclude by briefly noting what our own company has done to ensure that our business is conducted, here and abroad, in a legal and ethical manner.

First, we made it clear, publicly and within the company, that we insisted on a simple, unambiguous, and uncompromising standard of honesty in our operations. This always had been Bendix policy, but we took pains to reinforce it. No bribes, no kickbacks, no illegal contributions or improper payments of any kind.

Second, we organized the audits and other procedures which were required to determine how vulnerable we were on this issue. As it happened, we found the company in excellent shape.

Third, because our audits revealed some confusion as to definitions—the difference between a bribe, for example, and a *de minimus* payment such as a tip or a Christmas gift to a customer or a supplier—we refined our definitions, established more detailed guidelines, and carefully stipulated approval and reporting procedures.

Fourth, we began the task of spelling out these more detailed instructions and communicating them throughout the company.

Fifth, and finally, since we are a multinational corporation, Bendix Corporation conforms its policies and practices to the voluntary guidelines adopted on 21 June 1976 by the Organization for Economic Cooperation and Development. These guidelines, negotiated by the 24 member states of the OECD over a period of several years, define the rights and responsibilities of international companies with respect to such matters as investment, taxation, intercompany pricing, the environment, and employment.

This is what we are doing. I have outlined our program not because we are exemplary in this respect, but simply because I am more familiar with it than with the procedures of other companies. With our 80,000 employees around the world and the highly diversified structure of our company, it will be some time before we are entirely sure that everyone has got the word—and that everyone is living by it. In fact, we may never be entirely sure. But we can be sure we are doing what it is within our power to do.

In Toynbee's terms, there has been a challenge, and we are making our response. But, of course, the challenge did not begin with the problem of improper payments, nor will it end there. And the significance of the response, as I have tried to show, is that what was called a great crisis of morality and ethics, a threat to the survival of our business system, has been reduced—and properly so—to a series of practical problems.

Now, finally, what does this do for our moral and ethical climate? Well, that remains to be seen. Ernest Hemingway liked to define courage as *grace under pressure*. What we have been talking about is something akin to it, in a modest way: good sense under pressure. It does not solve all our problems, but I believe it will help to clear the air.

PURPOSEFUL SKIMMING COMPREHENSION CHECK: "The Moral and Ethical Climate in Today's Business World"

Answer the following questions:

1. According to the author, the moral and ethical climate in today's business world is:

   a. _____ troubled and getting worse.

   b. _____ troubled but getting better.

   c. _____ excellent.

2. List at least three ways the Bendix Corporation has attempted to conduct its business in a legal and ethical manner.

   1.

   2.

   3.

Check your answers with the Answer Key.

3
The Main Idea

INTRODUCTION

No doubt you have heard it said that some people cannot see the forest for the trees. This adage can be applied to many readers. When they read, they are able to identify and remember details (the trees) but they do not "see" the main point (the forest). One reason for this is that teachers, from grammar school to graduate school, have encouraged students to read for detail by asking questions that require a highly specific response. You probably remember such questions as: "Give me the date . . .," "Name the character . . .," "List the places . . .," "Identify the six characteristics of. . .." Even though such detail questions are often necessary, they discourage us from reading for main points, which, in the final analysis, is the message the writer expects the reader to get from his writing. The author usually gives details a secondary role; they are used to help explain and clarify main ideas.

In the section following, note that you are not told to locate the main idea by "finding the topic sentence." This approach is too mechanical and discourages the reader from mentally interacting with the writer. Furthermore, many writers do not use topic sentences; their main ideas are often implied. You are encouraged to use the technique described below for comprehending the main idea. When readers use this technique, they rarely miss the main idea.

HOW TO FIND THE MAIN IDEA

1. *Find the Topic*—Writers usually choose to write about people, things, or concepts. *Who* or *What* they write about is the topic. You can usually determine the topic of a passage by finding a word or phrase that is repeated several times.

2. *Find the Main Idea*—To expand on their topic, writers make a certain point or generalization. This is their main idea. You can usually determine the main idea of a passage by answering the question, "*What* does the author tell me about his topic?"

3. *Complete the Check Out*—Writers support or prove their main ideas by using facts, details, examples, illustrations, dates, and sometimes analogies. If you find none of these to help explain an author's main idea, then you probably have failed to state the main idea correctly. You can usually complete your check out by asking, "Does the author tell me more about the main idea? Am I told *When, Where, How,* or *Why?* Does the writer give me any examples?"

Now that you know the three steps, practice them. Let's go through the process together. First, read the passage below.

Most managers fail to seek ideas from subordinates. Many of those who do, fail to listen effectively when the ideas requested are offered. Discouraging as this conclusion may seem, there is ample evidence of its validity. If you have doubt, ask ten people below middle management in any organization; the results will be devastating. The reasons for this self-defeating behavior range from psychological to pragmatic implications. Some managers are simply self-centered and uninterested in the view of others—particularly their subordinates. Others honestly feel that on many matters the views of their subordinates would be neither relevant nor particularly helpful. Still others fear the impression of weakness that they suspect would result from asking the opinion of a subordinate. Some who solicit opinions with sincere intent find it difficult if not impossible to pay serious attention to the suggestions that are forthcoming.[1]

What is our topic? The word and its pronoun that is repeated is *managers*. Now that you know that *managers* is the topic, you should ask, "*What* does the paragraph say about managers?" The paragraph says that most managers fail to seek ideas from their subordinates. This is the main idea. Your answer to the question "*What* does the author say about the topic?" almost always will give you the main idea.

How can you be sure that your statement of the main idea is correct? Check it out by asking additional questions. "Does the author explain or tell me more about the main idea?" "Does the author tell me *Where, When, Why, How,* or give me some examples?"

Let's check out our main idea. In this paragraph, the author tells us *Why*. According to the passage, most managers fail to seek ideas from their subordinates because some are self-centered; others feel the views of subordinates are irrelevant; some believe seeking out ideas from subordinates is a sign of weakness. These, then, are details that tell us more or give us specifics about the main idea. We have checked it out and now know that the other information (details) in the paragraph did give us more specifics about our main idea.

This may seem like a lengthy process, but you will find that after you have practiced the technique a few times, the main ideas will come to you very quickly. You will also begin to see that whole paragraphs sometimes do nothing more than give details to support a main idea. In some cases, depending on your purpose for reading the selection, these paragraphs can be skimmed. Later, you will also see how main ideas fit into a writer's total organizational pattern. This will be an invaluable learning experience that will undoubtedly improve your reading rate and comprehension.

Now, try picking out the main idea of the thirteen short passages that follow. After completing four or five paragraphs, check your answers with the Answer Key. Any reasonable paraphrasing of the answers listed in the answer key should be considered correct. If you answered the first five correctly, you probably can skip the remainder of this chapter and move on to chapter four.

SELECTED PASSAGES

1. The fallacy of the SOB-type of management is that it has everybody running so scared that nobody will take a chance on making a mistake. When a man feels that, if he makes a mistake, he is out, he will spend his time trying to keep from making mistakes, not in trying to improve the work of his department. Let the man know that you want him to make decisions. Explain that he will make mistakes. You expect that. If he is right a certain percentage of the time, he is doing as well as management generally. I've seen figures that say if a manager is right in 58 per cent of his decisions, he is doing fine. That leaves a lot of margin for error, doesn't it? Don't expect all of your men to be up to your standards. They shouldn't be, you're the top man. Try to train them to come up to your standards, but don't rail at them if they can't make it. Admit your mistakes, you've been wrong at times and will be again. Use the "I made a mistake like that once" technique to help a man over a bad time after he has pulled a boo-boo. Men will make mistakes if they make decisions. Recognize this and encourage the decision making even though you know the mistakes will come.[2]

Topic:

Main Idea:

Check Out (Examples, When, Where, How, or Why):

2. You also have an organization weakness if one or more of the positions that your people hold require unique combinations of abilities. Some salesmen, for example, have excellent ability to open new accounts but poor ability to provide routine service to existing accounts. To resolve this problem, some firms have two kinds of sales positions: one with responsibility primarily for new business and the other with responsibility primarily for servicing existing business. In production, some managers have excellent ability to start up new facilities but poor ability to manage a going operation. To resolve this problem, some firms establish two kinds of production management positions: one with responsibility for start-up activities (and other special projects) and the other with responsibility for managing a going operation.

If you are with a nonprofit organization, you may face a similar weakness in your organization structure. For example, clergymen are often expected to function both as ministers and as administrators even though they may have little interest or training in administration. In universities, professors are sometimes expected to be both excellent teachers and excellent researchers.[3]

Topic:

Main Idea:

Check Out (Examples, When, Where, How, or Why):

3. The person who holds an "assistant" position often does not really know what his own responsibilities are, and those with whom he works are generally even more in doubt. An assistant may substitute for his boss or he may do detail work or he may carry out special projects or he may have clear-cut managerial responsibility. Too often an assistant functions at the pleasure of his boss. I know one firm that has several "Assistant Manager" positions each of which is supposed to have similar duties and responsibilities. In some instances the assistant is training to replace his boss and has line authority; in other instances, the assistant functions in a staff capacity by doing his boss's paper work. A good secretary can often perform most of the duties of the so-called "assistant manager."[4]

Topic:

Main Idea:

Check Out (Examples, When, Where, How, or Why):

4. Regardless of what field you are in, when you begin a new business, you must be concerned with your image in order to get where you want to get successfully and quickly. You must remember that you are competing with many established businesses that have proven track records, while you are an unknown quantity. In order to be able to compete effectively, you need an image, and you must carefully plan out the one you want. Don't wait for one to "happen" automatically. You'll eventually have an image whether you want one or not, but by conscientiously developing the right one, I strongly believe you will get what you want much more effectively and in a shorter period of time.[5]

Topic:

Main Idea:

Check Out (Examples, When, Where, How, or Why):

5. In spite of what often appears to be rampant promiscuity in our present American society, infidelity is still frowned upon by a great number of people. While I don't intend to discuss the moral aspects of such activities, I do believe that the subject of sex is quite relevant in this discussion of images. You must consider the reactions of others and how you appear from their point of view. If you are playing around, you must surely realize that there are a significant number of people who, when they become familiar with your promiscuous reputation, will mark you down as an individual of poor character. Just how much this attitude will affect you is anybody's guess, but even if only a handful of important people feel this way toward you, your career can be hindered or ultimately ruined. When you consider its consequences, promiscuity in business can create such a damaging image that your long-range success may be severely diminished. Although your sexual conquests may sound good in the locker room, do you really think you'll win any popularity contests by establishing a reputation as a tomcat? Do you personally have great respect for such an individual? Is this the kind of person you would trust? Many so-called modern-thinking people loathe such conduct, even though they pretend to go along with the swinger mentality.[6]

Topic:

Main Idea:

Check Out (Examples, When, Where, How, or Why):

6. After a three-and-a-half-month period of intense planning, the headquarters was blueprinted, built, and finally opened in March of 1971. Hailed by McDonald's as a new departure in "open planning"—and as a manifestation of the company's open attitude—it also got rave reviews from the outside. The magazine *Building Design and Construction* characterized the 110,000 square feet of workspace as "order without rigidity, vigor without frenzy, freedom without chaos, continuity without monotony." *Interiors* magazine saw it as "a breakthrough" in the open-plan corporate environment, and went on to praise its "status-free" atmosphere, in which those at all levels of the hierarchy shared 3,050 windows and got furnishings of the same top quality.[7]

Topic:

Main Idea:

Check Out (Examples, When, Where, How, or Why):

7. The first of these is that the process of job restructuring, reform, and general tinkering with the old principles is going out of public view at many companies. Increasingly, the situation in which a company like Volvo, General Foods, or Bankers Trust proudly lets the world know about its experiments is giving way to a situation in which companies are telling little, if anything, about their experiences. In fact, some of those who were eager to tell about their initial experiments—mostly small-scale—are now granting very little information as the lessons of those experiments are applied throughout the organization.

At first glance, it would seem that this silence is a reflection of the fear of letting the world know about something which may fail. While this is certainly a factor in some situations, the major reason is that change is proving to be such a windfall to those implementing it that the change process is beginning to be seen as an important proprietary development—akin to the discovery of a new product or industrial process. For many companies, finding a path to employee satisfaction, lower turnover, and higher productivity is looked upon as a highly valued discovery not to be shared with competitors. Some see little sense in giving away what they have pioneered at any price, while others have gone into the unlikely business of job consulting with others for a fee. Among those who have hung out shingles as job consultants are The Travelers, American Airlines, Lockheed and Ralston Purina.[8]

Topic:

Main Idea:

Check Out (Examples, When, Where, How, or Why):

8. In the long run, the most significant impact from zero-base budgeting will occur in the middle and lower levels of management, where managers will have to evaluate in detail their planning, operations efficiency, and cost effectiveness on a continuous basis. In industry, corporate profits should be improved because high priority new programs will be funded in part by improved efficiency and elimination or reduction of those current activities of lesser importance to the organization. In government, the taxpayer should benefit because high priority new programs can be funded at the expense of obsolete or redundant programs without significant reductions in service.[9]

Topic:

Main Idea:

Check Out (Examples, When, Where, How, or Why):

9. You can't always tell. While you can't find the time to run down every lead—and so must apply a certain amount of common sense screening—don't discard possibilities out of hand because of bias or set notions about the people who have provided them. Some of the most plausible volunteer counselors give you nothing but hot air while some of the most unlikely sources can render you invaluable service. So make a rough evaluation of leads and suggestions, yes, but concentrate on their intrinsic logicality, not the source from which they come.[10]

Topic:

Main Idea:

Check Out (Examples, When, Where, How, or Why):

10. This is why American businessmen are so frequently surprised by the less than reverent attitude toward organization charts manifested by their

counterparts in other lands. But the fact is that foreign companies are just not as hung up on the little boxes as we are in the U.S. And they seem to be doing all right. David Granick, in *The European Executive* (Doubleday, 1962), commented that "The French dislike for organization charts seems closely related to . . . the strong national emphasis on individuality at all management levels. A boxing in of responsibilities, authority, and personal requirements seems to leave no room for the individuality of the man filling the post. It lays his personality on a Procrustian bed, cutting or stretching it to size. In a social system where individuality is considered of prime importance, this approach appears as a violation of basic values."[11]

Topic:

Main Idea:

Check Out (Examples, When, Where, How, or Why):

11. Perhaps one day it will be possible to formulate scientific laws for the generating of creative ideas, but that day has not yet come. Nevertheless, if you look back on a number of creative movements there is one pattern which seems to repeat itself, the pattern of a leader who is himself a highly creative person working with a small nucleus around him, a creative group. It is by no means the only way to bring about change, or to seize and fashion to your own ends change which is happening, but it seems to have been consistently successful. There are numerous examples ranging from Charlemagne and Henry II to Lenin and John F. Kennedy. Sometimes, if the group is successful, it may grow until it appears to be very large; but if you look closely you find that only a small number belong to the central nucleus, however much power and responsibility other people may have in particular but limited areas of the enterprise. Groups of this same kind can be found in art, in science, in military history, in social reform and other areas of life. They also happen in industry; but not all that often in my experience, but if you have ever worked in or close to one, you recognize others at once; and if you observe them and talk to people inside and outside them, you find they share a number of important characteristics which also seem to have been shared by the creative groups of the past.[12]

Topic:

Main Idea:

Check Out (Examples, When, Where, How, or Why):

12. The future belongs to those leaders of organizations who can demonstrate the necessary managerial skill and imagination to cope with the enormous changes around them. All organizations in these changing times are confronted by the challenges of changing their structures, their patterns of management, and their leadership styles, if they are to function more effectively and attain their objectives. The days of the soulless corporation, the heartless capitalist, or the robber baron are gone. Their place has been taken by the enlightened management concerned with human behavior and social relationships—as well as technology and production.[13]

Topic:

Main Idea:

Check Out (Examples, When, Where, How, or Why):

13. The greater the distance between the leader and his followers the greater the danger of loss in credibility. What consultant has not listened to complaints about the unbelievable behavior of a top management that sits in an office a thousand miles from the operation. If the definition of leadership as a process of influencing is acceptable, then the gap between the leader and the led cannot be so great that it negates this influence. An excessive gap, either physical or psychological, renders the influence of the leader impotent. Some leaders have been known to argue that familiarity breeds stickiness and loss of respect. We have observed that those leaders who fear closeness are by and large the same people who doubt their ability to influence without resorting to the power of their position.[14]

Topic:

Main Idea:

Check Out (Examples, When, Where, How, or Why):

SOURCES OF SELECTIONS

1. Charles D. Flory, and R. Alec MacKenzie, *The Credibility Gap In Management* (New York: Van Nostrand Reinhold Company, 1971, p. 90 90.

2. Edward J. Hegarty, *How to Succeed In Company Politics* (New York: McGraw-Hill Book Company, 1964), pp. 235–236.

3. Raymond O. Loen, *Manage More By Doing Less* (New York: McGraw-Hill Book Company, 1971), p. 74.

4. *Ibid.,* p. 75.

5. Robert L. Shook, *Winning Images* (New York: MacMillan Publishing Company, Inc., 1977), pp. 15–16.

6. *Ibid.,* pp. 105–106.

7. Paul Dickson, *The Future of the Workplace* (New York: Weybright and Talley, 1975), p. 288.

8. *Ibid.,* pp. 345–346.

9. Peter A. Pyhrr, *Zero-Based Budgeting* (New York: John Wiley and Sons, 1973), p. xiii.

10. John J. Tarrant, *Getting Fired:—An American Ordeal,* (New York: Van Nostrand Reinhold, 1974), p. 57.

11. *Ibid.,* p. 127.

12. Anthony Jay, *Management and Machiavelli* (New York: Holt, Rinehart and Winston, 1967), pp. 104–105.

13. Alfred J. Marrow, David G. Bowers, and Stanley E. Seashore, *Management By Participation* (New York: Harper and Row, 1967), p. 247. 247.

14. Flory and MacKenzie, p. 77.

4
Organizational Patterns: Introduction

Examine the set of numbers that follow. Allow yourself twenty seconds to memorize them. Then write the set of numbers as accurately as possible. Check your answer for accuracy before continuing with the next paragraph.

1776555512126024365

How did you do? People who can accurately reproduce the numbers usually organize and reduce the group of numbers into meaningful units or associations. For example, 1776 is grouped and associated with the American Revolution; 5551212 is grouped and associated with the long distance information number; 60 and 24 are grouped and associated with minutes in an hour and hours in a day; and 365, the final group, is associated with the number of days in the year. Perhaps you made different associations.

Alan Sack of New York's College Skills Center calls this process the "law of reduction of units," a concept he learned from Irving Lorge at Teachers College, Columbia University. Thus, when you read articles, you can read them faster and with better comprehension and retention when you reduce the entire article into smaller, meaningful units. One way of doing this is to reduce the articles into units of main ideas. However, you will become an even more efficient reader when you can take the main ideas of several paragraphs, combine them into a few major points or generalizations, and associate them with the components of an organizational pattern. Readers who can do this read faster, comprehend better, and retain information longer.

Let's try another simple experiment. Study the four designs that follow for about thirty seconds. Then decide which of the four you could reproduce accurately without looking back at the designs.

No doubt you would find that you would be able to reproduce

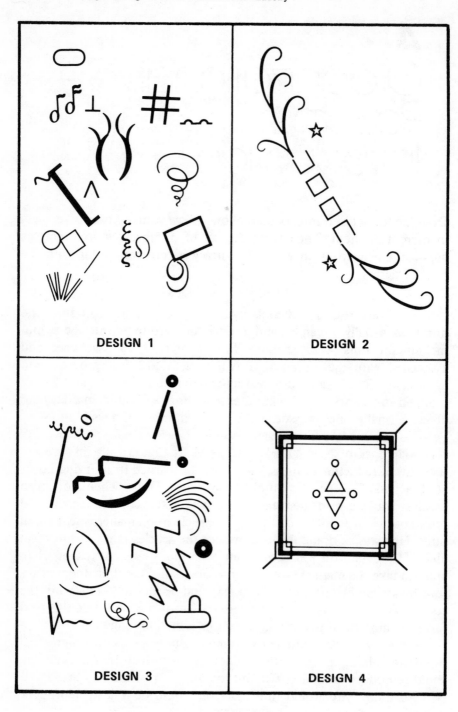

DESIGN 1   DESIGN 2

DESIGN 3   DESIGN 4

designs 2 and 4. Why? The reason is that each of these two designs follows a particular pattern; the markings have been grouped together so that they make some sense to you. Good readers are able to do this with ideas they encounter in their reading. Poor readers, on the other hand, fail to perceive the writer's organizational pattern. When they finish reading a selection, they end up with a bunch of unconnected ideas. What they have read appears confusing and senseless, just like designs 1 and 3.

The next three chapters focus on how to develop a more organized and efficient approach to reading by learning the basic organizational patterns, which are Problem-Solution; Persuasive; Data Pattern I: Informational; and Data Pattern II: Instructional.

5
Problem-Solution Pattern

INTRODUCTION

No matter where you work, problems are likely to arise. Discussion about any given *problem* inevitably leads to an analysis of the *effects* of the problem, the *cause* of the problem, and some alternative *solutions* to the problem. For example, one author wrote about a *problem* concerning poor employee morale. The *effects* were low worker output and a subsequent loss in the company's profit. The *causes* were that the workers were too closely supervised and that their goals were in opposition to those of management. The *solution* was for management to discover ways of involving workers in planning, organizing, and controlling their own work.

It is natural for a writer to analyze a problem by following the problem-solution pattern. This type of analysis appears often in business publications, popular magazines, and newspapers such as the *Wall Street Journal*. For example, in a recent *Wall Street Journal* article written in this organizational pattern, the *problems* were that it is difficult to get a phone installed in Paris, phone service is poor, and rates are high. The *effects* were that large numbers of people were frustrated and businesses lost money. The *causes* were that the post office and Telecommunications Ministry are unable to meet the public's demands. The *solutions* included the formation of the French Association of Telecommunications users, who will study the problem; meanwhile, some people use the local post office, which guarantees delivery of messages within two hours.

The problem-solution type of organizational pattern is easy to identify because the problem is often stated in the title of the article. For example, some of the titles of problem-solution articles included in the book are: "The Trouble With Drugs," "The Trouble With Open Offices," and "No Vacancy, Apartments Are Scarce." If the problem is not identified in the title, it will appear in the first few paragraphs of the article. Once you realize that the article deals with some type of a *problem,* your purpose in reading is to seek out the *causes, effects,* and *solutions* to the problem. The causes and effects are most often found in the middle of the article, and the solutions to the problem most often are found at the end of the article.

The diagram shown in Figure 1 illustrates how main ideas and details relate to the various components of the problem-solution pattern.

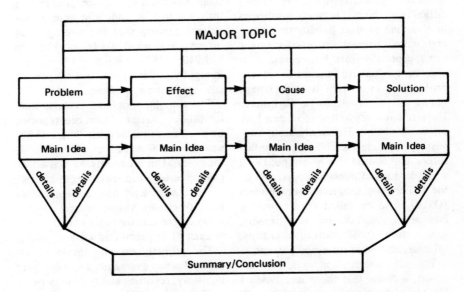

Figure 1 Relationship of Main Ideas to Problem-Solution Pattern

INSTRUCTIONS FOR ANALYZED READING: "Skyrocketing Product Liability Losses Worry U.S. Business"

Read the following problem-solution article at your normal rate and then study the analysis of it that follows. You should then be ready to meet the challenge of reading other problem-solution articles at a more rapid rate and with good comprehension.

Analyzed Reading

Skyrocketing Product Liability Losses Worry U.S. Business

The Editors, Commerce America

A major problem has developed for U.S. manufacturers in the field of product liability reflected in mounting damage claims, soaring court judgments, skyrocketing insurance premiums, rising insurance cancellations, increasing difficulty on the part of many companies in obtaining product liability insurance, and acute financial distress for many firms, especially small businesses.

A comprehensive discussion of the problem is embodied in a 233-page report on the results of a Commerce Department study to develop a data base on the problem. The study team canvassed 140 trade associations, manufacturers, and distributors by phone, using a standard set of questions approved by the Office of Management and Budget (OMB). Also consulted were insurance companies, state insurance departments, and a number of insurance groups, officials, and other informed persons.

The data, although meager, says the report, indicate that there is a product liability problem which is extensive and increasing. However, the lack of comprehensive data prevented the study team from performing a definitive analysis of the causes and effects of the problem and its severity, or to properly analyze any of the 21 remedies proposed by various industry and government groups.

The review established that many industries are experiencing difficulty in obtaining product liability insurance, especially in the case of small businesses. Industry sectors that have been severely affected include machine tools, industrial chemicals, pharmaceuticals, general aviation, and many sectors of capital equipment.

THE PROBLEM

The average loss per product liability claim has risen at a much greater rate than inflation. A leading insurance consultant reports that the average loss increased from $11,644 in 1965 to $79,940 in 1973, a jump of 686 percent in eight years compared to a 60 percent advance in the general price index.

The combined loss and expense ratio for product liability insurance reported by the Insurance Service Office (ISO) was about 200 percent in 1973. That is, for every $1 in premiums, $2 was either paid or reserved for payment of claims.

The cost of legal defense for product liability claims has increased so that today it accounts for more than 30 cents of each $1 of premiums written.

The property casualty insurance industry has just experienced its worst year in history, reporting statutory underwriting losses for 1975 which could exceed $4.2 billion. This follows 1974 losses of $2.6 billion, which were coupled with a $6 billion capital loss in the 1974 bear market.

Product liability insurance premium volume is already estimated to be more than that of medical malpractice. One report estimated the total at $1.5 billion for 1975, or double the $750 million for malpractice.

Loss of surplus by insurers coupled with substantial statutory underwriting losses in product liability have caused many insurers to restrict their underwriting in this area.

Miscellaneous liability produced a combined loss and expense ratio of 116.2 in 1975, or a statutory underwriting loss of $620 million. That is, for every dollar of general liability premium there was a statutory underwriting loss of 16 cents. Miscellaneous or general liability includes product liability, medical malpractice, and various other coverages.

Product liability insurance is estimated by various sources to account for about 40 percent of the total reported miscellaneous liability premiums. Using the estimated $3.7 billion miscellaneous liability premiums written for 1975, and adjusting this figure upward to reflect excess-surplus and package product liability protection, produces total written premiums for miscellaneous liability of at least $4 billion, not including product liability experience for self insurers.

Using 40 percent of this figure, total product liability premiums would have been about $1.6 billion in 1975.

ROOTS OF THE PROBLEM

In discussing the causes of the problem, the report points out that one of the most critical areas of concern for the business community has been its liability for products sold.

The trend towards increased litigation became more pronounced in the mid-sixties and has been increasing at an ever-expanding rate. Then too, as the number of suits has increased, so have the amounts of the judgments against manufacturers, processors, wholesalers and retailers. No one in the marketing and producing chain has been immune.

The reasons for this increase in product liability and product claims are probably three-fold: changing legal concepts, the growth of consumerism, and the relationship to employee injury and worker compensation.

The changing legal concepts, namely, diminution of the right of privity, the trend towards absolute liability, and the increased tendency toward class actions, have made it easier for a claimant to sustain legal action and to collect damages. These trends have served to make industry more responsible for its actions. Contingency fees paid to attorneys also are alleged to be increasing the number of product liability suits.

The growth of consumerism, or the increased demand on the part of the consumer for safer or cleaner products, has given impetus to changing legal concepts.

The shift towards strict liability of producers has occurred at a time when employees are electing to receive worker compensation benefits which must be provided by employers and then sue the producer of the equipment or product alleged to have caused the injury.

U.S. business has been faced with an upward spiraling growth of product liability claims while the amounts paid in damages for product liability losses have also been increasing.

Today, product liability provides that manufacturers or sellers of goods are charged with a duty of care to the users of these items. If this duty of care is not satisfied, the manufacturer or seller will be liable for any injuries sustained by the user of the product.

For many years, the legal principles of product liability remained relatively constant, with only minor changes. However, over the last few years there have been a significant number of changes which are causing problems for the manufacturer, the seller and the liability insurers. Changes in the thinking of our society have had a strong influence on judicial reasoning in product liability cases. There is without question a developing strong public interest in human safety which has assisted in the development of two growing concepts.

The first concept is that the manufacturer, and not the injured consumer, is in the best position to bear the burden of accidental injuries and commercial losses caused by a defective product. The manufacturer can purchase some form of insurance or go uninsured. He can also choose to absorb losses which occur, or pass them on to other consumers by increasing the cost of the product.

A second concept is the theory that anyone who enters a special field of manufacturing does not merely warrant that he will conduct his business as a reasonable man but is alleging that he possesses the knowledge and skill of an expert and that his product will be free of defect.

As a result of these concepts and due to the increasing public interest in human safety, the law of product liability is moving toward strict liability on the part of the manufacturer for any item he produces. There is a growing trend to impose liability on the manufacturer even if he exercised his best judgment and utilized the best material in making the product.

The report points out that the manufacturer's duty to warn of the dangerous characteristics of his product has been expanded to a point where it creates a serious problem for many manufacturers, since they must anticipate all possible and reasonable ways that their product could be misused.

It is important, the report adds, that the manufacturer recognize that many different persons of all ages and a variety of educational backgrounds may utilize his product, and thus the directions and warnings must be intelligible to all. When disputes arise, the court decides each case on its own facts, and in each instance the jury makes a careful examination of the label and the instructions that accompanied the product.

Lawsuits involving design defects are relatively new. Historically, the courts were most reluctant to impose liability because of design defects but today the situation is in the process of changing. In establishing the fact of a negligent design, the consumer usually must prove one or more of the following: (1) there are insufficient safety devices in the product; (2) there is an inherent danger in the product as a result of the design; and (3) to comply with the design, the manufacturer had to utilize materials which were not strong enough to comply with accepted standards.

The report states that manufacturers can anticipate a greater number of claims, and should also anticipate that many of these claims will be successful and that substantial judgments will be awarded.

REACTION

Increasing product liability claims and insurance problems have led manufacturers to take steps to reduce product liability exposure and to transfer premium costs to product prices. Such changes in manufacture, marketing, and product development have included: product redesign and testing; product recall and special equipment servicing; increased reports by manufacturers on product testing, product modification and service calls; retrofitting products with safety devices; increased emphasis on quality control; reducing expensive advertising claims and warranties; increased emphasis on safety engineering and loss control; improved reporting on product-related injuries.

The increasing number of product liability lawsuits, the report says, is affecting the legal system. Court case backlogs are lengthening because of the number of lawsuits, and the average time that product liability lawsuits remain open is increasing. Also, multiple product liability suits are becoming more prevalent. Wide variations in product liability case law among the states are further complicating the problem.

Irwin Gray, in his book entitled *Product Liability: A Management Response,* lists the following ways in which some firms have undertaken to protect themselves:

- Developed legal defenses by working closely with the Defense Research Institute, which provides help in locating expert witnesses, publishes material for management and defense attorneys, and aids in locating useful publications and records.

- Established national standards organizations; adopted federal or state agency standards as performance minimums; made increasing use of independent laboratory certifications, such as those of underwriters' laboratories.

- Adopted the standards of national societies such as American Society of Mechanical Engineers, the American Society for Quality Control, and the Institute of Electrical and Electronics Engineers; and set up manufacturers' captive organizations to perform independent testing or guaranteeing of merchandise.

- Lobbied to forestall consumer legislation. Other measures have included tightened up advertising; tightened up design; closer control on manufacturing methods and personnel; better quality control procedures; increased product liability insurance; expanded and improved legal staff; expanding the risk management function; establishing independent corporate level safety watchdog committees; and hiring independent consultants.

Insurance companies, the report explains, also have adopted a number of measures to reduce their exposure to product liability claims, such as: more stringent underwriting for existing and potential insureds; declining to write insurance for certain products and industry sectors; use of "prohibited" quotation lists; cancelling high risk policies; reduction in coverage limits; changes in policy wording and form to limit actual insurance coverage; introduction of layers of coverage; suggestions that manufacturers institute specific loss control procedures; suggestions to insureds to improve product design, safety engineering, quality control, etc.; introduction of deductibles; home office underwriting control on product liability policies quotation on renewal; and revisions in claim audit and review.

ANALYZED READING ANALYSIS: "Skyrocketing Product Liability Losses Worry U.S. Business"

In this article, the writer's topic had to do with a problem; therefore, the problem-solution pattern was chosen as the vehicle to communicate the message. The important main ideas and details from the article are presented below. Notice how they are associated with the different components of the problem-solution pattern.

Pattern Component	**Main Ideas and Details**
Problem	Product liability is becoming more and more of a problem for manufacturers.
Effects	Manufacturers are faced with high legal costs, an increase in the volume of liability insurance, and average losses in claims that exceed the rate of inflation.
Causes	Legal concepts are changing, consumerism is growing, and employees are taking advantage of worker compensation when injured on the job.
Solutions	Manufacturers must guard against liability claims by: reducing liability exposure, pretesting products, using safety devices, working with the Defense Research Institute, establishing performance minimums, adopting standards of national societies, lobbying to forestall consumer legislation, etc.

INSTRUCTIONS FOR UNTIMED READING: "How to Stop Time-Waste on the Job"

Read the following selection. It is written in the problem-solution pattern. The problem is stated in the title. Your main purpose in reading this article is to determine the cause(s), effect(s), and solution(s) to the problem. After reading the selection, jot down your answers to the questions that follow. Check your answers with the Answer Key.

Untimed Reading

How to Stop Time-Waste on the Job
O. Mark Marcussen

American businesses waste more than $300 billion each year through poor work force management.

If this statement is startling, consider the following:

The work force today totals more than 90 million. The average annual income of each worker is more than $12,000, extra benefits included. Therefore, this work force represents a total annual payroll of more than $1 trillion.

Studies have found that, on the average, only 4.4 hours out of eight working hours per employee are used productively. Another 1.2 hours are lost because of personal and other unavoidable delays, and 2.4 hours are wasted as a result of poor work force management.

WHY PRODUCTIVITY IS LOST

Since the waste totals about 30 percent of total work time, it is at least a $300 billion problem for business.

Poor management is caused by a central management problem. Front-line managers are notoriously unprepared for the responsibility of utilizing human resources. Selected on the basis of technical skills, untrained in management techniques, and unchecked by quantitative measures, they are victims and perpetrators of that $300 billion waste.

Typically, a first-level supervisor has only a general idea of the priority of each task, how long it should take to complete it, and what the checkpoints are. Thus he can, and will, set his own pace as long as it is not unreasonable. His poor scheduling accounts for 35 percent of the productivity loss.

In addition, when front-line managers assign tasks with vague instructions, the average employee does not know what is expected and how the work should be done. Imprecise assignment accounts for another 25 percent of the loss.

The inability of management to balance staff against volume, to staff for less than peak loads, or to adjust staff in nonbusy hours creates periods where there is no work available for some employees. This accounts for 15 percent of the hours wasted through poor work force management.

Poor coordination of resources with material flow and lack of work discipline—starting late and quitting early—account for the remainder.

A PLANNED CURE

The need to increase worker productivity is endorsed by every businessman. But productivity is traditionally defined as plant productivity, where big investments are needed to increase total output.

Unused work force productivity is different. It can only be increased by a finite amount—say, from 15 to 30 percent. But, unlike plant productivity, the costs are minimal, and the increase takes only a comparatively short time to achieve.

The process used to reduce this nonproductive time is known as work force management, and it can be adopted by any company. It requires planning and seven basic steps.

These are:

Assign Responsibility for Planning and Scheduling

The responsibility for day-to-day administration of scheduling should be identified and assigned.

Develop and Conduct Ongoing Training Programs for Supervisors

All supervisors should be trained in management controls and basic functions of management. Supervisors should know general management principles, measurement techniques, and systems of planning and control.

Review the Company's Organization, Layout, Methods, Procedures, and Work Flow

A company's division and distribution of tasks can result in duplication and poorly coordinated activity. Considering a department's mission, rather than its structure, will help identify how elements can best be joined to attain greater productivity. Analyzing methods, procedures, and work flows will lead to adjustments which will increase productivity.

In one chemical plant, for example, employees in one department were performing a task which was repeated by another department. The first department regarded the task as fill-in work, the second considered it important. Upon review, the company eliminated the duplication.

Establish a Reporting System

A successful work force management program requires analysis, reporting, and implementation. Set up an effective reporting system. One method of accomplishing and tracking improvements is a steering committee, consisting of a senior executive, subordinate managers (if any), and the supervisor whose work is reviewed.

Develop a Measurement Base

Proper planning and scheduling of work requires a data base of consistent time-to-work relationships. Develop scheduling targets by work sampling, by detailed study, and by employee self-reporting of activities and work volume.

Measurement of work content is viewed as something mystical, devious, or threatening. To measure is to establish a time-to-work relationship for effective planning and scheduling. Measurement of work is not an end; it is a tool for accomplishing other management functions.

In one company, for example, management was concerned that the employees would resist measuring and establishing work standards. The employees, however, regarded measurement as a progressive move. They saw that the standards were objectively derived and reasonable, and they accepted them readily. Some employees expressed relief at "knowing what is expected."

Develop Schedule and Control Mechanisms

Measurement of work itself has little value. It becomes valuable only when used to monitor performance against it. Establish a scheduling system that visibly avoids potential peaks and valleys in the work load.

Test Your System

To discover and correct the flaws, test the system in operation and modify it to conform to actual day-to-day operations. Do not mistake resistance to change on the part of your employees for a basic flaw. Test the system thoroughly.

Although straightforward, the process of increasing work force productivity demands attention. Total planning, estimating, scheduling, assignment, follow-up, and control can be designed effectively by recognizing the interdependence of all these elements. The output of one employee becomes input to the next. And the size of the work force can be adjusted to the amount of work to be done.

UNTIMED READING COMPREHENSION CHECK: "How to Stop Time-Waste on the Job"

Directions: Answer the questions below.

1. What is the *problem?*

2. What are the *effects* of the problem?

3. List the *causes* of the problem.

4. What is the process suggested by the author to *solve* the problem?

Check your answers with the Answer Key.

INSTRUCTIONS FOR PACED READING: "The Trouble With Drugs"

One way in which readers can increase their reading rate is to use a technique known as *paced reading*. A reading rate is predetermined, and then the reader is encouraged to read at a pace that approximates the predetermined rate. For example, in this article, the predetermined rate is 400 words per minute; therefore, to read at that rate you would have to finish the article in 6 minutes and 30 seconds, or a total of 390 seconds. Ask someone to stop you after you have been reading for 6 minutes and 30 seconds. Then complete the comprehension questions that follow the article.

If you complete the article in fewer than 390 seconds, you can determine your reading rate by dividing the number of seconds it took you to read the article into the number of words in the article (approximately 2,600) and then multiplying by 60. For example, if you finished the article in 300 seconds, your reading rate for this selection would be 520 words per minute.

$$8.66 \times 60 = 519.9 = 520$$

$$
\begin{array}{r}
8.66 \\
300 \overline{)2600.00} \\
2400 \\
\hline
200.0 \\
180.0 \\
\hline
20.00 \\
18.00 \\
\end{array}
$$

Paced Reading

The Trouble With Drugs

Doris M. Baldwin

Mothers take them, soldiers take them, students, dropouts, sick folks take them, and so do jolly good fellows. In increasing numbers, people are into drugs—wet and dry, legal and illegal, in small and large doses. Can anyone kid himself into believing that when America goes to work in the morning it sheds its drug habit, like its pajamas, at home? Unlikely.

True, some employers know exactly how the drug problem is hurting their company, and they're moving to turn the situation around. Others may suspect an erosion of profits from that direction, but don't know what to do. Still other employers, shelling out money to cover drug-related losses, may not know what hit them.

In any case, some effective courses of action are open today to any employer anxious to preserve the health of his company as well as the health of his employees. He can go to technical journals, not the popular press where sensationalism might cloud the facts; he can learn what other companies are doing; and he can call on other experts to help devise a system that works for his company.

GETTING THE BASICS

It is important to begin with an understanding of the scope of the subject.

What is a drug? As defined by the U.S. Special Action Office for Drug Abuse Prevention, a drug is "a chemical substance that has an effect upon the mind and body." The most used and abused of legal drugs is the wet drug, alcohol; for many people, alcohol is addictive. (See *Job Safety & Health,* Dec. 1974). The major addicting dry drugs are members of the opium family, with heroin the heavyweight among them. By no means are all drugs addictive, but all may be harmful when taken to excess. Most abused are tranquilizers, pep pills, marihuana, cocaine, solvents that are sniffed, and hallucinogens like LSD.

All of these chemicals are mind-bending and mood-altering. In certain combinations or overdoses, some drugs are killers. But their initial attraction is undeniable: They make a person feel good at the start. With the current easy availability (and social approval) of fine booze and sophisticated drugs, plus the persuasiveness of commercials, it becomes more and more accepted to "cope chemically" with life's difficulties.

There may be no harm in that method of coping, up to a point. Legal and limited, drugs are often prescribed by doctors and can have a good effect. Illegal and overused, however, drugs can cause chaos of the costliest kind, especially on the work scene.

What can drug abuse among employees cost an employer? According to the size of the company and the degree to which drugs are used, losses could run into millions of dollars in absenteeism and lateness; slowdowns; sloppy work performance leading to flaws in the quality of produced goods; a contagion of drug taking; human injury; work days lost for medical treatment; damage to equipment and materials; higher insurance rates; and a sharp rise in crime, especially theft, on the premises.

Yet with all these threats hanging over his head, an employer shouldn't panic and overreact. Professional response to the presence of drug abusers in the plant should be kept in line with normal management reaction to any other potentially dangerous situation. The question is: How can the long-and short-term interests of the company best be served?

INDUSTRY OPTIONS

Two different answers are being heard from industry.

In the first, employers are actively excluding known users of dangerous drugs from their labor force by using reasonable means—usually an interview and a physical examination—to identify them. Should this type of employer discover an illegal drug user on the payroll, he's likely to fire him if possible.

In the second kind of response, an employer may also try to learn whether a worthy job applicant is or has been on dangerous drugs. If the drug use seems under control, this employer is likely to hire the person, train him and treat him like everyone else, and expect him to stay clean. In this type of plant, a rehabilitation program may be offered to anyone on the payroll who admits he has a problem he can't handle without help.

Reportedly only about 100 U.S. corporations out of 1.5 million have an active drug abuse control program. The number should increase as other companies learn of the success of most control programs in keeping valued workers on the job. But at present, management concern is expressed unevenly across the country.

One survey of the employee drug problems, conducted by *Industrial Rela-*

tions News, showed that of the companies responding—ranging in size from 275 employees to over 80,000—only 34 percent had any official policy on drugs. Among companies with a policy: 81 percent were using some means to try to find whether a job applicant had a history of drugs; and 51 percent fired an employee on the spot if they caught him violating company drug rules.

Obviously, no one on drugs is going to show up high at a personnel office or for his physical exam if he really wants the job, any more than an alcoholic would show up drunk. Hard-drug addicts have grown wise about concealing surface evidence of their habit, and adept at lying their way out of situations where an accusing finger might be pointed. One way of identifying drug users is by pre-employment screening.

"Most employers are anxious to eliminate the possibility of problems," says Julius Simon, associate director of the Laboratory for Chromatography, an independent laboratory in Flushing, N.Y., devoted to drug screening for industry. Of the 300 accounts the laboratory currently handles, "most are large companies and most are strongly unionized."

Simon continues: "Few companies have rehabilitation programs. If a pre-employment screening of urine shows positive results, employers generally do not hire the applicant, and they feel no obligation to hire him. The company is bound primarily to protect its property and employees." He says there is virtually no in-service testing, partly because unions ordinarily object to mandatory testing once a person is hired. The exception would be if an employee becomes ill on the job; should a supervisor have reason to suspect that the employee is on drugs, the company then may take steps to determine whether this is the case.

A few of the larger companies, Simon reports, have rehabilitation programs set up with the help of unions and funded by the government. Employees undergoing rehabilitation are kept on the job "as long as they're clean."

In the past five years, the Laboratory for Chromatography has amassed some half million statistics that could prove valuable to anyone doing a deep study of the subject; the collected data provide a complete demographic breakdown, plus the age and sex of people screened, the various drugs found, and in what percentages.

Statistics indicate that the drug situation is not declining, according to Simon. Users are moving from some of the hard drugs that are scarce to the soft drugs. Poly-drug or multiple-drug use is up; people who try one drug are likely to try several, sometimes in rotation, sometimes in combination. There's evidence of an alcohol/drug cycle, where a person depends on a couple of pills to get him to work in the morning and a couple of drinks to get to sleep at night.

"There's a basic difference between the alcoholic and the drug addict," Simon points out. "The alcoholic generally is a loner. But the drug addict requires company; he usually feels a need to bring others into his milieu." While the user may or may not try selling drugs around the plant to get money for his habit, he is likely, according to Simon, to be active in persuading others to take drugs with him.

The Laboratory for Chromotography provides clients with a checklist explaining how to handle results when the lab report comes back to the company's medical department. Not all laboratory discernment of drugs implies illegal drug use, or drug abuse; persons undergoing medical treatment for hypertension and diabetes, for example, may take drugs in substantial quantities. And it is important for the employer's personnel department to know about any such medication for these and other chronic diseases; the ailing employee might then be placed in a job where he is least likely to cause unnecessary risks to himself or fellow workers. In some areas, insulin or oral hypoglycemic agents used for the control of diabetes are considered in the same category as dangerous drugs; flying privileges, driving, or the operation of dangerous machinery may be prohibited to the user.

STAKES ARE HIGH

What exactly is it about drugs that makes them such a threat to employee health and safety?

According to the kind of drug taken, its quality and quantity, and its effect on the taker, human reaction to drugs can include any or a combination of the following, and one must imagine these effects in an employee working around high places, moving machinery, rolling stock, sharp instruments, or hazardous materials; drowsiness, euphoria, depression, hallucinations, panic, hyperactivity, irritability, belligerence, anxiety, irrational behavior, confusion, tremor, staggering, impairment of coordination, dizziness, distortion of space or time, abdominal cramps, nausea, convulsions, and unconsciousness.

Some drugs, like the barbiturates, can cause death from withdrawal. Others—morphine, heroin, codeine, cocaine—cause death from overdose.

Not all mind-bending drugs are bought in a drugstore or in the street. Some are provided by the employer. For example, paint thinners and other volatile solvents used in industry contain various chemicals of a dangerous nature. When sniffed extensively, these produce a clouded mental state that can develop into a coma; temporary blindness has

been reported. Death can occur when the solvent is inhaled without sufficient oxygen. Damage to bone marrow, kidneys, and lungs has also occurred.

How about the plant security problem presented by employees habituated to drugs?

In New York City, a study was made of crimes committed by drug addicts against employers and fellow workers. Participants in the study were 95 volunteers from residential communities for the treatment of drug abusers and addicts. All had been on drugs at the time the crimes were committed; the jobs they held ranged from messenger to college registrar, rigger to plant manager, stock clerk to security officer.

Asked whether they'd used drugs on the job, 91 or the 95 said yes; 40 explained that they hid in the lavatory to take their drugs.

Did they get other employees involved? Forty-eight of the 91 on-job users said they'd sold drugs to other employees; one steel mill worker used an abandoned area of the plant to peddle marihuana.

Thirty-seven admitted to stealing goods from the plant or office and selling them outside. Twenty-eight also said they stole money, checks, and bank deposits. One man forged a payroll. The pharmacy clerk stole prescriptions; an air conditioning installer burglarized customers' apartments; a truck driver stole from workers' lockers.

None of the employers of these addicts seemed aware of their drug involvement. Thirty of the addicts in the study were fired from their jobs, but only ordinary-sounding reasons were given for dismissal: lateness, absenteeism, inadequate job performance.

Some of the addicts—especially the older ones—got away with their peculiar behavior by saying they'd had too much to drink. This excuse was always acceptable to the boss.

With precaution, an addict can hold a job for a long time without attracting attention. However, as with alcoholism and other diseases, in the late stages of the disease of drug addiction, concealment becomes difficult and finally impossible.

By the time the ravages of disease are obvious, it's often too late to reclaim an employee to health and renewed productivity.

EARLY SIGNS

In a number of companies, the trend is to throw lifelines to people who may not be able to help themselves. The idea is to look for signs of illness early, while it's treatable and there's hope for rehabilitation.

In the course of a seminar "Drugs as a Management Problem," the American Management Association, New York, named some of the factors that may identify the user: slipping job performance, absenteeism, lateness, frequent trips to the washroom, AWOL from the work station. There may also be psychological or physiological manifestations, such as unexplained changes in behavior, dress, and disposition.

The employee's problem could be drugs or drinking; or it could also be other kinds of illness or personal anxiety over money, marriage, legal troubles. Maybe the employee simply doesn't like his boss, his working conditions, or the job he's been given to do!

PATHS AND PITFALLS

A leading expert on drug control plans insists that if a company program is limited only to alcoholism or dry drug abuse, discovery of abusers will be confined to advanced stages. Louis Presnall,

manager of the Behavioral Science Division of the National Loss Control Service Corporation, James S. Kemper Institute, Long Grove, Illinois, says the problem should be handled through the company's regular occupational health system.

According to Presnall, if a company program is aimed at just one ailment, and that one socially stigmatized—such as drug abuse or alcoholism—the sufferer may be embarrassed to acknowledge his need.

Where the work performance review procedure is good, that same central referral system should serve to uncover any ill or troubled person who isn't meeting job requirements. "Don't substitute any new procedures when you have a system that works for other problem areas," says Presnall. If a company doesn't have a good system for evaluating work performance, then it should create one.

Regarding an appropriate name for a drug control plan, Presnall says, "Call the program anything. It doesn't make any difference what you call it. What matters is how you run it. Announce the policy, begin the program, then mishandle just one early identified case—or let someone lose his job over drug use—and you lose the integrity of your program, for a while at least."

There's a danger that management will "red circle" certain jobs for rehabilitated drug abusers, a discriminatory practice, according to Presnall. Hiring and placing rehabilitated users should be integrated with all other hiring and placement.

Sometimes discrimination works in reverse: Sick people are coddled. Instead of a supervisor being helpful in requiring a good job performance of everyone, "some well-intentioned supervisors get their kicks from playing big daddy," says

Presnall. Attempts at playing counselor to the drug user, instead of sticking to the supervisory role, can delay getting an employee the help he needs.

As far as management is concerned, continues Presnall, "the scope of the problem and the scope of the control program extend only to the boundaries within which the worker's problem affects production and work performance." If a worker uses marihuana evenings or weekends and it doesn't interfere with his job, then it's out of bounds of company action.

"It's a false step to discharge an employee suspected or known to be on a drug," says Presnall. "Rather, consider how would you react if the misdemeanor were minor, and in another area of behavior. Don't let fear or hysteria cause you to overreact."

Instead of launching a "witch hunt," the wiser course of action is to bring the subject out into the open, like any other matter deserving public consideration.

One such cool approach was used by the L&N Railroad Company, Louisville. To open lines of communication with employees, drugs and their effects have been discussed at regular safety meetings. Foremen and supervisors were trained in preparation for the sessions. Pocket-sized narcotics identification guides were distributed among the various sections, divisions, and work crews as part of the educational process.

When a formerly taboo subject is introduced this way by management representatives, and views are exchanged, a lot of the scare is taken out and there's an opportunity to dispel myths and to encourage users to seek help.

The illegal aspect of certain drugs presents a problem. Louis Presnall suggests: "Deal with the legal aspect of drug abuse as you might with any other illegal act on company property. The company is not in the law enforcement business per se. Ask yourself: Can you *prove* possession or pushing of drugs? Do you want to prove it?" There is no pat answer, he says, but there should be no legal difficulty if a company follows guidelines consistent with any other violation of civil law on the premises.

In initiating a company policy for the rehabilitation of drug abusers, the concept of counselling available to all troubled people seems to work well. A certified physician or psychologist can generally assure patients that any discussion of drug abuse problems will be kept confidential. Persons actively under treatment also are usually assured of legal safeguards relating to the confidentiality of their treatment.

PACED READING COMPREHENSION CHECK: "The Trouble With Drugs"

Directions: Answer the questions below. Base your answers on the information included in the reading.

1. The *problem* discussed in this article is:

   a. _____ drinking on the job.

   b. _____ sleeping on the job.

   c. _____ the use of wet and dry drugs on the job.

2. The *effect* on the employee is:

   a. _____ a change in one's mood and a bending of one's mind.

   b. _____ loss of job.

   c. _____ loss of self-respect.

3. The *effect* on the employer is:

a. _____ great loss of money.

b. _____ great loss in prestige.

c. _____ great loss of interest in the company.

4. Select two statements that represent *causes* of the problem.

a. _____ Drugs are accessible in the street and drug stores.

b. _____ Workers go to bed too late.

c. _____ Drugs are accessible on the job.

d. _____ Employers are indifferent to employees' problems.

5. Select five statements that represent *solutions* to the problem.

a. _____ Develop an Alcoholics Anonymous program.

b. _____ Develop an official policy with respect to the problem.

c. _____ Potential problem employees can be prescreened.

d. _____ Provide rehabilitation programs.

e. _____ Make pep pills available to employees.

f. _____ Immediately fire the problem employee.

g. _____ Look for early signs of illness.

h. _____ Create a good system for evaluating work performance.

i. _____ Avoid discussing the problem.

j. _____ Stay away from quack counselors.

Check your answers with the Answer Key.

INSTRUCTIONS FOR PACED READING: "No Vacancy"

The pacing rate for this *Wall Street Journal* article is 450 words per minute. This means that you should finish reading the article in 4 minutes and 25 seconds, or a total of 265 seconds. Ask someone to tell you when the time has expired. The article contains approximately 2,000 words.

Be sure to examine the *Journal*'s headlines and subheadlines; the information contained in them provides many of the article's important ideas. For example, you can identify the problem, some causes, and one solution in the headlines!

Paced Reading

No Vacancy
Apartments Are Scarce, But the Outlook Dims For New Construction
Higher Interest, Other Costs Prevent Some Building; Rents Fail to Keep Pace
Staying With Mom and Dad

Anthony Ramirez

For two years Mattie Presley has been trying to move out of her sister's house. But in Seattle, where the 24-year-old office assistant lives, almost 99% of the apartments are occupied, and waiting lists are long. The apartments that are left are too expensive for Miss Presley. "I'm stuck," she says.

In many other cities the apartment supply is almost as tight. The occupancy rate in some parts of Los Angeles is 98%. Rodney Lucio, a 23-year-old law student there, shares a cramped $433-a-month apartment with two roommates. That's better than last year, when he lived out of his Toyota Celica sedan for three weeks waiting for an opening at an apartment complex.

In Detroit, where occupancy is 97%, retired nurse Ann Jordan lives with her daughter's large family. To make room for her, two of her grandchildren and a three-year-old great grandchild must sleep on the living room floor. "It pains me to see my family crowded so," says the 67-year-old Mrs. Jordan. But government-subsidized apartments for the elderly have five-year waiting lists, and non-subsidized housing is far too costly.

DOUBLING UP

Around the country there is a growing shortage of apartments. One result is that many people, usually the young and those on fixed incomes, must move in with relatives or take on roommates. The shortage is likely to worsen as the recent steep rise in interest rates drives even more builders away from apartment construction.

"I'm sitting on land that's already zoned for multi-family use," says Robert Brody, a Detroit-area developer, whose view is typical of many builders. "I'm not going to build a thing on it until those rates come down."

Since the first of last year, the prime rate, or minimum interest rate on business loans, has soared to 11¾% from 7½%. Because rates on construction loans range from prime to 4½% above prime, depending on the borrower's creditworthiness and other factors, a builder today could wind up paying more than 16% in annual interest on construction money.

But some builders say that as long as they can get money, they'll keep building. "I don't adjust to interest rates," says Ray Huffman, a San Diego builder. "My material costs 1% more each month. I can't afford to lose rent and lose depreciation by not building. Do you think General Motors stops building cars because the prime goes up?" What's more, Mr. Huffman is betting on the arrival of prohibitively high single-family-home prices. "More and more people are going to want apartments," he says, "because they can't afford anything else."

CHEAPER LOANS RUN OUT

The rise in interest rates has led many analysts to forecast a construction downturn this year, probably by summer, as units built with previous years' cheaper loans reach completion and fewer new projects are begun. The Commerce Department expects a 9% decline this year to 500,000 multi-family units. (The government doesn't break down the figure into privately built apartments, government-subsidized units, and condominiums.) Some private analysts are predicting a plunge of 25% or more.

Most of the drop will come in private construction, analysts say. "Private builders have been getting out of the multi-family market for the last five years," says George Sternlieb, a Rutgers University professor of city planning who helped prepare a study for Congress on multi-family housing demand.

Indeed, the only real growth has been in subsidized housing, Mr. Sternlieb says, because increasingly only the government can afford to build apartments. He estimates that the federal government builds two apartments for every one built by a private developer.

REDUCING THE SUPPLY

Condominium conversion is also growing, and this trend worsens the apartment shortage by reducing the supply of rental apartments and driving up rents of the remaining units.

Basically, the shortage has two causes: increasing construction and operating costs and owners' decreasing ability to raise rents. Between 1972 and 1977, the consumer price index rose more than 41%, but building costs rose almost 50%. Biltmore Homes Co., a Detroit builder, was forced to cancel a 108–unit luxury apartment complex when it turned out that the firm would have to charge $705 a month in rent to recover its investment. "Who's going to pay that?" asks Abraham Ran, vice president-construction.

Costs to operate a building once it's built have also skyrocketed. A Southern California landlord, Maxine Trevethen of Rancho Palos Verdes, complained in a letter to the Los Angeles *Times* that her gains under Proposition 13 were "nonexistent." The sharp property-tax cut "merely allows me to cut my losses and help pay a plumbing bill of $5,000," she wrote. Increasingly, builders are requiring tenants to pay for heat and electricity. They install separate air-conditioning units for each apartment, even though centralized systems would be more energy-efficient.

Meanwhile, rents haven't kept pace with costs. "Rents have risen only about half the general rate of inflation," says Kenneth Rosen, a Princeton University economics professor who studies housing. The 1973–74 recession hobbled multi-family housing starts by 77%, dropping them from 917,000 in 1972 to 208,100 in 1975. Developers found they were grossly overbuilt and had to resort to such measures as giving away one month's free rent to attract tenants. Rents have lagged ever since.

All of which is little consolation for the apartment hunter.

"I get mad every day," says Kathy Rowe, who's been looking a month for an apartment in Atlanta, where the occupancy rate is about 98%. "If the newspaper ads say call after 6 p.m., and you call at 6:15, you miss the apartment." Miss Rowe, a 23-year-old psychology-research assistant, tries to outfox rival apartment seekers by buying the first edition of the Sunday newspaper on Saturday night for an early peek at the ads. "But that's probably what everyone else is doing," she concedes.

"I'm just biding my time," says Miss

Presley in Seattle. At one complex, she's next in line for a $185-a-month, two-bedroom apartment. She's waiting for a couple to move out when their new home is completed.

WORRYING ABOUT THE RENT

But she worries about paying the rent, which would be nearly 43% of her $435 a month take-home salary. She's unmarried and has a five-year-old son. "I'm just going to have to let a lot of things go," she says, like eating out, a weekly bowling night, and an occasional $2.75 movie ticket.

In Hackensack, N.J., 22-year-old Rosemary Imbemba is living with her parents to save money. Rent for an apartment by herself, she figures, would eat up half of her $8,000 take-home salary as a housing counselor. If she moved out of her parents' house, she says, "I'd have to take a part-time job, forget graduate school, forget new clothes, forget purchasing a car and forget socializing."

For some young people having to live at home has yielded unexpected rewards. "I appreciate my parents a lot more," says Jeanne Mori, a 23-year-old fine-arts graduate student at UCLA. "I'm not into the big independence struggle anymore, and living at home has made me realize that my parents are really okay."

For the elderly, though, it's often frustrating to live with their children. "I've always been independent," says Mrs. Jordan in Detroit. "My family doesn't want me to live alone, but I prefer to be alone." Mrs. Jordan has traveled all over town looking for low-rent housing, where older citizens pay $100 or less in rent. At one such apartment complex, she was told the waiting list had 800 names. Rents on one-bedroom apartments in Detroit range between $200 and $300 a month.

LESS HELP FROM UNCLE SAM

Prospects for more subsidized housing aren't good, analysts say. President Carter wants to keep a tight lid on spending in the fiscal-1980 budget, and that may mean the knife for domestic programs, including housing.

The Department of Housing and Urban Development estimates that it will build or rehabilitate 50,000 units in the fiscal year ending Sept. 30, down 21% from the year-earlier level of 63,651. But this year's housing will cost 78% more, or an additional $297 million. Rental subsidies will rise 11% to about $1.03 billion in fiscal 1979, HUD says.

In the short run, analysts say, the supply of apartments will continue to lag behind demand, but the projected downturn in apartment construction isn't likely to be as sharp as the 77% collapse of the mid-1970s. "The market isn't overbuilt the way it was in the last recession," explains Mr. Rosen, the Princeton housing analyst. "So it doesn't have very far to fall."

Life-insurance companies are another stabilizing influence, analysts say. These companies are stepping up their lending activity, and in a credit crunch they would help replace saving and loan institutions and banks as sources of mortgage money. Such long-term money is used by apartment developers to pay off short-term construction loans.

NO MONEY SHORTAGE YET

Insurance companies are flush with cash, analysts say, because their money comes mainly from premiums paid by policyholders, a fairly constant money flow. Banks and S&Ls, on the other hand, get their money from depositors. In the past, federal ceilings on what banks and S&Ls could pay for savings led to scarce loan money for apartment developers. But now savings banks and

S&Ls are offering special six-month savings certificates that pay a rate slightly higher than the Treasury-bill rate and commercial banks are allowed to match the bill rate. So far, institutions haven't had serious trouble attracting deposits, and apartment developers can still borrow construction money, though it is expensive.

What happens to the market for apartments is closely related, analysts say, to developments in the market for single-family homes. In recent years, high demand for single-family homes has encouraged house construction, but not apartment development. To fill orders, home builders bid up the price of wallboard, plywood and other building materials that are also used in apartment construction. In some regions, shortages developed, slowing apartment completion, and adding to construction costs.

In the long run, population trends appear to foreshadow a decline in apartment demand. Mr. Sternlieb estimates that since 1975, demand has averaged about 416,000 units a year and will decline almost 12% to 367,000 units a year in the 1980s. The post-World War II "baby boom" generation sharply expanded the rental market in 1966, but that generation is now between 30 and 35 years old, the prime housing-buying years. Additionally, births began to fall sharply in the mid-1960s.

"The age patterns were still favorable to rentals in 1974 and 1975," says Citicorp Real Estate Inc., a Detroit-based research unit of Citicorp. But the recession intervened, cutting demand, the firm says. Now, it says, "the age pattern has turned against the rental market."

PACED READING COMPREHENSION CHECK: "No Vacancy"

1. What is the *problem?*

   a. _____ Apartment rental costs are exceeding the rate of inflation.

   b. _____ Apartments are poorly managed.

   c. _____ Apartments are in short supply.

2. Select two *effects* of the problem.

   a. _____ Health hazards develop.

   b. _____ People live out of their automobiles.

   c. _____ Family relatives live together.

   d. _____ People seek loans to pay rents.

3. Select three *causes* of the problem.

   a. _____ Builders delay construction because of high interest rates.

   b. _____ Apartment owners are greedy.

   c. _____ Some private builders are getting out of the apartment market.

   d. _____ Apartment owners hire a poor managerial staff.

   e. _____ Many apartments are being converted to condominiums.

   f. _____ Apartment owners refuse to pay the managerial staff well.

4. A positive effect of the problem is that:

   a. _____ banks are making greater profits.

   b. _____ apartment dwellers are becoming more self-sufficient.

   c. _____ young people appreciate their families more.

5. In the short run, we can expect apartment supply to:

   a. _____ exceed demand.

   b. _____ lag behind demand.

   c. _____ be determined by interest rates.

6. Select two *solutions* to the problem.

   a. _____ Improve the training of apartment managers.

   b. _____ Population trends will solve the problem naturally.

   c. _____ Fight for rent control.

   d. _____ Reduce inflation.

   e. _____ Attain construction loans from life insurance companies.

   f. _____ Demand better services.

Check your answers with the Answer Key.

INSTRUCTIONS FOR SKIM READING: "All Deposits, No Returns—The Story Of Suzie's Bank"

Using the skimming techniques you learned in chapter 2, skim the following article in order to identify the problem, effect(s), cause(s), and solution(s). Time yourself to find your skimming rate; you should finish the article in no more than 1 minute and 15 seconds. Write down your time in the space provided at the end of the article.

Answer the questions following the article, then check your answers in the Answer Key. (Remember, a score of 50 percent or higher is acceptable when skimming.) Determine your skimming rate from the Words Per Minute: Skimming Chart, then record your skimming rate and comprehension score on your Skim Reading Progress Chart.

Skim Reading

All Deposits, No Returns—
The Story Of Suzie's Bank

Kenneth Gallo

ALL DEPOSITS

At 3:05 PM Suzie had her register drawer open after completing a customer sale. She carefully took a ten dollar bill out of the register drawer, dropped it on the floor by her feet, kicked it close to the counter, stepped on it—then closed her drawer. Calmly reaching into her pocket for a tissue she touched it to her nose, looked around, dropped the tissue to the floor by the counter and scooped up the ten dollar bill inside the tissue. She then put the tissue and money in her pocket.

Ten minutes later she was given her regular coffee break by the manager. When the break came, Suzie went to the office asked the assistant manager for her pocketbook and went to the ladies room. She added the ten dollar bill to the 20 dollar bill she had stolen prior to her lunch break. It was after 3:00 PM, but Suzie's bank was still open for business. Suzie is underringing sales.

NO RETURNS

When Suzie cashed out at the end of her shift, was the money missed? No! Will the money she's been stealing ever be missed? Only after the store inventory, which could be days, weeks, or months away.

The actual cash money Suzie is stealing will never be noted as missing in any of her cashier balance sheets. It will be absorbed into the overall store shrinkage. In other words, if and when an accurate inventory is taken—it will be noticed that *something* has created an inventory shrinkage. Yet even then

Suzie's contribution to the losses will have been absorbed into the general shrinkage picture without her actual involvement being visible.

AUDITS, AUDITS, AUDITS

A bad inventory is like an anonymous call to the police about a floating crap game. The police now know there is illegal gambling going on—but where is the action?

Underringing sales, or the deliberate failure to properly enter customer purchases into register tapes for the purpose of misappropriating company cash, is, along with unauthorized discounts, becoming an ever-increasing factor of corporate losses and an increasingly larger hole in the bucket of company profits. Suzie has her way of stealing money, others may vary the process, but the end results are the same, SHRINKAGE!

In the normal, busy operations of a retail store, unless previously suspected, the chances of a cashier being observed by a supervisor underringing sales are not as high as could be desired. (Even if observed by a fellow cashier—how many of these other cashiers, knowing they are still members of the same peer group, would voluntarily come forward and state what they have seen?) What are the answers?

One very definite answer is the unannounced cash register audit. Without prior notification, walk over to the cashier's register and with her present, advise her that you are going to audit her drawer. Take a register reading, subtract her opening reading and the starting cash and compare this to her cash on hand (which you counted in her presence) — remembering to add or subtract pick-ups, voids, and refunds.

Why audit? Simple. Most cashiers who are underringing sales do NOT "pocket" this money immediately after committing the violation. Whether they are building a "bank" by continually underringing sales or intended only to underring that one sale, they will wait. Wait for an opportune time to take the next major step of removing the cash from the register and hide it on their person. They first must be sure that no one has seen those "zeros" in the register window, or saw that $.57 in the window instead of $10.57. They must be sure that the customer did not notice the "error" and report it to the manager. As long as the cash is still in the register drawer, most cashiers feel that they can "explain" its presence—"Oh, I must have made a mistake."

This is why unannounced audits on an irregular but frequent basis are important. Those times the register shows major overages—you must question those overages with raised eyebrows. Maybe you have just caught and/or stopped that invisible thief. Keep in mind, additionally, that a register shortage at time of audit can be equally important as an overage. Remember, some cashiers in their haste to steal the cash take too much! If they underring a total of $8.62 they will not take the chance of stealing a five dollar bill, three singles, and sixty-two cents in change. They will take a ten dollar bill causing a shortage, or a five dollar bill leaving an overage. Sure, honest mistakes can be made, but this one loss preventive procedure might discourage those dishonest employees whose actions might otherwise go unnoticed.

When is the proper time to audit? Anytime during the shift. However, try some of these times—just prior to coffee, relief, or lunch breaks; just before change of shifts; on truck days or when the manager is usually tied up for extended periods; one hour or so after the store opens or before it closes.

Who should be audited? Anyone who runs the cash register. No matter if it is a manager auditing a cashier or a supervisor auditing a manager. Not everyone will commit dishonest acts, but most everyone is capable of doing so if an unusual opportunity persists.

Audits are an indispensible deterrent against cash shrinkages when properly administered and practiced. They are a proven control of cash shortages when inaugurated into your loss prevention program. It takes just a few minutes to complete an audit and it might save you hours of investigation later on.

Finishing time:_____

SKIM READING COMPREHENSION CHECK:
"All Deposits, No Returns—The Story Of Suzie's Bank"

1. What is the *problem* discussed in this article?

   a. _____ Some employees do not ring up sales.

   b. _____ Some employees under-ring sales and pocket the difference.

   c. _____ Some employees over-ring sales.

2. What is the major *effect* of this problem?

    a. _____ The company loses profits.

    b. _____ The record keeping system does not work properly.

    c. _____ Customers do not get the correct change.

3. What is the major *cause* of the problem?

    a. _____ Customers do not count their change.

    b. _____ Companies have poor record keeping forms.

    c. _____ The illegal actions of employees go unnoticed.

4. What is the *solution* to the problem?

    a. _____ Encourage customers to count their change.

    b. _____ Improve the record keeping system.

    c. _____ Implement the unannounced cash register audit technique.

Check your answers with the Answer Key.

SKIM READING: "Investigators Tackle Computer Crime"

Using the skimming techniques you learned in chapter 2, skim the following article in order to identify the problem, effect(s), cause(s), and solution(s). Time yourself to find your skimming rate; you should take no longer than 40 seconds to finish the article. Write down your time in the space provided at the end of the article. Answer the questions following the article, then check your answers in the Answer Key. (Remember, a score of 50 percent or higher is acceptable when skimming.) Determine your skimming rate from the Words Per Minute: Skimming Chart, then record your skimming rate and comprehension score on your Skim Reading Progress Chart.

Skim Reading

Investigators Tackle Computer Crime
Tim A. Schabeck

Computer crime can be defined as a crime which either directly or indirectly involves a computer system as a means or as a target in the perpetration of the crime. The types of computer crime are: embezzlement, espionage, extortion, fraud, larceny, malicious mischief, sabotage, and theft.

Computer related crime is, by far, the most lucrative of all crimes. In 1975 the average bank robbery netted $19,000 while the average computer related crime netted $450,000. The computer crimes that *have been reported* are responsible for the loss of over $100,000,000 annually in the U.S. It has been estimated that 85% of all white collar crimes are not reported to police.

Consequently, if we were to project the dollar loss attributed to unreported (not to mention undetected) computer crime, the nation's businesses could be losing in excess of one billion dollars annually.

Many routine police forensic science/chemistry techniques may be applied while investigating a computer crime. However, with the advancement of computer technology paralleled by the rapid increase in the use of computer systems, new and unique crime lab techniques must be used to assist the investigator in the apprehension and conviction of the computer criminal.

Documentary evidence exists in the computer environment in the form of source input documents and computer printed output. Input documents have been forged or altered in order to embezzle from private industry and government. Source documents can be traced back to an individual by utilizing various techniques such as: handwriting analysis; ultraviolet radiation for determining forgeries and document age; or fingerprint recovery such as electronagraphy, magnabrushing, or ninhydrin.

Stolen computer generated reports containing mailing lists, research data, *etc.,* can be traced back to the computer printer which produced the report. Tracing methods include: ink analysis via the spectrophotometer; paper stock analysis; and the analysis of the printed characters.

Magnetic tape is the most widely used form for the storage of computerized data. A standard reel of magnetic computer tape can hold over 40 million characters of information. Destroyed, stolen, or copied tapes containing mailing lists, research data, computer programs, and financial data have resulted in the loss of millions of dollars and the downfall of many businesses annually.

Magnetic tape can be traced back to its originating tape unit via various methods. Particles of dust, smoke, oil, grease, cleaners, perspiration, hair particles, and clothing lint that can be found on magnetic tape can be analyzed by gas-chromatograph/mass spectrometer. Tool marks caused by the buildup of oxide on the tape unit recording head can be found on the surface of the tape and traced back to the originating tape unit via magnetic tape comparison techniques.

Teleprocessing systems are being widely used as a means of computer input and output. Substantial monetary losses have resulted from the manipulation of computer terminals to gain unauthorized access to a company's computer for the purpose of espionage, sabotage, or theft.

Active or passive electronic eavesdropping of teleprocessing networks such as timesharing systems or automatic teller banking terminals can be accomplished with relative ease using the proper equipment. Radio frequencies emitted by Cathode Ray Tubes (display terminals) and the computer's central processing unit can be monitored.

Electronic countermeasure equipment must be used to detect these types of intrusions.

Finishing time: _____

SKIM READING COMPREHENSION CHECK: "Investigators Tackle Computer Crime"

1. What is the *problem* discussed in this article?

   a. _____ Computer crime is proliferating.

   b. _____ Investigators do not know how to handle computer crime.

   c. _____ The computer criminal cannot be prosecuted.

2. What is the *effect* of the problem?

   a. _____ Computer crime is not deterred.

   b. _____ Law enforcement agencies lose their status.

   c. _____ The nation's businesses lose large sums of money.

3. Check *two causes* of the problem.

   a. _____ We have poor criminal laws.

   b. _____ Computer terminals are manipulated.

   c. _____ Investigators have been poorly trained.

   d. _____ The criminal's techniques are fool proof.

   e. _____ Employees tamper with input and output data.

   f. _____ There is no way to stop the crime.

4. What is the *solution* to the problem?

   a. _____ Use new lab techniques and electronic equipment.

   b. _____ Improve the training of investigators.

   c. _____ Establish new criminal laws.

Check your answers with the Answer Key.

INSTRUCTIONS FOR RAPID READING: "The Trouble With Open Offices"

Read this article as fast as possible while trying to maintain a comprehension score of at least 70 percent. Time yourself. When you finish the article, write down your reading time in the space provided at the end of the article. Answer the comprehension questions following the article, then check your answers in the Answer Key. Determine your reading rate from the Words Per Minute: Rapid Reading Chart, then record your reading rate and comprehension score on your Rapid Reading Progress Chart.

Rapid Reading

The Trouble With Open Offices

The Editors, Business Week

A workers' revolt was the last thing that executives at Paul Harris Stores Inc. expected when they modernized their dingy Indianapolis headquarters in 1976 with a sleek, $90,000 open-plan office. The partly enclosed work spaces made with low, brightly colored partitions and modular funiture had been working well for many U.S. companies for at least eight years.

But Paul Harris management had overlooked a crucial element: the nature of the work being done. The retailer's fashion buyers, accustomed to their private, closed offices, raised a nerve-frazzling din on their telephones. As their tolerance wore thin in the open offices, purchasing decisions normally made in minutes began to lag a day or more. "Everybody went right to the president and said they couldn't work," moans the manager who recommended the open plan. Within a week, $30,000 worth of the new components was carted away, and nearly all of Harris' office staff were soon back in closed offices.

Record Shipments

While Paul Harris' experience with open-plan—or "landscaped"—offices is more dramatic than most, it serves warning that, as one interior designer notes, "the open plan was overpromoted to the point that it sounded like everybody's magic solution." And by the law of averages, more managers may be learning that such offices are not for everybody.

Open-plan offices now account for roughly 10% of all existing office space in the U.S., and the trend to them is definitely upward. Makers of office furniture, who expect record shipments this year—more than $1.9 billion worth, up at least 13% from 1977—say that sales of modular units for open plans are increasing twice as fast as sales of ordinary office furniture.

The majority of open-plan offices is largely successful; managers claim that most employees are content, productivity is up, space savings abound, and rearrangement costs have been slashed. But a significant minority of managers is discovering problems that can drive top executives up the very walls that only they are likely to have:

MORALE

It can plummet when employees who have traditionally judged their status by walls and doors find themselves in a status-less environment. Polls at Smith-Kline Corp., the Philadelphia drugmaker, show that 10% of office workers there actively dislike their open offices. The number includes "the person who just got a promotion, who's been struggling for that office, for those doors," explains Robert R. Ferguson, manager of pharmaceutical facilities. "Then they go into the open plan, and those hard-won walls disappear." This is particularly a problem when workers' superiors have closed offices, researchers learned when they recently evaluated modular furniture for the General Services Administration (GSA). "Having senior people in private offices is a powerful deterrent to worker satisfaction with open planning and systems furniture," the researchers noted.

LACK OF PRIVACY

It can inhibit the communication that open plans are meant to spur. International Harvester Co., after converting several sections of its Chicago headquarters to an open plan, had to go back and wall in the personnel and corporate planning sections. Delicate and secret discussions within them could be overheard elsewhere.

'WHITE SOUND'

A hum or hiss that sounds much like an air conditioner is generated electronically in many open offices to mask background noise. But it can be a no-win proposition. Paul Harris had to shut it off because employees found it "irritating." Yet Linda S. Feldman, senior designer at KP Associates in Philadelphia, reports on an office where it was too successful. The white sound went off and "everyone thought the air conditioner had broken down," she recalls. "Everyone got warmer and warmer. Finally they had to go home because everyone was so hot." Such disparities lead Lawrence Lerner, president of SLS Environetics Inc., a major interior design company, to term white sound "an excuse for a lousy job" of controlling acoustic problems through design.

TOGETHERNESS

Not everyone likes the closeness fostered by the open plan. Although proponents say it encourages interemployee communication, a Michigan secretary who used to sit near only her boss says that the constant chatter of her peers has cut her productivity. "I wasn't in the mainstream before," she says. And the furnishings that allow the tight squeeze—one manufacturer has some clerks in spaces as small as 6 × 7 ft.—can

rattle employees. A General Motors Corp. materials analyst, whose desk is suspended from a partition, complains that "when the guy on the other side closes a drawer, the whole thing shakes."

Of course, employee reaction depends largely on what kind of environment the open office replaces. Those who worked in an old-style "bullpen" generally welcome the 5½-ft.-high partitions and furniture that wrap around two or three sides of an employee's space. Numerous studies do indicate that improved communications and paper flow result when associated workers are assembled in one large room with no ceiling walls. At the 100% open-plan offices of Caudill Rowlett Scott, the Houston architects, engineers, and planners, "communication is better because people can't just walk off and shut themselves up in their offices," says Chairman William W. Caudill. And at American Can Co.'s Greenwich (Conn.) headquarters, 12 out of 100 managers recently abandoned four-sided modular offices in favor of three-sided spaces, "to have the feeling of openness," says Nicholas Marchak, vice-president for corporate administration.

Beating the System

Since many workers are not enamored of wide-open space, the more ingenious of them find a way around it. Some employees at Smith-Kline in Philadelphia have hung doors across their work-station entrances. The doors serve no practical function, but when swung shut they signal that the office occupant wants to be left alone. A writer at another large company also took matters into his own hands. When his memos to executives about office noise were ignored, he started visiting the company nurse. She gives him earplugs. Other workers use rubber plants, hanging mobiles, ceramic ducks, or cardboard cutouts to stuff the unwanted space above their partitions, for at least a psychological sense of privacy.

Still other workers just grumble. "The executive [who implements an open plan] has to know that some people are going to complain," cautions designer Feldman. Sometimes the complaints take an extreme form. Mid-level supervisors at the Health, Education, & Welfare Dept. in Washington banded together and refused to move when they learned that they were to be booted from closed offices as soon as an open-plan conversion was finished. Their boss relented. Only 40% of the department's space in the Hubert H. Humphrey office building will be open-plan now; 60% had been planned on.

On the other hand, managerial firmness can counter some complaints. At the McQuay Div. of McQuay-Perfex Inc., a Minneapolis maker of heat-transfer devices, accountants have occasionally complained that their offices are smaller than those of secretaries who run many office machines, but who earn only one-third what the accountants make. "We try to ignore that," says W. Clark Jenney Jr., the company's administrative services manager. "We give people what [space] they need and don't assign them by status."

Flexibility and Savings

Of course, many open-plan users are delighted with their systems. Any vice-president whose division works in open offices at Eastman Kodak Co.'s Rochester (N.Y.) headquarters sits in an open office himself. Kodak management relishes the ease with which a small crew can rearrange an average of 15 offices at Kodak headquarters every work night to adapt them to new projects. At Pizza Hut Inc.'s rapidly growing home office in Wichita, "the overriding factor is flexibility," says one executive. "It's so easy to expand, and that seems to be the primary priority on the bottom line."

In Michigan, a state government official calculates that "in three years we can pay for the open-plan furnishings with the money we saved in space we would have had to rent otherwise." And McQuay claims that time measurements show productivity increases averaging 10% in its open offices, mainly because workers are less distracted. That provides an effective savings of some $200,000 a year for the $156 million company.

Visibility may be a key factor. Mervin G. Morris, president of Mervyn's, a department store chain based in Hayward, Calif., theorizes that boosts in productivity result from "the hidden feature about open planning." As he explains: "The mere fact that you are out there, that all eyes are on you, causes you to spend less time lighting cigarettes and visiting."

The Price Tag

There is a danger, though, that executives can have their heads turned to the open plan too easily by the promising potential of higher productivity and future savings. Initial costs for modular furniture are far higher than those for ordinary office furniture. A desk and chair may go for $600, but a clerk's work station furniture runs from $750 to $1,400, and a manager's modular components can total between $2,400 and $5,000. Shipping and installation add as much as 20% to those prices.

So do provisions for running electrical and communications wires through panels—those offered for the first time this year in Steelcase Inc.'s "9000 Plus" system bring the price of each divider panel up by $60. And local union workers may balk at installing prewired panels. It is also necessary to order spare pieces of furniture to accommodate changes or additions, and computers and their programs may be needed to keep track of the inventory.

Once the furniture is in place, problems that arise can usually be traced back to top management's lack of care in devising the office plan. "A large number of people go into open plan without investigating what it's all about," says Larry G. Blundell, Canadian sales manager for Sunar Ltd., a Waterloo (Ont.) modular furniture maker that sells into the U.S. market. Then, for example, "they discover that traffic situations and the flow of people are cumbersome," Blundell notes.

Interviews with office staffers about their job needs can minimize such pitfalls, many advisers suggest. GSA researchers urge contact with every employee—questionnaires are the cheapest method—because "it is not appropriate to allow supervisors or others to state what an individual needs." But M. Arthur Gensler Jr., A San Francisco architect and co-author of *A Rational Approach to Office Planning,* says that polling only 10% of employees in most cases provides an adequate sample, while cutting research costs and time and avoiding "over-customization" of work stations.

Getting Advice

The concepts that make the system work seem simple, but the details can be mind-boggling. At least 129 manufacturers make modular furniture. Their catalogs list hundreds of components, ranging from file cases and pencil drawers to electrical outlets and tackboards. The combinations are infinite. "I'm not sure a layman, a businessman, will ever understand them," says Neils Diffrient, a partner with Henry Dreyfuss Associates, a New York City industrial design firm creating one new modular system. "The difficulty is in the conversion of the [workers'] need to the understanding of the hardware," notes Diffrient.

The standard way of obtaining help, of course, is hiring an architect or interior designer experienced with open plans. Then, too, aid may be available from a new source as early as this fall. The Philadelphia-based Landscape Users Group, an informal organization of some 40 planners who have developed open plans within their companies, plans to form a council of volunteer advisers—working for expenses and an honorarium totaling perhaps $3,000—who will visit companies to analyze problem offices or suggest ways of avoiding pitfalls in new ones. The volunteers will not actually design offices but just respond to "the continuing series of requests for more discussion about landscape offices," says R. A. Park, the group's chairman.

Furniture manufacturers themselves are responding to open-plan users' complaints, too. Steelcase and Herman Miller Inc., for instance, offer modular systems that will enclose space on four sides with partitions to provide an executive his necessary privacy. Storwal International in Toronto takes that approach a step higher by capping executive enclosures with nylon "umbrellas." Several companies offer components made of wood or covered with leather, intended to convey status to an executive reluctant to shift to an open office. Miller is also studying ways of making open offices more accessible to handicapped workers.

But while improved hardware may mitigate the more obvious problems of some open offices, nearly all experts stress that no desk or chair can make an ill-conceived office work. For example, a static company that has little anticipation of an increased work force may be wasting its money on a flexible office. And a company that employs many engineers, geologists, or other staffers who need vast wall spaces for drawings and maps may discover that an open plan would be a disaster.

What is possibly most important is that no change in physical environment can mask a bad managerial environment for very long. As Gensler sums it up: "If you're an aggressive manager who wants to communicate and reassign people to different tasks as work changes, then open plan is the ideal situation." But, he warns, "if you run a crummy operation and don't pay attention to your people, it's not going to help."

Finishing time:_____

RAPID READING COMPREHENSION CHECK: "The Trouble With Open Offices"

1. The *problem* discussed in the article has to do with:

    a. _____ the heating of some open offices.

    b. _____ the sound systems in some open offices.

    c. _____ the confusion of some open offices.

2. Select four *effects* of the problem.

    a. _____ Workers become too intimate.

    b. _____ Decisions lag.

    c. _____ Background music puts workers to sleep.

    d. _____ Productivity is lowered.

    e. _____ Morale can decline.

    f. _____ Workers develop back problems.

    g. _____ Workers are too cold in the winter.

    h. _____ Communication is suppressed.

    i. _____ Workers are too warm in the summer.

3. The *causes* of the problem are:

    a. _____ inappropriate selection of heating system and poor planning on the part of top management.

    b. _____ inappropriate selection of sound system and poor planning on the part of top management.

    c. _____ inappropriate selection of furnishings and poor planning on the part of top management.

    d. _____ over promotion by sellers and poor planning on the part of top management.

4. Select four *solutions* that were mentioned in the article.

    a. _____ Substitute music with the white sound.

b. _____ Remove the sound systems completely.

c. _____ Interview office staffers before implementing the program.

d. _____ Consult advisers before implementation.

e. _____ Use ear plugs.

f. _____ Get help from an architect.

g. _____ Refuse to purchase modern furnishings.

h. _____ Consult heating engineers before implementing the program.

Check your answers with the Answer Key.

INSTRUCTIONS FOR RAPID READING: "Dermatitis: Causes and Cures"

Read this article as fast as possible while trying to maintain a comprehension score of at least 70 percent. Time yourself. When you finish the article, write down your reading time in the space provided at the end of the article. Answer the comprehension questions following the article, then check your answers in the Answer Key. Determine your reading rate from the Words Per Minute: Rapid Reading Chart, then record your reading rate and comprehension score on your Rapid Reading Progress Chart.

Rapid Reading

Dermatitis: Causes and Cures
Doris Baldwin

What is it that a person sees every day, couldn't live without, yet often treats badly? It measures 17 feet square, weighs six pounds, and is the body's largest organ. It also is the only organ touching all there is in life to be touched.

It's the human skin. Vital but vulnerable.

Whatever might damage the skin can be a serious health hazard, for the skin has many important jobs to do. It's the body's first line of defense against bacteria. Skin blocks the passage of disease germs and harmful chemical substances. The pigmentation of skin serves as a protective screen against sunlight. Skin also acts as a thermostat, assisting the central nervous system in regulating body temperature automatically. It's a cleaning agent that gets rid of much of the body's wastes. It secretes oils to keep itself soft and pliable.

Skin is a kind of protective rain slicker; waterproof, it guards the body's substantial water content. The skin handles a third of the body's circulating blood. Its millions of nerve fibers transmit messages to the central nervous system, which makes a person move instantly to avoid cuts, burns, and other physical threats. Skin renews itself, growing new cells, junking old ones.

From the cradle to the grave, a healthy skin does all these things naturally, with no conscious assist from its occupant.

What does man do in return? Sometimes he pampers his skin. More often, skin is neglected or abused. Abuse is especially common on the industrial work scene, where skin frequently is exposed to environmental irritants and poisons.

Dr. Marcus Key, former director of the National Institute for Occupational Safety and Health (NIOSH), recently zeroed in on the severity of this hazard to skin. He reported that data from New York State, California, and the Bureau of Labor Statistics Reporting System under OSHA bear out the fact that "occupational skin diseases continue to be one of the most important groups of occupational diseases in this country. . . . OSHA statistics for the last six months of 1971 compiled by the Bureau of Labor Statistics show that approximately 34 percent of all reported occupational illnesses were occupational skin diseases or disorders."

In New York State, reported Dr. Key, "43 percent of the occupational disease cases compensated from 1966 through 1970 were dermatides. Dermatitis constituted 17 percent of the total compensation costs for occupational diseases in the state for this same period. An analysis of California's Doctors' First Report of Work Injury statistics for 1966 through 1970 indicates that 40 percent of the total occupational disease cases were skin conditions."

In the past, available data on this job health problem were not comparable between states, nor were they even particularly reliable. Different methods were used to gather information. Few states used the same definition of occupational disease. Also, because of varying waiting periods before compensation began, many occupational skin diseases never got on the books.

Today, OSHA provides the states with a uniform reporting system for all occupational diseases, including dermatoses. The new system is expected to yield more widely useful data leading, hopefully, to more widely effective means of tackling the problem.

Despite a history of inadequate documentation, skin diseases are held to be the most common of all occupational diseases. They are known to be costly in many ways. Even when affected employees don't lose time from the job, they're not doing their best work when the skin on their faces, hands, or arms hurts. Painful hands aren't eager to grasp work tools and materials firmly; they're a health problem on the way to becoming a safety problem.

Although most dermatoses are preventable, the job isn't an easy one, nor are total and permanent success guaranteed. Some of the difficulties lie in the constant introduction of new chemicals and new work processes, and the need to revise, update, and reinforce preventive measures continually.

Dr. Key spells it out by comparing approaches to skin diseases and respiratory problems: "The main thrust of the Occupational Safety and Health Act of 1970 is to control hazardous occupational exposure through enforceable standards, supplemented by employer-employee education. There are environmental limits for some 450 contaminants in the workroom air, which provide an effective mechanism for preventing occupational respiratory diseases and systemic toxicity. However, the limits are of little help in preventing occupational skin diseases."

The best ways to control dermatoses, says Key, are: substitution of materials, enclosure of hazardous processes, personal protective measures, cleanliness, and early detection.

Before these methods are attempted, however, management or the industrial hygienist must become familiar with the causes of occupational skin diseases.

The five direct causes are: (1) mechanical agents—friction, pressure, abrasion, and blows; (2) physical factors—moisture, electricity, heat, cold, and radiation; (3) plant poisons, found in certain leaves, sap, vegetables, wood dusts, resins, and lacquers; (4) biological agents—bacteria, viruses, fungi, parasites, and insects; and (5) chemical agents.

Chemicals, the greatest single cause of industrial dermatosis, can cause trouble two ways: as irritants and as sensitizers.

Primary irritants have the power to damage normal skin on contact, if left on long enough and in sufficient concentration. Examples of primary irritants are inorganic acids, anhydrides, alkalis, heavy metal salts and tanning agents, bleaches, and chlorine compounds. This type of irritant causes 80 percent of the contact dermatitis reported in industry.

About one out of five cases is caused by the second type of chemical action, called sensitizing. This means that certain chemicals may appear harmless to an individual at first, but produce a reaction after a number of contacts. Dyes, photo developers, rubber accelerators, certain soaps, insecticides, cosmetics and oils, resins, coal tar, explosives, and plasticizers are all known sensitizers of some people.

Employees ought to be instructed to report immediately any skin lesions, sores, or burns observed, whether or not they know how they got them. It is the responsibility of employers to see that employees with damaged skin, requiring medical attention, do not return to work until authorized by a physician.

It is a cardinal medical principle in the treatment of skin disease that the patient be removed as soon as possible from the irritant substance, and that his inflamed skin be protected. "Any other course," says Dr. Donald Hunter, physician at the London Hospital, "may lead to intractable skin disease associated with sensitivity to many agents." Sometimes it is necessary to transfer the affected worker to a job where he will never again be exposed to the offending agent.

The ideal place to begin prevention of contact dermatitis and sensitization dermatitis is while a new plant is still in the design stage. Here, processes and materials handling can be planned with employees' health as a prime consideration.

Take, for example, the plant where industrial irritants will be manufactured or used. Such irritants ought to be handled only in enclosed systems. If liquid chemicals are to be brought to the plant, they ought to come in sealed tank cars, be transferred to storage tanks by pumping through closed systems, and removed from the tanks by a valve-operated closed system. Filters and dryers should be enclosed, and operated mechanically. Wherever drums or bags are used for shipment of irritants, filling methods also should be enclosed so that no harmful liquid, dust, or fume can come in contact with the workers by touch or inhalation. Good general ventilation in the plant ought to be provided; in addition, wherever there's a hazardous operation, a local exhaust system should be installed to draw potential irritants away from the work area immediately.

These same two important design features—extensive use of enclosed systems and extra care given to ventilation—can be provided, to at least some degree, in existing plants when a new substance or process might lead to skin irritation or disease.

Besides direct causes of occupational

dermatoses, there are predisposing causes to be considered. Some people will be threatened in a situation not particularly dangerous to another person. Factors such as age, sex, skin type, hair coloring, allergy, and pre-existing skin infections may indicate that selective placement of employees will cut down the incidence of skin disorders requiring medical treatment.

A chemist representing the Calgon Corporation comments on some of these predisposing conditions:

"Skin pigmentation may affect the development of dermatosis. Negroes are generally less susceptible to skin irritants than Caucasians. Mongolians tend to have drier, less oily skin; are more prone to ichthyosis (excessively dry and flaky skin); and are greatly affected by friction and pressure. Individuals of any race may differ greatly in resistance or susceptibility to specific irritants.

Contact with many external irritants will intensify the young worker's predisposition to acne-like lesions, the chemist says. Working with chlorinated naphthalenes, for instance, could aggravate the susceptibility.

Some people perspire more heavily than others. While perspiration can be cleansing, the effect could be the reverse when the material dealt with—caustics, soda ash, slaked lime, for example—characteristically becomes an irritant in solution. Heavy perspiration, then, would serve to activate the irritant.

Sex can make a difference, too. Many reports indicate that women suffer less from dermatitis than men do. There are several possible reasons. One is that women may not be handling substances as offensive as those that men are assigned to handle. Another is that some women may be more meticulous about the appearance of their skin and will be quicker to report minor irritations and

get medical attention. The fact remains, however, that women's skin tends to be less oily than men's, which makes women's skin more sensitive to many irritants, especially solvents.

At plants where exposure to chemicals or other skin irritants can be expected, the preemployment physical ought to include a check for existing skin problems. It has been found that people with a history of certain skin diseases (atopic eczema, for instance) are likely to develop industrial dermatoses—either new skin problems or heightened aggravation of pre-existing conditions.

It is estimated that 20 percent of occupational dermatitis is caused by allergy. Allergy, says the Calgon chemist, "is the altered degree of susceptibility in an individual . . . just the exposure to the allergen will produce reaction symptoms which frequently result in dermatosis." So personnel policy might permit the allergic individual to avoid a worksite that could cause him grief.

Obviously, the best overall hope for a low incidence of occupational dermatosis lies in a scrupulously clean work environment. A clear workplace minimizes chances for a worker to develop contact dermatitis by touching or breathing an irritant. Not only the machinery, but floors, walls, ceilings, lighting fixtures, and windows must be kept clean.

Washrooms must be equipped with adequate wash basins, showers, lockers, and cleaning supplies to make employee cleanliness easy. In addition to washrooms, hand cleaning and skin reconditioning products can be made available throughout the plant.

Where supervision of washing facilities is lacking, use of the wrong kind of cleaning agent can cause a new kind of trouble. In many cases, dermatitis is caused not by the materials used on the job but by cleaning with degreasing agents and other materials that can harm the skin. Washing soda, naphtha, and turpentine are among the worst offenders. Where a painter, for instance, might be tempted to use turpentine to clean his hands, he'd be well advised to substitute cottonseed oil or another mild but effective cleaner.

A number of firms are developing products which would offer skin protection in the face of many different hazards. Packaged systems of this sort could save employers many headaches in figuring out for themselves what assortment of products they need—contact prevention creams or lotions, effective cleansing agents, and skin conditioners. Skin care products manufacturers—among them 3M Company, Mine Safety Appliances, Randustrial, Ayerst Laboratories, American Optical, the Milburn Company, E.D. Bullard, and the Calgon Corporation—are expert in helping employers and industrial hygienists set up whatever systems are needed to protect workers from the risks of a particular workplace.

Protective apparel often is recommended to supplement other controls such as plant design, substitution of materials, and proper washing. Gloves, sleeves, aprons, and neck and face shields may be appropriate; in all cases the materials used in the manufacture of the apparel must be right for the hazard to be dealt with.

Protective clothing is not without its dangers, if simply wearing it gives a false sense of security. The hapless employee wearing a punctured rubber glove, for instance, may not realize that a harmful substance has seeped through and contaminated the inside of the glove where it may remain in contact with the skin for many hours. To prevent such "accidents," daily inspection and cleaning of protective equipment is [sic] essential.

There must also be provision for removal and laundering of clothing saturated with cutting oils and other harmful substances. Soiled garments should never be reused before cleaning. Home laundering is not recommended because the washing method may be inadequate to decontaminate work clothing and irritant infection may be spread to other members of the family.

Industrial hygienists, nurses, and physicians may encounter some employee resistance to skin protective programs. "He-men," for instance, may hate to be told to pamper their skin. So, in addition to providing the best possible housekeeping and making skin care both easy and pleasant, the employer would do well to present some form of education on the subject.

Finishing time:_____

RAPID READING COMPREHENSION CHECK: "Dermatitis: Causes and Cures"

Directions: Answer the questions below. Base your answers on the information included in the article.

1. The *problem* discussed in this article has to do with the occupational illness of:

   a. _____ skin disease.

   b. _____ psychological stress.

   c. _____ food poisoning.

2. What are two *effects* of this problem?

   a. _____ Loss of time from the job.

   b. _____ Irrational behavior.

   c. _____ Vomiting.

   d. _____ Irregularity.

   e. _____ Poor job performance.

   f. _____ Moodiness.

3. What is the greatest *cause* of this problem?

   a. _____ Biological imbalance.

   b. _____ Chemicals.

   c. _____ Poor personal planning.

4. About what proportion of this illness is caused by allergy?

   a. _____ 20 percent.

   b. _____ 30 percent.

   c. _____ 40 percent.

5. Select four statements that represent *solutions* to the problem.

   a. _____ Provide education on the subject.

   b. _____ Have periodic checks on industrial cafeterias.

   c. _____ Encourage employees to report skin problems immediately.

   d. _____ Provide proper ventilation.

   e. _____ Remove employees from stressful situations.

   f. _____ Hire a consulting psychiatrist.

   g. _____ Provide protective apparel.

   h. _____ Administer chelating agents.

6. Which of these solutions can lead to further problems because it gives the employee a false sense of security? (Circle one)

a   b   c   d   e   f   g   h

Check your answers with the Answer Key.

6
Persuasive Pattern

INTRODUCTION

As you read this book, a local or national political campaign may be taking place. Even if one is not taking place, you undoubtedly remember ads such as the following:

> **FRANCIS X. O'NEIL IS YOUR**
> **CANDIDATE FOR COUNCILOR**
>
> He has business experience.
> He has an M.B.A. degree.
> He is an outstanding family man.
> He is a member of 15 prestigious organizations.
> He cares about you.
>
> **Vote for O'NEIL on election day!**

Every day you come across various business ads in the newspapers like this one:

> **UNISEX BANK IS SPECIAL**
>
> You get:
> Friendly, personalized service
> Free checking
> Highest possible interest rates
> Free gifts for opening new accounts
> Loans of every kind
>
> **Do your banking at UNISEX**

Ad writers try to "sell" their product, whether it be the selling of a political candidate or the selling of a bank.

Many writers like to "sell" their ideas. When this is their purpose, they organize their material in much the same way as advertisers organize their ads. First, the writers make an *assertion*. An advertiser may write "Unisex Bank Is Special"; an author may write "Because managers at Unisex Bank adapt their leadership style to various situations, they are more effective in reaching personal and organizational goals."

How are these assertions supported? The bank advertiser may support the assertion that the bank is special by noting the bank's personalized and varied services. The writer may support the assertion regarding leadership style by conducting interviews, completing research, quoting authorities, or providing personal, subjective reasons.

What outcomes does the bank advertiser expect? The advertiser expects J. Q. Public to bank at Unisex. The writer, on the other hand, expects the readers to accept the theory or opinion and, in some cases, to act on it. For example, if you were a manager, you might in fact decide to adopt the adaptive leader behavior model espoused in the article.

Thus, the writer who wishes to persuade the reader will first make an *assertion,* which is a positive and forceful opinion, theory, conclusion, or declaration. Next, the writer *supports* the *assertion* with subjective reasons, objective research, interviews, or expert testimony. Finally, the writer often includes the *expected outcome,* which may be either stated directly or implied. You may simply agree with the author's ideas or you may take some action. On the other hand, you may have read the article critically and noted some flaws in the writer's reasoning or research. In such cases, you reject the writer's assertion and do not act or think as the writer would like. The writer, therefore, has not been successful in attaining the expected outcomes.

The diagram shown in Figure 2 illustrates how main ideas and details relate to the various components of the persuasive pattern.

INSTRUCTIONS FOR ANALYZED READING: "The Corporation in Crisis"

This article is written in the Persuasive Pattern. Read it and note how it has been analyzed.

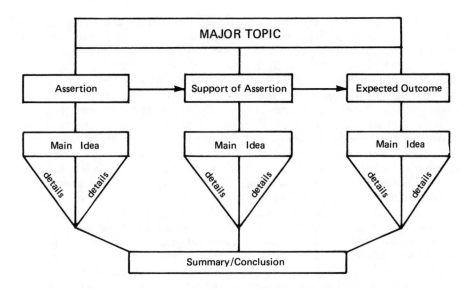

Figure 2 Relationship of Main Ideas to Persuasive Pattern

Analyzed Reading

The Corporation in Crisis

John C. Perham

Can the corporation survive? That may seem like a foolish question about an institution that has provided so much of this nation's wealth and power, but even business' most ardent champions admit that it is a legitimate one. The corporation, and the system it represents, is being attacked as never before. It is under assault from the government, charged with everything from bribery to price-fixing, from polluting the air and water to turning out unsafe products in unsafe working conditions. Dissident stockholders echo those charges and further contend that companies are neither living up to their social responsibilities nor giving their owners enough information about corporate activities. Most vociferous of all are the economic doom-sayers, who predict that the corporation will indeed be toppled from its leading role as the main driving force in the U.S. economy.

Business leaders generally are confident that the business form defined by Chief Justice John Marshall more than 150 years ago will prevail. But they acknowledge that they face a tough fight against many strong forces. Strongest of all, of course, is the federal government, which over the years has wielded ever-increasing power over business through a growing maze of laws and regulations.

Currently, moreover, business is confronted by perhaps the most anti-business Congress since the New Deal. According to the U.S. Chamber of Commerce, there are some 56 major issues before Congress that are of direct concern to business—from national health insurance to federal economic planning. Among the major bills now in the Senate hopper are two aimed at the oil industry, another that would require every major corporation to have two independent members on its board of directors to watch out for bribes and payoffs, and Ralph Nader's proposal to make all large companies federally chartered.

To critics who find many aspects of modern America abhorrent, the corporation, which seems so impersonal and inhuman, makes an inviting target. It is especially inviting to the doomsayers, who believe that the prevailing market system, in which millions of individual buying and selling decisions determine the direction in which the economy moves, must be replaced by some kind of socialist setup in which government makes the big decisions. Well-known economist J. Kenneth Galbraith, for one, has written thousands of words arguing that what he calls America's private affluence and public squalor can only be relieved by putting corporations under much tighter government controls. Liberal idea man Richard Goodwin, who was a speech writer for Presidents John F. Kennedy and Lyndon B. Johnson, is convinced that the major corporations will inevitably be absorbed by the state, with government bureaucracy taking over the planning role. And Socialist Michael Harrington, in his latest book, *The Twilight of Capitalism,* argues that today's businessmen, and the economists who advise them, are so self-serving that they themselves are the greatest threat to free enterprise.

Perhaps the most widely circulated of the recent doomsday books is *Business Civilization in Decline* by veteran economist-writer Robert L. Heilbroner. According to Heilbroner, capitalism will probably disappear within a century. Our natural resources are becoming exhausted, he says, and therefore neither national nor industrial growth can continue at their historic rates. "The end of corporate growth," Heilbroner writes, "will bring the progressive elimination of the profits that have been both the means and the end of the accumulation of private property." He foresees a vast increase in national economic planning, in which the corporation's role will grow continually smaller, that of government correspondingly larger. What will eventually emerge is a static but tightly controlled society where, he says, "the traditional pillars of capitalism—private property and the market—have been amended beyond recognition."

In response, business can argue that the U.S. must have growth, even if not at the hectic pace of fifty or 100 years ago. Only by increasing production, and therefore jobs, can the nation generate the tax dollars to pay for all the demands of its citizens, whether it be better health care, cleaning up the environment or reversing urban decay. As for natural resources, experts now believe that the world's resources are much more adequate than they predicted three years ago. And while some domestic resources, like oil, are being rapidly depleted, the U.S. coal supply is centuries away from exhaustion. But the technology to find new and better uses for coal and other resources will also cost a great deal of money.

Unfortunately, corporate leaders have always been notoriously unsuccessful in taking their case to the public, and pervasive myths about business—and the profit motive—still persist. In several recent public polls, for instance, most respondents estimated that the average manufacturer's after-tax profit was 25% and even 30%. The actual figure is about 5%.

Clearly, business must improve its

communications with the outside world. Above all, corporate leaders must explain more effectively the efforts they are making to help solve the problems of society—and the tremendous costs of those efforts. For example, while no corporation today can afford to be indifferent to the job of protecting the environment, it has to somehow reconcile its responsibility to control pollution with the hard necessity of continuing to make a profit.

U.S. corporations will spend $9.5 billion on pollution control this year, according to a recent McGraw-Hill survey. These outlays yield no direct return on the bottom line. Nor is it true, as some people argue, that spending on pollution-control equipment creates just as many jobs as any other kind of capital investment. According to a U.S. Steel study, an investment in new steel capacity, like the $75 million pipe mill announced by Big Steel in May, creates thirty times as many jobs as the same amount put into pollution-control equipment because of its multiplier effect on the economy.

With the government calling the tune on not only pollution control but energy, occupational safety, equal opportunity and many other vital issues, the biggest problem for most corporations is to achieve a better working relationship with the Washington bureaucracy that administers the laws. Corporations are going to have to live with government agencies, like it or not. What is needed is a better dialogue and a more reasonable division of responsibility.

INSTRUCTIONS FOR ANALYZED READING ANALYSIS: "The Corporation in Crisis"

In this article, the writer voices an opinion or theory that he wants to convey; thus, he chose to use the persuasive pattern to convey his message. The important main ideas and details in the article are listed below. Notice how they are associated with the different components of the persuasive pattern.

Pattern Component	Main Ideas and Details
Assertion	The corporation is under attack from the government, stock holders, and economists.
Support	The government is establishing more and more laws and regulations. Congress is anti-business. Galbraith and Goodwin call for greater government control of business. Harrington believes businessmen are a threat to free enterprise. Heilbroner predicts greater economic planning on the part of government.

Expected Outcomes

If you are a businessperson, you should improve communication with both the public and the government in order to improve your image and to soften the attack.

INSTRUCTIONS FOR UNTIMED READING: "What Does Your Briefcase Tell About You?"

In this amusing article, the authors have an opinion of what your briefcase can tell about you. Read the article in order to determine their opinion on this subject and how they support this opinion. Think about what the authors might expect you to do *(expected outcome)* if you were to agree with their opinion or assertion. After reading the article, answer the questions that follow it. Then check your answers with the Answer Key.

Untimed Reading

What Does Your Briefcase Tell About You?
The Editors, Administrative Management

People who carry briefcases are usually a subject of envy among those who don't. There's a certain mystique to a briefcase. The key question is what's inside? the closed case presents no hint of what might reside within, whether diplomatic documents—or lunch.

What we'll do here is snoop into briefcases, exterior and interior, until we poke enough holes in the mystique that neither the briefcase nor the mystique could hold document one . . . or a salami.

Let's start with the basics. A briefcase is carried from one point to another to avoid losing what is being transported. You don't have to take a complete inventory when you get up, you just grab a handle and move.

There's a certain status involved with briefcasemanship. To begin with, if it's heavy, you're out. Important folks only carry light things, the theory being that someone else has done the staff work and you're just making the final decisions.

The current fad is to carry only an envelope or a folder. This makes you look like you're on business instead of on your way to lunch, but nobody's going to mistake you for the plumber. A comfortable and neat-appearing little item is an underarm folder that has a zipper on three sides. Something like you had when you were a kid but without the three binder snap-rings at the bottom. You don't lose anything, it presents a good, professional appearance and is totally useless. One *Time* magazine and a ham sandwich and you've wiped it out. About the time you buy a good leather one, your job will change and you'll be carrying more stuff than you can possibly fit into it.

A heavy cardboard envelope fulfills the same purpose, and you can get more into it. It presents absolutely no image. As far as your overall appearance goes it's a neutral object. The viewer's eyes focus elsewhere for hints as to what you're about—your tie, for example, but all to virtually no avail. You can maintain your anonymity, if that is your goal.

Moving up in size from envelopes and the underarm style, we come to the real, live briefcase—the job with a handle on it.

The most popular one in the United States is the attache case, the kind you lay flat on the desk before opening. The biggest problem with this type is that when you open it upside down, your whole world falls out. Amazing things accumulate in the bottom of a briefcase, which becomes the top when an attache case is opened upside down. How would you like it if a bottle of Scotch which you innocently picked up to take home fell out at your job interview?

OPEN WITH DRAMA

Just the opening of the two snaps of an attache case has in itself a certain mystique about it. The sole function of opening the fasteners is, of course, to open the case. Done with a little drama, however, it can strike fear into the heart of the observer.

('We have a report on your actions, Johnson, and I must say we're not totally satisfied,'' the man from New York said. The snapping open of his black attache case was like two rifle shots.)

(I have a check for $100,000, O'Reilly . . . if you can complete one condition,'' he said. He slowly unsnapped his briefcase, each distinct ''click'' opening O'Reilly's eyes further in anticipation.)

Snapping them closed can be a lot of fun too, and may be extremely unnerving.

Make a decision, then close just one side with a loud snap. You've told your counterpart that you've made the final decision and that his arguments are not getting through. However, you are open to any solid last arguments he may have.

Close both sides and you communicate that your decision is final and hell or high water won't make you change it, especially if you accompany the snapping sounds with a little shuffle of preparation, indicating the meeting is over.

As a communications device, it's great.

Size is a problem. Get one item that's too big and you've had it. Attache cases don't bend. The ultra-thin two-incher model always look embarrassed if it has a handle. A single Sunday newspaper loads it to capacity. A bit too cute for men, it's all right for women.

The three-and-a-half-inch case is adequate for most needs, unless you carry more than one or two books or a Thermos with your lunch.

The five-inch model is large enough to be very practical but prestige goes downhill. Don't be surprised if someone mistakes you for the plumber. Many tool kits are made in this size, a spin-off from when IBM got smart and called its repairman ''customer engineers'' and gave them ties and briefcases.

You also run the danger of having people ask you where you're going for the weekend. This size does make a handy overnight bag, and is only a bit smaller than one.

The next size up is the sample case. The only people who get away with carrying these monstrosities are pilots. If you're addicted to flying boots and don't mind mumbling to yourself about the weather between here and Paris loud enough to be overheard, you might make it . . . maybe.

The other style of briefcase, small enough for status and popular in Europe but not here, is the top-loader. In the States, they're considered old-fashioned . . . or very in. If the carrier of a top-loader has been to Europe and wants to subtly advertise this fact, he'll carry a French or Italian top-loader. It probably won't be recognized for what it is except by others who've been around, but that's okay . . . it's a very in-group thing.

TABOOS AND TASTE

On a descending scale of how concerned you are about your status, colors are brown, black and sometimes gray.

The expert briefcaser will choose brown. Any shade. A brown briefcase connotes dignity and even if it isn't leather, it pays homage to it's leather forebears.

A good second choice is black, but this color has a few problems. For some reason, it connotes aggressiveness.

Gray sends out one of those neutral signals that makes the observer look at your tie for his impressions. It means you're not a briefcaser, the whole mystique of briefcasemanship confuses you, and you'd prefer the viewer to admire your nice new suit. It's a very safe thing, sort of like a short haircut.

Contrasting stitching. The plague would be my answer if asked to play word association games. Contrasting stitching connotes cheapness. You don't have it on your business suit; you don't need it on your briefcase. End of subject.

The material you select also sends out vibes, both good and bad. Quality leather sends out good vibes; obvious plastic sends out bad.

If you can afford it (sell the Porsche), buy leather. Good leather. It should even smell like leather a block away. There is nothing better in the art of briefcase one-upmanship than a quality leather briefcase. Bally brand, or Gucci, if possible and if you can find them (sell the Volvo, too). No decorations or designs on the sides, please! Some leathers, like alligator, present an appearance you don't really want. This appearance is hard to define. Just don't sit next to me on an airplane.

Needless to say, embossed leather is a no-no, with the possible exception of your initials, small and conservative. No bucking broncos, Mexican eagles, or three little pigs having an orgy.

Most briefcases are carried by conservative people and most of those on the market are conservative. Buy a conservative briefcase and take out your frustrations elsewhere.

UNTIMED READING COMPREHENSION CHECK: "What Does Your Briefcase Tell About You?"

1. Select the authors' *assertion*.

   a. _____ Your briefcase can be a status symbol and an image builder for you.

   b. _____ Your briefcase can help you get a pay raise.

   c. _____ Your briefcase reflects your personality.

2. Select the authors' *support* for this *assertion*.

   a. _____ The size, color, and texture of your briefcase reveal personality characteristics such as aggressiveness and motivation.

   b. _____ The size, color, and texture of your briefcase affect your image and are indications of your status in the company.

   c. _____ By picking a briefcase that has the 'right' size, color, and texture, you will probably get promoted.

3. If you agree with the authors' *assertion,* you will probably buy:

a. _____ a large, gray, plastic briefcase.

b. _____ a small, brown, leather briefcase.

c. _____ a moderately large, black alligator briefcase.

Check your answers with the Answer Key.

INSTRUCTIONS FOR UNTIMED READING: "The Business of Business Schools; Part I: The Attack"

The next reading, reprinted from *The Wharton Magazine,* represents one of two conflicting theories on the efficacy of business schools. Your purpose in reading is to identify the writer's theory and how it is supported. You should also determine the author's expected outcomes. Later in this chapter, you will have an opportunity to skim read an opposing point of view. After reading the article, write down your answers to the questions that follow.

Untimed Reading

The Business of Business Schools; Part I: The Attack

C. Jackson Grayson

I am increasingly concerned that business schools are not *business* schools. That is, the universities are not turning out students well trained to conduct business. They put too much emphasis on "understanding" business and seriously neglect the "practice" of business. Therefore, I lay the "dead cat" of this situation—the gap between studying business and doing business—primarily at the door of the business schools. (The saints, burly sinners, and castrated buffaloes of the title will appear later.)

The serious choice ahead, in my opinion, is whether universities are really going to have *business* schools—or have something else instead. And I am not just talking about a name shift to a "School of Management." The gap is still the same whether their graduates go to work in a business, a government agency, or a hospital.

A few years ago I conducted a survey of leading businessmen on this developing problem. They said that while business schools in general are doing some good, their "products' are missing the mark in many ways. They cited these shortcomings:

1. Too much emphasis on talking about action and not enough on actually taking action.

2. Inability to communicate—both verbally and in writing.

3. Inability to accept responsibility for a project and carry it through to completion.

4. Over-emphasis on "solving" problems before they are fully identified and understood.

5. Inability to get along with and motivate people.

6. Inability to set personal goals and design plans to achieve them.

7. Too much theoretical knowledge and not enough practical orientation.

As I travel around these days, and talk to businessmen as ex-dean of a business school, the problem is still just as bad. Furthermore, academic surveys also keep turning up results that illustrate the mismatch between business schools and business:

- Professor Lewis Ward at the Harvard Business School found that the median salaries of Harvard's MBA graduates plateau 15 years out and don't increase afterward. Another study at Harvard showed that men attending its Advanced Management Program, after having had 15 years experience, but practically no formal training in management, earn a third more than men who hold MBA degrees.

- Professor Gordon Marshall at the Harvard Business School looked at the records of 1,000 of its graduates and concluded that "academic success and business achievement have relatively little association with each other."

- Tom Harrell at the Stanford Business School found little correlation between its students' grades and their financial success in business after graduation. And the same lack of correlation was true for scores on the ATGSB (Admission Test for Graduate Study in Business) and financial success. Yet these tests constitute the prime method by which most business schools continue to select promising business leaders!

There is only one way that most of these shortcomings and mismatches could be significantly improved—our business schools must consider themselves more *of* business, *by* business,

and *for* business. The same discipline that has honed our business system needs to be applied to our business schools: responsiveness to consumers' needs (instead of placing the faculty's needs ahead of students' needs); conducting research that is relevant (instead of just theoretical and interesting); greater freedom of entry (instead of traditional student credentials); creative destruction when necessary (instead of creeping incremental change); and efficient and effective management instead of scholarly deliberation that defers taking responsibility and action).

Now it's true that at least part of this dead cat (perhaps one foot, an ear, and part of the tail) needs to be awarded to business, government organizations, and consulting firms for their benign neglect of business schools. More on them later. But the main carcass belongs to the business schools themselves. I believe that for any significant improvement to occur in the present state of affairs, *the greatest changes have to take place in the students and faculties of the business schools.*

I am well aware that this point of view is not a consensual agreement, and that my words are not typical of most business school deans or professors. I do not claim them to be. I am also aware that there are some legitimate reasons and concerns why business schools should be wary of becoming completely "by business, of business, and for business." Errors exist in swinging the pendulum too far the other way.

Having stated this, I am still of the opinion that we, at business schools, are far from where we should be. We are not turning out as useful a product as we should be, and I include in the term "product" both people and ideas. If I am right, what explanations can be offered?

The problem originates from a

schizophrenia that has plagued universities, in general, since their very beginning: Is their mission to discover and transmit "truth and understanding" or to prepare people with "knowledge, skills, and attitudes for practical application"? Education or training?

This dichotomy, in my own view, is spurious and dysfunctional. The two are inter-dependent. But universities have operated too much as though the two processes are independent. A whole system of traditions, attitudes, norms, taboos, and curricula have grown up to perpetuate a division between the liberal arts "understanding" and the professional schools "practice."

Business schools inherit this division. "Understanding" connotes an intellectual, impersonal knowledge of theory and techniques, a cognitive, scholarly, detached process. "Practice" connotes application of this understanding in a situation where there is operational responsibility, personal involvement, emotional engagement, consequential judgment, situational anxiety, outcome, and feedback. The twain exists even inside professional schools where one might think that at least a shotgun wedding would occur.

At the heart of the problem are the *faculty* of business schools. Too many are blocking, or certainly not aiding, the essential symbiosis between understanding and practice. The primary reason is the cultural separation between business managers and university faculty members. The individuals are different in goals, personality, life styles.

Faculty members are not managers. They choose the academic life because they prefer it to the action-oriented life of a manager. Few have had direct experience with any real organizations. By that I mean experience in which they have had real operating responsibility for any extended period of time including diagnosis, analysis, decision-making, implementation, the use of power, and political confrontation. Consulting and staff positions do not qualify. Academics have not learned from experience to increase even their "understanding" of the most critical elements of a successful businessman's concerns. Instead, most of their understanding has come from listening to other scholars, reading books, and reasoning in a logical manner.

In the classroom, faculty members are not exemplars of practice. The model they offer to students is one of contemplation, analysis, detached thought— scholarly traits that lead to understanding, not practice. They are more Yogi than Commissar. Students are led to mirror their attitudes, knowledge, and skills because that is the model offered to them—and the payoff structure rewards such behavior with good grades.

Managers, on the other hand, select their careers because they want to make things happen. They want to organize things that work, to take responsibility, to be measured on performance. An idea to them is something to be tested to see if it will work, not to be defined and refined in the laboratories of the mind. They prefer to deal with intangible, intuitive modes of behavior and ill-structured risk-taking situations. Their world is populated with people, power, and politics—"messy" complications that interfere with orderly analysis and implementation.

The faculty culture also inhibits "practice" by continuation of the traditional didactic methods of teaching. The lecture-seminar is still predominant and the faculty member "teaches" his knowledge with descriptions of theory, followed by example, followed by textbook exercises. The case method is a departure from the passive lecture-seminar, but it, too, suffers from a lack of practice orientation. Even in a case discussion, the student still sits in a classroom and intellectually discusses problems and implementation of the solution. Whether lecture, seminar, or case method, the result is still an intellectual process with little emotional involvement or personal responsibility beyond the excitement of cognitive understanding and, of course, the professor's approval.

Another factor in this gap is that business students are usually defined as 18 to 28-year olds. Managers are not considered to be students; they are "participants" in management development programs. And because the culture concentrates so hard on degrees and 18 to 28-year olds, programs for practicing managers usually are merely tacked onto the main program. Faculty often participate in them only for extra income, so they do very little to adapt themselves to the more experienced, results-focused practitioner.

The faculty posture usually is: "Here is a concept or technique that I find exciting. I hope you find it useful." Very few say: "What are your problems? Maybe I can be of some help." What comes across is an attitude that ranges from intellectual arrogance to complete naivete. What's missing is knowledge about how business really operates, or could operate. Most business managers don't really feel at home with most business faculty. They often walk away unsatisfied, angry, and damned sure they aren't going to put any of that "theoretical" stuff into practice.

Are there any faculty members in business schools who are more oriented toward practice—by training, instinct, preference, and personal history? Yes, there are some. But too often even these

faculty members—let's call them "practice-oriented" professors—are also not really in touch with practice. They have relied for too many years on past knowledge and have effectively isolated themselves from current practice. What they call "involvement" means having lunch with managers occasionally, inviting some managers to lecture in their classes, or taking students on field trips.

Furthermore, some of these practice-oriented faculty members, after unsuccessfully bucking theoretical trends for years, have become disgusted and tired of fighting the current. They have, in effect, resigned "in the saddle," effectively protected by tenure and their outside consulting, teaching and/or textbook royalties.

The drift away from practice is not being stemmed by academic administrators either. One reason is that many deans and department chairmen were once discipline-scholars themselves and they perpetuate the trend. Also, many deans and chairmen consciously, or unconsciously, are setting the reward system in such a way that it signals the direction away from practice. This is done in a variety of ways:

- giving light teaching loads to those who perform journal-publishing research, and heavy loads to their practice-oriented brethren ("they may as well teach since they aren't doing anything else");

- giving promotions primarily to those with research and publication records despite lip-service to the contrary;

- awarding praise, recognition, and other status symbols for "scholarly" behavior;

- allocating resources to discipline-oriented departments.

Finally, even if the dean believes that

the pendulum is swinging too far away from practice, too often he is unwilling or unable to take reversing actions for the following reasons.

1. He is unwilling to "manage" the direction of the school because it is against his scholarly philosophy of the role of a dean or chairman.
2. He is unwilling to buck the direction being set by powerful faculty members for fear of being labeled "anti-intellectual" and "trade-school oriented".
3. He is unable to buck the direction because the faculty have sufficient power to take the school where they want.
4. He is too busy on other matters—money-raising, university committees, or outside activities—to take firm action to resist the trend.

How much fault in this situation lies with the business community itself? As stated before, at least an ear, one foot and part of the tail of the dead cat.

Some "real world" managers agree with the theoretical emphasis. But most deplore the trend, and then do little about it. They complain in the country-club locker room, at board meetings, on the golf course, in speeches. But they do not involve themselves in the schools. They don't know how to go about it and/or they don't want to take the time. Some have been rebuffed in a few attempts and don't care to try again. They have written off business training as mostly useless: "We'll teach them when they get here."

Even though some managers try to be involved—by serving on a school advisory committee, teaching a course, or visiting campuses as a lecturer—their time commitment is low, and they are not effective agents for change. Also, if they suggest a redirection of the school more toward practice, they are often outflanked by academic strategists. One company president serving on a prominent school advisory committee said:

I told them they were turning out students that didn't know a damn thing about business. They smiled and said I didn't understand. They were turning out the people with good analytic training that would prepare them for tomorrow, not today. Hell, I understand that. But we'd be in a helluva situation if we let our company R&D department isolate iself to that extent and set the major direction for the firm. But that's their business—not mine.

And what about the students?

Though many people think that students would be delighted if universities would only involve themselves more with practical applications, it isn't necessarily so.

For one thing our entire U.S. educational system is geared more toward the knowledge-seeking, reflective, theoretical, aesthetic student as opposed to the action-oriented, pragmatic, and intuitive student. Those who score highest in their high school classes and on the admission tests are those who exhibit scholarly aptitudes. As Sterling Livingston stated it: "Over-reliance on scholastic learning ability has caused leading universities and business organizations to reject a high percentage of those who had the greatest potential for creativity and growth in nonacademic careers."

Most students have been exposed to only passive intellectual classroom learning all through their educational life in elementary schools, high schools, and universities. Some of them blossom, given an opportunity to become more involved in unstructured, experiential learning, with the responsibility shifted more to them. But a surprisingly large number are frightened, anxious, even downright hostile. They sometimes become anxiously dependent, paralyzed by any demands for self-reliance. They resist attempts to alter the curriculum and educational setting, preferring instead the comfortable, passive classroom process with which they are familiar. Small wonder that many founder when they move from the classroom to the work arena.

One last process and institution that tends to suppress change is the "hallowed" institution of accreditation. The AACSB (American Association of Collegiate Schools of Business), like most accrediting societies, was initiated to correct some evils and shortcomings. But over the years, it has become so institutionalized and conformity-demanding that real innovation is largely impossible, despite lip service to the contrary. In the name of raising standards, they are denying diversity.

Now that I've succeeded in one way or another in antagonizing almost everybody, I'll balance my remarks a little and also offer some positive suggestions. First, the balancing:

- Faculty members are not all neatly divided into theoretical and practice-oriented groups. There are all degrees of mixes.

- If we only concentrated on today's practical problems we wouldn't be preparing business organizations or students for tomorrow.

- Curricula in the past *were* too descriptive, impressionistic, outmoded, institution-oriented, and factionated. The curricula did need change.

- Disciplines and theories do have ideas and methodology very useful to practice.

- Not all faculty, deans, chairmen, managers, and students fit my broad brush indictment. Some are actually engaged in some of the suggested actions right now.

- Managers do not speak with a unified voice about the people they want business schools to produce. There are still debates on whether they should be theoretical staffers or results-minded leaders, creative managers or entrepreneurs, analysts or general problem-solvers.

However, I will not back away from my overall observation that most business school faculty and students have drifted away from practice in recent years and are continuing in this direction—to the detriment of both management and the business schools. Can you imagine such a situation existing in medical schools? Suppose that most medical school faculty members had never practiced medicine, and that the doctor about to practice on you had only sat in classrooms for his training, or discussed medical cases abstractly.

What can be done to alter the situation? Some of my recommendations will sound impossible to do. But unless such steps are taken, I predict there will be little change in the present situation.

My first recommendation is that business schools shift more of their curriculum to *learning by doing*—experiential learning as some call it. By this I mean that a substantial portion (not all) of a student's education about business and himself should be done by interaction with faculty and businessmen around a live business situation (including hospitals, government agencies, etc.). This goes beyond the case method, which despite its simulation of reality, is still a classroom process.

Such learning would not be a capstone at the end of a business education, but the main process throughout the program. For example, by working on the design of an accounting system for a small restaurant, all those involved would be driven to seek information about accounting knowledge and theory. The accounting faculty would be resources, offering course modules, programmed instructional material, lectures, guides to literature, etc. Evaluations would be based on performance, not on ability to transcribe memory onto an examination paper. Students would enter the system at different levels and times depending on their knowledge, abilities, and experience; and they would leave at different times depending on different performance.

A second recommendation is to change the mix of faculty members to include a much higher percentage (50 percent and up) who have had and continue to have direct practical experience with operating organizations. Recruit them from business, government, and the military. Forget whether they have a Ph.D. or *any* degree. Recruit on the basis of demonstrated capacity to mix "understanding and practice."

Require, through performance objectives, some demonstration that faculty members are involved in practical applications in both research and teaching. Examples: live research projects with students and managers, internships with organizations, sabbaticals in companies, etc. Criteria for reward, promotion, praise, and raise should follow the same lines. We must require that faculty leave the university at periodic intervals for some direct experience. As Whitehead observed: "The second-handedness of the learned world is the secret of its mediocrity."

Here are a few additional ideas for increased student-faculty-business interaction outside the business school:

1. Have the business school own a business and have students and faculty learn by operating the business. (Quite a few people have thought of this, but no one has done it to my knowledge.)

2. Have students "adopt" an ongoing small business where they become responsible for observing and counseling. Students in some medical schools "adopt" a family.

3. Have students take over a "night shift" operation of a business when otherwise it would shut down.

Learning by doing is not "laissez-faire" education. Students must be prodded, encouraged, corrected, shaped, and evaluated. Projects must be supervised and monitored and there must be formal conceptualization during the process. Faculty members can teach concepts and techniques and assign books far more effectively than in the traditional way. In fact, they have a more demanding role than in the traditional method, a fact which in itself has probably blocked extensive development of this method.

Are these things difficult? Hell, yes. When I propose this method of learning, both to managers and to faculty, I am usually met by a barrage of objections:

1. How can you get the live problems? (That's the job of the faculty and managers. It can be done. We did it at SMU).

2. Organizations won't be willing to have students running all over the place and looking at confidential data. (They don't "run all over the place." Confidentiality, though a problem, is not as big a problem as most people think it is.)

3. Such a learning process is much more expensive and inefficient. (It's more expensive only if the faculty persist in offering the curriculum as they have in the past. It is inefficient only if you measure efficiency by knowledge covered in the classroom from the professor's course outline—and ignore retention, use of knowledge, motivation, etc.)

4. Students will be graduated who may not have all the basic skills. (Behavioral objectives insure some basic skill acquisition. But it isn't clear that all students should acquire all basic skills. Don't forget that even in the traditional system, they may not have really acquired skills even though their transcript says they had a course in "Stochastic Processes.")

5. Faculty can't do research, because they will be so involved with students and time-consuming practical problems. (True, if research is defined as being (a) divorced from students and (b) on problems remote from practice. But if research is done on real problems, involves students and businessmen, and is a way of teaching, then everyone benefits, and so does the quality of the research.)

My final recommendation has to do with the selection of students. We are now admitting students largely on scholastic criteria created over the centuries for selection of the intellectual, cognitive, analytic student. These criteria predict that the student will do well in the next academic progression, but not necessarily at work. We shouldn't be surprised at the outcome!

I fear that we are screening out the action-oriented, creative, intuitive students who may not score well on the traditional academic tests, but who often are the best when it comes to application. Many such students do not even apply to universities, and particularly business schools, because they believe the traditional structure would bore them, be a waste of time, or actually harm them. Searching them out means searching for creativity, drive, energy, ambition—all the attributes that most businessmen say they want in their managers.

Now that I have accounted for most of the "dead cat," how about the rest of the title?

The "castrated buffalo" comes from a story about an Operations Research group that was studying the survivability of buffalos and their eating habits on high plains grasses. Because the male buffalo was difficult to manage during the study, he was castrated. The research group did not appreciate a question about whether the castrated buffalo was going to act very naturally. We have a lot of castrated-buffalo teaching examples in universities in the United States.

Regarding saints and sinners, John Dewey argued that it was better to err on the side of active participation in the real problems of the age than to maintain an immune monastic sterility. "Saints engage in introspection," he said, while "burly sinners run the world."

I do not think that introspective saints and burly sinners need be mutually exclusive; I believe that they are and can be inter-dependent. Another way to put it is that we must get more learning into practice, and more practice into learning. To produce men of understanding *and* practice means, in my opinion, that we have to do something very different.

At least that's the view from one introspective sinner in a university.

UNTIMED READING COMPREHENSION CHECK: "The Business of Business Schools; Part I: The Attack"

1. What is Grayson's *assertion* or theory?

2. How does he *support* his theory?

3. What *reasons* does Grayson give that led him to present his theory?

4. If Grayson's *theory* is generally accepted, what are some *expected outcomes?*

Check your answers with the Answer Key.

INSTRUCTIONS FOR PACED READING: "Workweeks and Leisure: An Analysis of Trends, 1948-75"
The pacing rate for this article is 500 words per minute. This means that you should finish reading the article in 5 minutes and 45 seconds, or a total of 345 seconds. Ask someone to tell you when the time has expired. This article contains approximately 2900 words. After reading the article, write down your answers to the questions that follow.

Paced Reading

Workweeks and Leisure: An Analysis of Trends, 1948-75
John D. Owen

Employed American adults have had no net gain in their leisure time in 30 years—since the end of World War II. That was the somewhat surprising result of analysis of data published by the Bureau of Labor Statistics from the Current Population Survey on hours of work.

There was a rather modest decline in the measured average weekly hours of nonagricultural employees; they went from 40.9 in 1948 to 38.1 in 1975. However, this drop appears to reflect changes in the composition of the labor force rather than a reduction in the hours of work of the individuals or groups that compose the work force. As a result of postwar trends, a larger proportion of the work force are women and students: women nonagricultural employees made up 29 percent of the work force in 1940 and are 40 percent of it today; students made up 1 percent or less in 1940 and 2.5 percent after World War II, but now are at a level of about 6 percent. In the same period, the proportion of nonstudent males in the nonagricultural work force dropped to under 57 percent.[1] Because of group differences in hours worked—women average 34 hours, male students 22 hours, and nonstudent males about 43 hours per week—the declining proportion of nonstudent males in the labor force has produced a statistical decline in average weekly hours. However, these compositional shifts may not reflect a real reduction in working times. This article explores these shifts and tests a hypothesis as to why hours have not declined.

THE POSTWAR EXPERIENCE

Hours data for the majority group, men not in school, are very probably the most reliable indicators of average work input, partly because this group has changed relatively little in composition, partly because the work effort of this group has been measured more carefully over the years than the input of what were once considered "marginal" workers. The following tabulation shows hours of work of nonstudent men employed in nonagricultural industries:

Year	Unad-justed	Adjusted for growth in vacations and holidays
1948	42.7	41.6
1950	42.2	41.0
1953	42.5	41.4
1956	43.0	41.8
1959	42.0	40.7
1962	43.1	41.7
1966	43.5	42.1
1969	43.5	42.0
1972	42.9	41.4
1975	42.5	40.9

This tabulation actually shows a slight increase in hours from 1948 to 1969 (2 years of relatively full employment), and a slight decline in 1969–75, largely resulting from cyclical factors. Over the whole period, there was no net change.

In 1948–75, the hours of male students, however, increased by about 4 hours per week. Those of women declined somewhat, and the difference between the weekly hours of men and women roughly doubled. However, these changes reflect changes in the composition of the women and student groups rather than any change in the hours of work of individuals. For example, there was a steady increase in the average age of male student workers in nonagricultural industries; the proportion under 18 years of age fell from 62 percent in 1947 to 38 percent in 1972. (This decrease in very young male workers reflects the increased proportion of young people finishing high school and going on to college in more recent years.) Since older students generally

work much longer hours than do younger students—those 20–24 years of age average about 28 hours per week, while those age 14–15 average only 10 hours and those age 16–17 average about 18 hours—the increasing average age of students has produced an increase in their average hours of work. Within age categories, however, there has been no significant change in students' weekly hours of work.

Similarly, the decline in hours of working women is largely the result of changes in the composition of the female labor force. Among employed women, the proportion who are married with husband present increased from 30 percent in 1940 to 58 percent in 1975. The proportion of working mothers with children under 18 years of age rose from 24 percent of all women in the labor force in 1950 to 37 percent in 1975. The rising proportion of wives, and especially of mothers, tends to reduce average hours for women, since wives and mothers generally put in fewer hours of work than other women of comparable age. On the average, employed wives work about 1.4 fewer hours a week for every child under age 15 at home.[2]

Changes in the statistical procedures used by the U.S. Government have also altered the measurement of hours of women and students and helped to generate the statistical trends described above. The measurement of part-time work has been improved in the postwar period, in an effort to eliminate the undercounting of part-time workers that had once been common. This has tended to reduce the average hours of women workers, many of whom are part time. On the other hand, the decision, in 1967, to exclude 14- and 15-year-olds from the labor force base used to calculate average hours has increased the reported average age of the labor force somewhat and the average hours of student workers in the Current Population Survey.

In summary, a decomposition of the measured statistical decline in average working hours does not indicate that any significant reduction in paid work actually took place in the total work force. Further, and perhaps more important, the various compositional shifts in the labor force responsible for this apparent decline in hours of work may well *not* have yielded any net gain in leisure time. Indeed, one could more reasonably interpret the increased employment of groups with extensive nonmarket work responsibilities as tending to reduce free time. Students must go to school, attend classes, and prepare assignments; the additional time many of them now spend at part-time work leaves the conscientious student who is also employed with very little leisure available.

More statistical data are available for the time allocations of women. Employed women in the United States have been estimated to spend about 33 hours per week in unpaid work or worklike activities (which includes commuting time as well as time spent in housework), leaving about 6 hours less free time for recreation and other leisure activities than employed men have. The longer workweeks of employed men are offset here because they spend fewer hours in housework and related activities. Employed women have about 12 fewer hours a week for free-time activities than full-time housewives.[3]

Hence, the shift from full-time housewife to employed wife which so many women have undergone was probably associated with a decline, not an increase, in their available free time. This interpretation gains support from a well-known study of changes in housework over time, which found that the average worktime of full-time housewives stood at about 54 hours a week over a 40-year period, despite the numerous time-saving devices and products which have been purchased by housewives.[4]

The hours of work series for nonstudent men probably provides us with a better indicator of net changes over time in the leisure of the working population than could be constructed from available data on women and students. However, it is still flawed in two respects. First, as an indicator of leisure time it may be biased upwards, insofar as the rise in female labor force participation over the past 30 years has been accompanied by an increase in the amount of housework done by men. A comparison of a nationwide statistical study of time use in 1965 with earlier studies suggests that there have been only minor changes in this area since the 1930's.[5] However, scattered reports indicate that in the last 10 years men's contribution to household tasks may have increased more significantly.

The second flaw in the series is that it is, in fact, biased downward as an indicator of changes in leisure over time because it omits the effects of increases in holidays and vacations. On the basis of available data on vacations and holidays, the weekly hours series can be adjusted to reflect this growth,[6] as has been done in our earlier text tabulation. When this adjustment is made, no significant change is found in hours in the 1948–69 period, although a slight decline is observed in the next few years, as unemployment levels increased.

CONTRAST WITH EARLIER YEARS

The leveling off in hours of work in the past 30 years is a sharp contrast with experience before World War II. Hours had been declining in the United States for about 100 years. Let us discuss the course of hours of employees in the nonagricultural sector since the turn of the century. Since weekly hours tend to rise and fall with the course of the business cycle,[7] only full-employment peak years are useful in the interest of isolating the long-term movements more clearly. World Wars I and II are also excluded because of the special labor market conditions characteristic of the war years. There has been a decline from 58.4 hours a week in 1901 to 42.0 in 1948, and little or no change since.[8]

Labor economists have explained the long-term downward movement in hours as largely a result of secular increases in real hourly earnings. In a number of countries, as industrialization progressed, hours of work declined with a rise in hourly wages. The economists' explanation of this correlation was that higher wage rates increased the worker's potential living standard, enabling him to increase his leisure time or his consumption of goods and services. In practice, most of this rise in standard of living—three-quarters to four-fifths or more in the United States—was reflected in purchases of consumer goods rather than leisure.[9] Nevertheless, over a period of decades, the cumulative effect was to cut working times very considerably.

If this pattern had been maintained, there would have been an accelerated rate of hours reduction after the war. Real hourly earnings of nonfarm employees rose at an average annual rate of 2.7 percent, a somewhat higher rate than that achieved in the prewar decades. If the same reduction in hours per unit increase in hourly wages had occurred in the postwar years, there would have been a decline of over one-half day per week. For example, the 40-hour week in manufacturing might by now have been reduced to 35 hours, with proportion-ately shorter schedules in white-collar work.

WHY DID HOURS OF WORK LEVEL OFF?

Upon closer examination, the divergent pattern of hours movements since the end of World War II is not difficult to explain. The post-World War II years followed upon a decade-and-a-half of depression and war. Consumption needs of all sorts had gone unmet in those years of unemployment and shortages; in the first few years after the war, workers tried to catch up on purchases of clothing, household appliances, and other consumer goods. There was very little demand for a reduction in work-times.

But there were also somewhat longer lasting effects of the catching-up process. Birth rates at a very low level in the 1930's, rose sharply with the return of better times in the war and postwar periods. This type of "catching-up" had long-term effects on American work and consumption patterns because (unlike a purchase of a refrigerator or a car) a decision to have a child imposes costs that extend for two decades.[10]

The effects of this sudden increase in childrearing costs was further exacerbated by another postwar development—the "education revolution," which increased the average years of schooling by about 3 years and increased the proportion of those going on to college to a near majority. This vast increase in education investment is believed by some observers to be a reaction to labor-market conditions, which generated a higher level of demand for college-trained labor and an increasing level of unemployment for those with below-average schooling. In any event, the extension of schooling greatly increased the average cost of raising a child.

As the combination of the "baby boom" and the "education revolution" increased the costs of childrearing very considerably in the postwar period, the enormous outlays required diverted resources from other consumption and savings in the average household and made a shortening of the working hours of adults—with the loss of earnings that such a reduction would entail—less attractive.[11]

IMPLICATIONS FOR THE FUTURE

Hours reduction is influenced by a complex of forces: economic factors like the unemployment rate and the growth rate of real hourly wages and such social variables as the birth rate and the average school-leaving age. Because any forecast of such a range of causative variables is uncertain, it is prudent to present several scenarios (possible future histories) for the future of hours of work in the United States.[12] Three different scenarios appear to be plausible, one in which working times are rather gradually reduced over the next 25 years, one in which hours are cut quite sharply within the next 5 to 10 years, and one in which no significant reduction in working times takes place.

First Scenario: A Gradual Reduction in Hours of Work

The baby boom has long since ended. Birth rates began to decline in the 1950's, and are now at an extremely low level. The average number of years of schooling has temporarily leveled off. If these trends continue, childrearing costs should increase much less rapidly. If, at the same time, the upward trend in real hourly earnings continues, the long-term analysis of hours movements presented here indicates a gradual reduction in working times in the years ahead. The prewar trend would resume, and workers would once again divide the potential gain in living standards made possible by rising real hourly wages between increased consumption of goods and services and increased free time for the enjoyment of those goods and services. In all probability, by far the larger share of the potential gain would still go to consumption, but over a period of two or three decades, a significant cumulative reduction in hours could take place.

In the short run, this scenario might imply a small *increase* in average hours if an improvement in economic conditions were accompanied by the usual cyclical upturn in hours of work. However, in the medium run, a return to more prosperous conditions might be followed by a renewed interest in practical methods for reducing workhours—for example, compressed workweeks.[13] Some workers might want to work 4 days for 9½ hours, and others might prefer a workweek consisting of 4½ days of 8 hours each. On the other hand, many workers might opt for a shorter workday with no reduction in the number of days worked per week. Continued gains in vacation and holiday time would also be expected in this scenario.

Second Scenario: A Rapid Decline in Hours of Work

Some pessimists believe that the recent high levels of unemployment will continue to plague us for at least the next 5 years. If this dismal forecast is correct, one could expect to find very considerable support emerging for a 30-hour week as a way of sharing the available work opportunities in a more equitable manner. Individual company efforts and agreements negotiated with trade unions could be supplemented at a later date by measures to reduce the workweek at the local, State, and Federal levels of government. This was, of course, the pattern of hours reduction in the 1930's, but economic conditions would probably not have to be nearly as depressed as they were in the 1930's to generate the collective action needed to share the work by reducing hours.

Third Scenario: No Reduction in Hours of Work

A second group of pessimists regards a prolonged period of high unemployment as unlikely but does not believe that we can expect the upward trend in the purchasing power of the average American's take-home pay to continue because of the growing energy and materials problems which may face the Nation, the expectations of a "capital shortage," and the likely costs of budgeting for future social and military programs. In addition, because of the very recent apparent upturn in birth rates, some point out that another baby boom may well be underway. The statistical analysis presented here would suggest that such a constellation of factors—little or no growth in real hourly earnings and, possibly, another spurt in childrearing costs—would definitely work against a further reduction in hours of work.

One can rank these three scenarios in order of their probability. The first would be regarded by many observers as more likely than the second, and the second as more likely than the third. However, an analysis of past events indicates that none of the three can be ruled out altogether as a plausible "future history" for hours of work and leisure.

FOOTNOTES

[1]Unless otherwise noted, data on hours of work and on student employment are derived from two publications of the Bureau of Labor Statistics, *Employment and Earnings* and *Special Labor Force Reports*. Data on employment of women are from *Statistical Abstract of the United States, 1975*.

[2]Calculated from a multiple regression using the May 1973, Bureau of Labor Statistics, Current Population Survey data tape. The other independent variables in the regression were race, schooling, age and other family income.

[3]See J.P. Robinson and P.E. Converse, *66 Basic Tables of Time Budget Research Data for the U.S.* (Ann Arbor, University of Michigan, Survey Research Center, 1967).

[4]See Joan Vanek, "Keeping Busy; Time Spent in Housework, United States, 1920-1970" (Ph.D. dissertation, University of Michigan, 1973).

[5]See Robinson and Converse, *66 Basic Tables;* M. Komarovsky, G. A. Lundberg, and M. A. McInerny, *Leisure, A Suburban Study* (New York, Columbia University Press, 1934); and Angus Campbell and Philip E. Converse, eds., *The Human Meaning of Social Change* (New York, Russell Sage Foundation, 1972).

[6]See Peter Henle, "Recent Growth of Paid Leisure for U.S. Workers," *Monthly Labor Review*, March 1962, pp. 249-57; and John D. Owen, *The Price of Leisure* (Montreal, McGill-Queens University Press, 1970).

[7]See Robert W. Bednarzik, "Involuntary part-time work: a cyclical analysis," *Monthly Labor Review*, September 1975, pp. 12-18.

[8]Full-employment years are defined as those in which unemployment is less than 4.5 percent. When several such years occur in sequence, only the peak year was chosen. See Owen, *The Price of Leisure*, for further detail.

[9]The traditional explanation of this lopsided division is that, with a high and rising market price for his time, the American worker has been tempted by higher wages to take most of the gain as an increase in consumption. Thus, it was argued that if the national productivity dividend had been distributed differently—for example, if the U.S. Government had given checks for identical amounts to each citizen—a much larger reduction in hours might have been observed. See Lionel Robbins, "On the Elasticity of Income in Terms of Effort," *Economica*, June 1930, pp. 123-29; Gary S. Becker, "A Theory of the Allocation of Time," *Economic Journal*, September 1965, pp. 493-517; Owen, *The Price of Leisure;* and Staffen B. Linder, *The Harried Leisure Class* (New York, Columbia Unversity Press, 1970).

[10]Richard A. Easterlin, *The Baby Boom in Historical Perspective* (New York, National Bureau of Economic Research, 1962).

[11]For statements about the expected positive relationship between hours of work and investment in children, see T. A. Finegan, "Hours of Work in the United States," *Journal of Political Economy*, October 1962, pp. 452-70; Owen, *The Price of Leisure;* C. M. Lindsay, "On Measuring Human Capital Returns," *Journal of Political Economy*, August 1971, pp. 1195-1215; and Y. Barzel, "The Determination of Daily Hours and Wages," *Quarterly Journal of Economics*, May 1973, pp. 220-38.

[12]For an application of the scenario method to the more general problem of predicting the future of work, see Denis F. Johnston, "The future of work: Three possible alternatives," *Monthly Labor Review*, May 1972, pp. 3-11.

[13]See Janice N. Hedges, "How many days make a workweek?" *Monthly Labor Review*, April 1975, pp. 29-36.

PACED READING COMPREHENSION CHECK: "Workweeks and Leisure: An Analysis of Trends, 1948-75"

1. What is the writer's *assertion* or *theory?*

   a. _____ The amount of leisure time has remained about the same for American adults for the past thirty years.

   b. _____ In the last thirty years, American adults have decreased their leisure time.

   c. _____ In the last thirty years, American adults have increased their leisure time.

2. The writer *supported* his theory by analyzing data from:

   a _____ the annual work and leisure study.

   b. _____ the Harvard Business School.

   c. _____ the current population survey.

3. One of the author's purposes in writing the article is to examine why there has been:

   a. _____ an increase in working times.

   b. _____ no real reduction in working times.

   c. _____ a substantial decrease in working times.

4. With respect to students within various age categories, their weekly work hours have:

   a. _____ increased.

   b. _____ not changed.

   c. _____ decreased.

5. When compared to that of employed men, employed women's free time for recreation is:

   a. _____ greater.

   b. _____ the same.

   c. _____ less.

6. As the availability of time-saving devices for housework increases, the average worktime of full-time housewives:

   a. _____ stays the same.

   b. _____ increases.

   c. _____ decreases.

7. As the standard of living rises, there is an increase in:

   a. _____ television viewing.

   b. _____ leisure time activities.

   c. _____ purchases of consumer goods.

8. After World War II, reduction in worktime became less attractive because:

   a. _____ workers wanted to buy luxury consumer goods.

b. _____ childrearing costs increased.

c. _____ hourly wages decreased.

9. The average weekly work hours began to level off in:

a. _____ 1948.

b. _____ 1958.

c. _____ 1968.

10. Which, according to the author, is the most likely scenario with respect to future hours of work:

a. _____ A gradual reduction in hours of work.

b. _____ A rapid decline in hours of work.

c. _____ No reduction in hours of work.

Check your answers with the Answer Key.

INSTRUCTIONS FOR PACED READING: "NFL Coaches and Motivation Theory"

The paced rate for this article is 500 words per minute. This means that you should finish reading the article in 4 minutes, or a total of 240 seconds. Ask someone to tell you when the time has expired. The article contains approximately 2,000 words. After reading the article, write down your answers to the test that follows.

Paced Reading

NFL Coaches and Motivation Theory

Kelly Kerin and Charles N. Waldo

In the worlds of business and professional football, highly motivated participants are sought and much effort is put forth to achieve high levels of motivation. For instance, George Allen, former coach of the Washington Redskins and the Los Angeles Rams, has this to say: "Mental health and team morale are 90 percent of football."

Peter McColough, chairman of the board of Xerox Corporation, echoes Allen's thoughts: "At Xerox one doesn't lead or supervise because of their status in the company. It's generally because of their natural effectiveness, persuasiveness, personality or character and their *motivation* to achieve."

There is, however, no universal agreement as to which theories work best. And a wide spectrum of theories exists in both worlds.

To what extent, if at all, do professional football coaches use currently popular management theories and concepts of motivation in their coaching strategies?

Does it make any difference which theories of motivation are used? In football, do coaches holding to one method of motivation win more frequently than coaches holding to other views? Popularity, at least in terms of appearances in the management literature and frequency of courses and seminars, suggests that certain theories on motivation have rung a bell and are being used successfully in business. Is this true for pro football?

It is hard to classify a pro coach as successful or unsuccessful. Overall win-loss records are an indicator. But taking a losing team and turning it into a winner, even though the career win-loss record is not impressive, could constitute success. And some coaches who have had decent regular season records have been unsuccessful in the playoffs and have been fired.

Furthermore, the authors have been unable to satisfactorily separate talent from motivation in the formula that makes for victory. Despite George Allen's words, if a coach comes into a situation in which his predecessor or the team owner has done a poor job in the draft or has made some poor trades, or in which key players have been injured, the team may not be able to compete. Motivation and mental preparation, *alone,* will not always carry the day. It helps to have the horses.

All coaches of the National Football League during the 1976 season were the sample. The NFL level, as opposed to college or high school, was chosen because several theories revolve around the effectiveness—or lack thereof—of money as a motivator to high performance. We wanted to see how coaches believe pay (above the board) affects motivation.

A questionnaire was developed in which the respondent could indicate agreement or disagreement, in varying degrees, with 25 statements about various methods of motivating and handling players. These statements, while phrased in football terms, covered different aspects of motivational theory. For instance, the statement, "The player's present salary is his number one motiva-

tor for the present season," can be related to a key element of Herzberg's Motivator-Hygiene Theory that current pay is generally not a prime motivator.

The questionnaires, with an explanatory letter asking for help and a self-addressed, stamped envelope, were sent out to each NFL coach early in the 1976 season. A follow-up questionnaire was sent to nonrespondents four weeks later. A second and final follow-up questionnaire was mailed several months later. In all, twenty of the twenty-eight NFL head coaches sent in usable replies.

The twenty who responded were Bill Arnsparger, Monte Clark, Don Coryell, Chuck Fairbanks, Forrest Gregg, Lou Holtz, Bill Johnson, Chuck Knox, Tom Landry, John Madden, John McKay, Jack Pardee, Bum Phillips, Tommy Prothro, John Ralston, Lou Saban, Bart Starr, Hank Stram, Dick Vermeil, and Paul Wiggin.

The following theories, concepts, and understandings regarding motivation and behavioral change have been widely researched, written upon, and discussed by management practitioners and academics alike. However, there is no universal agreement as to which ones are most valid or which ones bring about the highest levels of output under specific conditions. Of the twenty-five questions used in the survey, for brevity's sake only eleven were chosen for discussion here. These indicate how the coaches regard each theory in their coaching/motivational bag of tricks. The following are the theories and the statements used to test them.

Skinner's Behavior Modification

"The use of game film review, praise and/or criticism is a prime way of motivating the ballplayer to perform to his optimum potential."

and

"Players need to be constantly reminded of their importance to the team."

MacGregor's Theory X

"The threat of being cut, benched or traded will cause the player to perform better."

and

"The threat of physical hardship (example—harder practices) motivates players to perform better."

MacGregor's Theory Y

"For the most part the player is capable of motivating himself—consequently motivation does not play a big role in my coaching philosophy."

and

"The players should have a high degree of say in regards to the establishment of policies and rules governing them off the field."

Herzberg's Motivation-Hygiene Theory

"A clean, modern environment (stadium, locker rooms, practice areas) is conducive to motivating the athlete to perform to his potential."

and

"The player's *present* salary is his number one motivator for the *present* season."

Transactional Analysis

"Emotionally, the player resembles a child and is actually just a big kid playing a little boy's game."

Maslow's Hierarchy of Needs

"The best method of motivating football players is to appeal to certain human needs which crave for recognition, prestige and status."

RESULTS

Because of the small sample and the way the data ran, results will be displayed in a simple, straightforward manner using only absolute counts. No statistical tests or correlation analyses were done.

Data are presented in terms of the theory statements and the way the coaches expressed agreement or disagreement with the statements.

Statement 1: Skinner's Behavior Modification

"The use of game film reviews (praise and/or criticism) is a prime way of motivating the ballplayer to perform to his optimum potential."

Strongly agree	5
Agree	12
Undecided	1
Disagree	0
Strongly disagree	2

Adoption of Skinner's theory would suggest that the answers ought to be in the "Agree" areas.

Statement 2: Skinner's Behavior Modification

"Players need to be constantly reminded of their importance to the team."

Strongly agree	5
Agree	15
Undecided	0
Disagree	0
Strongly disagree	0

This statement also could have been placed under Herzberg's Motivator-Hygiene Theory or under Maslow's Hierarchy of Needs. Agreement with the theories suggests that answers ought to lie in the "Agree" areas.

Statement 3: MacGregor's Theory X

"The threat of being cut, benched or traded will cause the player to perform better."

Strongly agree	1
Agree	12
Undecided	3
Disagree	4
Strongly disagree	0

Modern theory suggests that answers should be in the "Disagree" areas. But a majority of coaches believe that at least some Theory X motivation can and should be applied to their players.

Statement 4: MacGregor's Theory X

"The threat of physical hardship (example—harder practices) motivates players to perform better."

Strongly agree	0
Agree	2
Undecided	3
Disagree	11
Strongly disagree	4

Modern theory suggests that answers should be in the "Disagree" areas, and this is how most coaches answered. There is, though, a shading to Theory X.

Statement 5: MacGregor's Theory Y

"For the most part, the player is capable of motivating himself—consequently, motivation does not play a big role in my coaching philosophy."

Strongly agree	0
Agree	2
Undecided	0
Disagree	9
Strongly disagree	9

Believers in MacGregor's theory would answer in the "Agree" areas, but NFL coaches apparently feel that outside resources must be called upon to motivate players. So, in addition to blocking,

tackling, and strategy setting, a head coach pays close attention to motivation. It would be interesting to know if readers can guess the names of the two successful coaches who do agree with Theory Y.

Statement 6: MacGregor's Theory Y

"The players should have a high degree of say in regards to the establishment of policies and rules governing them off the field."

Strongly agree	1
Agree	3
Undecided	3
Disagree	9
Strongly disagree	4

Acceptance of Theory Y suggests that answers should be in the "Agree" areas. There are some divided feelings on this question but, overall, the coaches indicate players cannot have great say regarding off-field policies. Coaches generally deny Theory Y's full application in this area.

Statement 7: Herzberg's Motivator-Hygiene Theory

"A clean, modern environment (stadium, locker rooms, practice areas) is conducive to motivating the athlete to perform to his potential."

Strongly agree	5
Agree	13
Undecided	2
Disagree	0
Strongly disagree	0

Agreement with Herzberg's theory suggests that answers should fall in the "Agree" areas, and so they do.

Statement 8: Herzberg's Motivator-Hygiene Theory

"The player's *present* salary is his number one motivator for the *present* season."

Strongly agree	1
Agree	1
Undecided	1
Disagree	10
Strongly disagree	7

Adherence to Herzberg would indicate answers should be in the "Disagree" areas and, with little exception, they are. In this case, Herzberg seems to hold up in coaching and motivation strategy.

Statement 9: Herzberg's Motivator-Hygiene Theory

"A chance for a boost in pay *next* season will motivate a player to perform better *this* season."

Strongly agree	0
Agree	10
Undecided	4
Disagree	4
Strongly disagree	2

In this statement an incentive is presented in the form of monetary increases next season for good performance this season. While half of the coaches agree with the statement, there is still enough disagreement to raise questions about the validity of money as a strong motivator.

Statement 10: Maslow's Hierarchy of Needs

"The best method of motivating football players is to appeal to certain human needs which crave for recognition, prestige and status."

Strongly agree	2
Agree	10
Undecided	1
Disagree	7
Strongly disagree	0

Theory suggests answers should be in the "Agree" areas, but feelings are very much mixed, although weighed slightly toward "Agree." In retrospect, the words *a powerful* in place of *the best* would have improved this statement. It could well be that some coaches were asked to make an either/or choice they couldn't make. Had the wording been different, more answers might have been in the "Agree" areas.

Statement 11: Transactional Analysis

"Emotionally, the player resembles a child and is actually just a big kid playing a little boy's game."

Strongly agree	2
Agree	5
Undecided	1
Disagree	8
Strongly disagree	4

TA theory doesn't suggest any particular direction for this answer. In fact, Transactional Analysis is much more descriptive than prescriptive and seeks to explain and understand behavior or outlook. Surprisingly, seven of the twenty coaches agreed with this statement. This was consistent with the way coaches felt about players setting the policies that governed them off the field (statement 6). How can kids manage themselves?

CONCLUSIONS

Professional football coaches, in the main, but not totally, accept modern motivational theories, even if they don't refer to them in the same terms as would a manager or business professor.

Physical rewards or punishments (money, harder practices) don't seem to be considered nearly as effective as mental rewards or punishments (being made to feel important or being benched).

Pro football coaches are much like pro business managers—they are individuals and operate in different ways to try to achieve positive results. Even though they may try to operate the same, results are not always the same. We suspect, but can't prove it from the study, that successful coaches probably operate more from a fluid, contingency approach than do unsuccessful coaches. Other variables determining success, often out of the coach's control, enter the picture.

We note in closing that coaches, especially successful ones, wrote in comments to the effect that no all-inclusive statements can be made about how to motivate all the players all the time. Each player is an individual and must be understood as unique, and, to the greatest degree possible, handled as a distinct person. Coaches emphasized that impartiality must rule at all times.

PACED READING COMPREHENSION CHECK: "NFL Coaches and Motivation Theory"

1. What *assertion* or *theory* do the authors present?

   a. _____ Football coaches consciously apply motivation theory.

   b. _____ Only successful football coaches use motivation theory in their coaching strategies.

   c. _____ Football coaches may apply motivation theory in their coaching strategies.

2. How did the authors *support* or try to prove their theory?

   a. _____ By sending a questionnaire to 1976 NFL coaches.

   b. _____ By telephoning and interviewing 1976 NFL coaches.

   c. _____ By reading the press releases of 1976 NFL coaches.

3. One difficulty in determining a coach's successful application of a motivation theory is that:

   a. _____ there is no real way to measure success.

   b. _____ it is not possible to separate talent from motivation.

   c. _____ most theories are not stated clearly.

4. How many motivation theories were investigated?

   a. _____ Six

   b. _____ Eleven

   c. _____ Twenty-five

5. "The threat of being cut, benched or traded will cause the player to perform better." With respect to this statement, most coaches:

   a. _____ strongly agreed.

   b. _____ agreed.

   c. _____ disagreed.

6. The two coaches who agree with MacGregor's Theory Y are considered to be:

   a. _____ successful.

b. _____ unsuccessful.

c. _____ neither successful nor unsuccessful.

7. Had the authors changed the wording of their statement, probably more coaches would have agreed with the theory of:

a. _____ Herzberg.

b. _____ MacGregor.

c. _____ Maslow.

8. "The player's *present* salary is his number one motivator for the *present* season." With respect to this statement, most coaches:

a. _____ agreed.

b. _____ were undecided.

c. _____ disagreed.

9. A conclusion of this study is that coaches:

a. _____ consciously apply modern motivation theory.

b. _____ use transactional analysis.

c. _____ accept modern motivational theories.

10. Football coaches who read this article probably will:

a. _____ use different motivational theories to match different conditions.

b. _____ seek raises for their players.

c. _____ use threats to motivate their players.

Check your answers with the Answer Key.

INSTRUCTIONS FOR SKIM READING: "The Business Of Business Schools; Part II: The Defense"

Using the skimming techniques you learned in Chapter 2, skim the following article. Time yourself to find your skimming rate; you should finish the article in no more than two minutes. Write down your time in the space provided at the end of the article.

Answer the questions following the article, then check your answers in the Answer Key. (Remember, a score of 50 percent or higher is acceptable when skimming.) Determine your skimming rate from the Words Per Minute: Skimming Chart, then record your skimming rate and comprehension score on your Skim Reading Progress Chart.

Skim Reading

The Business of Business Schools; Part II: The Defense

Kermit O. Hanson

Jackson Grayson's flailing of dead cats and his protestations to introspective saints and burly sinners may provoke a stampede among castrated buffaloes, but these exhortations are unlikely to stimulate constructive dialogue between business school deans and faculty on the one hand and business executives on the other. This I regard as unfortunate, because I do believe—as I am sure Grayson believes—that a continuing constructive dialogue between business educators and business executives can contribute to the quality of both business education and business leadership. However, before maximum benefits can be derived from this interchange it is essential that each party to the dialogue understand the nature and objectives of universities and their business schools—and the proper roles for saints and burly sinners.

Universities are educational institutions, not training institutions. Programs in the academic disciplines are designed to introduce students to fields of knowledge and to develop the capacity to think and to continue learning—in a wide range of careers that cannot be predicted with any high degree of accuracy for individual students. Within universities, professional schools have a higher degree of career orientation than schools of liberal arts, but their basic roles continue to be educational in nature. This is true for schools with a clinical approach such as medicine as well as in business, engineering and law.

I do not agree that business schools should engage to any substantial degree in "training for practice." This learning experience can be provided much more effectively by business firms and other organizations that employ business school graduates. Learning does not (certainly *should* not!) stop with the awarding of a degree from a professional school. Each institution or organization on an individual's career path contributes to his or her learning and professional development. These learning experiences are the responsibility of both the institutions and the individuals involved. Excessive concern with "practice" in a business or professional school is an unwise use of both school resources and students' investment of time and money.

Grayson's reference to the schizophrenic nature of business schools deserves further comment. Business schools, as important units of universities, must have faculty who maintain close linkages with other faculty in underlying disciplines such as economics and behavioral sciences. Admittedly—and very appropriately—theoretical considerations bulk large in these linkages. Concurrently, it also is important that some members of the business school faculty (not necessarily the same members) maintain connections with representatives of the organizations that employ graduates of business schools. Each of these faculty groups (theory-oriented and practice-oriented) must be respected by the groups they maintain contacts with—and each must have respect for the contributions which the other brings to the success of the professional school. Maintaining a balance among these linkages is exceedingly difficult. Herbert Simon put it very aptly when he wrote:

... organizing a professional school ... is very much like mixing oil with water; it is easy to describe the intended product, less easy to produce it. And the task is not finished when the goal has been achieved. Left to themselves, the oil and water will separate again. So also will the disciplines and the professions. Organizing, in these situations, is not a once-and-for-all activity. It is a continuing administrative responsibility, vital for the sustained success of the enterprise.

I agree with Grayson that faculty are critical to the success of a business school. However, business schools, from an historical perspective, are recent newcomers to the university family whose lineage can be traced to 1100 in Europe and 1636 (Harvard) in the United States. Indeed, the establishment of The Wharton School in 1881 was the first successful venture in higher education for business. Most business schools have been established only since World War II. In an effort to establish credibility and achieve academic "respectability" among other units of the university it is not surprising that faculty in many business schools have been more concerned with linkages to basic disciplines and concentration upon theory. During much of this period business was singularly unsupportive of business schools. A report by the Committee for Economic Development in 1964 stated that:

There is a widespread but mistaken notion that schools of business are better off financially than other schools or departments of colleges and universities, thanks to generous private contributions by businesses or well-to-do alumni. On the contrary, of more than $900 million in voluntary support accorded to higher education during 1962- 63, only *1.7 percent was specifically directed to business schools,* although about 20 percent of all students are in such schools.

Contrary to Grayson's views, I have noted much favorable change in recent years. Business schools have advanced very markedly in the "pecking order" among the schools and colleges that make up universities. While connections with underlying disciplines have been strengthened significantly, connections with the business and professional community also have been improved and are stronger than at any time in the relatively short history of business schools. I concur most wholeheartedly with Grayson that these connections need to be improved, but I differ with him about the direction in which the pendulum is swinging.

I differ also with respect to concern over students. Keeping in mind that business schools are educational in nature, it seems quite appropriate that admission criteria are related to probability of success in educational programs. Students, faculty and employers should be aware that satisfaction of these criteria does not insure success in business.

Skeptics of the usefulness of education for business cite, among other things, the success of business people who were educated in other disciplines, or were self-educated, as evidence that undergraduate programs in business are of questionable value. This is spurious reasoning. Management is an art as well as a science; entrepreneurship is a quality not possessed by everyone. Can "art" be "taught" in the sense that every art student is likely to become a great artist? Or every music student a virtuoso? Educational dropouts and self-educated persons have succeeded and will continue to succeed in many endeavors including business. But one should not overlook the large number of persons with degrees in business and management (both undergraduate and graduate) who hold senior executive positions in business and government; the roster of members of Beta Gamma Sigma (national honorary society for business students) who hold positions as presidents and board chairmen is impressive.

It is also significant that student demand for admission to business schools and demand for their graduates by both businesses and other kinds of organizations has never been higher. A survey of university and college freshmen in autumn 1976 revealed that 20.9 percent selected business as the probable major field of study for bachelor's degrees. The next ranking probable majors were far below: education, 9.3; engineering, 8.5; and health professions (non-M.D.), 6.9 (*Chronicle of Higher Education,* January 10, 1977). A recent survey of educational levels of bank presidents revealed that as recently as 1963, only 57 percent of bank presidents held bachelor's degrees; in 1974 this proportion had increased to 85 percent and a third of these held advanced degrees, the MBA being the most common (*The Banker Magazine,* Winter, 1976). I feel confident in predicting that the attitude of executives toward business schools will continue to improve as the proportion of executives who hold bachelor's and MBA degrees continues to increase. This in turn should facilitate the maintenance of linkages between business schools and executives.

Grayson also indicted the AACSB (American Assembly of Collegiate Schools of Business) as an inhibitor to change and innovation through its standards of accreditation. Unfortunately this myth continues to persist even among presumably knowledgeable people. The accreditation of schools with as diverse masters programs as Harvard, MIT and Wharton (and others not as eminent) should be rather striking evidence that accreditation does not force business schools into a fixed standard mold. Reference to the AACSB standards on curriculum and faculty provides conclusive evidence regarding the latitude individual schools have in shaping their curriculum:

... there is no intention that two schools must meet the common body of knowledge in the same way, nor that two concentrations within a school necessarily must meet the common body of knowledge in the same way.

With reference to mix of faculty, AACSB standards specify that the percent of academic staff holding the Ph.D., DBA, or other appropriate doctoral degree shall be not less than 40 percent of the minimum number of faculty required at the undergraduate level and not less than 75 percent of the minimum number of faculty required at the graduate level. These relatively low minimum limits provide business schools with ample opportunity to engage burly sinners with excellent business and managerial experience. Lack of adequate salary levels is a far more serious handicap than are the AACSB standards with respect to faculty mix.

The reader will not be surprised when I confess unabashed pride in the progress of business schools to date. However, to keep things in proper perspective, I should underscore my deep concern for continued progress, particularly in improving the linkages between business schools and the organizations which employ their graduates. These linkages could strengthen both the research and instructional capability of the schools while concurrently enhancing the analytical and managerial capability of the organizations. Such connections will not develop if either potential partner remains withdrawn; initiative must be shown on both sides. Developing strong linkages—"partnerships" in a sense—has never been easy; oil and water—and saints and burly sinners—left to themselves will separate!

Finishing time:_____

SKIM READING COMPREHENSION CHECK: "The Business of Business Schools; Part II: The Defense"

1. What is the author's *theory?*

   a. _____ The main purpose of business schools is to train students in the "practice of business."

   b. _____ Business schools should accept and train only the best students.

   c. _____ The main purpose of business schools is to train students to think.

2. Select two statements below that the author used to *support* his theory.

   a. _____ Students must be prepared for a wide range of careers.

   b. _____ Business schools can achieve academic respectability by stressing the practical.

   c. _____ Only the best students can comprehend the theory of business.

   d. _____ There are too many practitioners on business school faculties.

   e. _____ Many presidents and board chairmen have graduated from schools stressing theory.

   f. _____ Executives have a poor attitude toward business schools because they graduate poor students.

3. If the author's theory is generally accepted, what would be the *expected* outcome?

   a. _____ Business schools will become more practical.

   b. _____ Business schools will continue to focus on a theoretical approach.

   c. _____ The admissions standards of business schools will change.

Check your answers with the Answer Key.

INSTRUCTIONS FOR SKIM READING: "American Workers Evaluate the Quality of Their Jobs"

Before you skim this article, preview the questions that follow it. This is a very long article, and previewing the questions will help you to skim faster. Time yourself to find your skimming rate; you should finish the article in no more than 6 minutes. Write down your time in the space provided at the end of the article. Answer the questions following the article, then check your answers in the Answer Key. (Remember, a score of 50 percent or higher is acceptable when skimming.) Determine your skimming rate from the Words Per Minute: Skimming Chart, then record your skimming rate and comprehension score on your Skim Reading Progress Chart.

Skim Reading

American Workers Evaluate the Quality of Their Jobs
Graham L. Staines and Robert P. Quinn

A new survey designed to measure the quality of employment in America shows that U.S. workers have experienced declines both in job satisfaction and in the desire to stay with their present employers. The survey, the third conducted by the Survey Research Center, provides an overview of conditions of employment in the United States in 1977, as reported by workers. Data are compared with results of surveys conducted in 1969 and 1973, thus providing trends over an 8-year period.[1]

The 1977 survey, for the first time, asked questions about the relationships between worklife and certain domains of life away from the job, particularly the relationships between employment and family life and between employment and leisure activities. A third of the married workers reported that their jobs interfered with family life "somewhat" or "a lot." Much of the conflict involved time—the amount of time spent at work, inconvenient work schedules, or uncertainty about work schedules. Available energy for family life was also a factor, especially for working wives with children. Most married workers (80 percent) reported spending at least half of their free time with their spouses. A third of all workers said their work interfered with leisure activities "somewhat" or "a lot."

These results confirm important connections between life on and off the job. Changes in employment patterns are inducing major shifts in family life, leisure, and other activities away from work. For example, the rise in the proportion of working wives has installed the dual-earner household as the modal family type. This shift from housewife to working wife has a multitude of potential implications for life off the job: fewer volunteers available for charity work, greater demand for after work and weekend shopping and business hours, steadily rising purchases of fast foods and easily prepared foods as well as the increasing tendency for families to eat out, and, finally, more socializing with people from work and less with other families in the neighborhood. Clearly, the investigation of the interplay between work and leisure-time activities has only begun.

INDICATORS OF WORKER WELL-BEING

Following are indicators of the well-being of workers that are known to be associated with employment conditions.

Job Satisfaction

In all three surveys, job satisfaction was measured in two ways: first, with a set of general questions phrased so the worker could invoke any considerations of his or her choice; second, with a series of questions about specific aspects of the worker's job and employment conditions (pay or hours, for example). Responses to the general questions were averaged to form a "general satisfaction" index. The specific responses were indexed by topic and statistical similarity, and were averaged to form a "specific satisfactions" index. The topics included: comfort, challenge, financial rewards, relations with coworkers, resource adequacy, and promotions. The overall index combines the "general satisfaction" and "specific satisfactions" indexes.[2] (See table 1.)

Table 1. Job satisfaction Indicators, 1969, 1973, and 1977

[Mean overall job satisfaction in 1969 = 0]

Indicator	Mean		
	1969	1973	1977
Overall job satisfaction index[1]	0	−2	[2]−24
General satisfaction values	3.75	3.79	[2]3.66
Specific satisfactions values	3.24	3.20	[2]3.05
Comfort	3.14	[2]3.03	[2]2.87
Challenge	3.26	3.21	[2]3.06
Financial rewards.	3.06	3.10	[2]2.89
Relations with coworkers	3.41	3.34	[3]3.40
Resource adequacy	3.45	3.44	[2]3.28
Promotions	−	2.63	[2]2.46

[1]The overall job satisfaction index is an equally weighted combination of the general and specific satisfaction values, transformed arbitrarily to a mean of zero in 1969.

[2]Statistically significant changes from 1973 to 1977 and, in the case of comfort, from 1969 to 1973.

[3]The derivation of the relations with coworkers index is somewhat different for 1977 than for the prior years, and its comparability has not yet been ascertained. However, versions of this index were constructed for comparing 1969 and 1973 and for comparing 1973 and 1977. Neither difference was statistically significant.

There was no change in overall job satisfaction between 1969 and 1973; in contrast, there was an appreciable drop between 1973 and 1977. The full story on job satisfaction, however, requires separate consideration of the various components of the overall job satisfaction index and also of the various demographic subgroups of workers. Over the 8-year period from 1969 to 1977, particularly between 1973 and 1977, the specific satisfactions index exhibited a marked and significant decline, whereas the general satisfaction index declined slightly but significantly. The decrease was about equally distributed among five areas—comfort, challenge, financial rewards, resource adequacy, and promotions—but was absent for the sixth, relations with coworkers.

Analysis of the decline in the general satisfaction index requires a review of analogous data from other years and other surveys. A 1974 report concluded that there was no evidence of significant changes in job satisfaction over the 15-year period, 1958–73.[3] This conclusion was based on data from 15 comparable national surveys, conducted by four different agencies. All surveys included a similar question which asked, "How satisfied would you say you are with your job?" This question was asked in the three surveys discussed in this article. Job satisfaction, as measured by this question, did not decline significantly between 1969 and 1977.

This finding indicates the limitations of a single-question measure of job satisfaction. Despite the considerable face validity of this general job satisfaction question, it fails to show much change over periods when other more elaborate measures detect a substantial decline in satisfaction. This insensitivity to change may be attributable, in part, to the gross generality of the question (because such measures reveal less decline than their more specifically stated counterparts) and, in part, to its distinctive wording (because other general questions do show the decrement in job satisfaction over time). In contrast, the indicators shown in table 1 have a high degree of consistency in their representation of change.

The decline in job satisfaction has been pervasive, affecting virtually all demographic and occupational classes tested. (See table 2.) Still, there are some differences and similarities worth noting. Men, for example, reported greater declines in satisfaction between 1969 and

1977 than did women. Satisfaction of workers under age 21 was unchanged, whereas that of older workers changed. The decline was virtually identical for white and black workers, although black workers continued to remain less satisfied than did whites. Satisfaction dropped in all educational achievement categories, but the drop was larger among workers with a college degree. The self-employed had a relatively slight decrement in satisfaction, compared with wage and salary employees. Workers in the higher skilled occupations (professional, technical, and managerial jobs) exhibited a smaller decline than did those in lower skilled occupations (operatives and laborers).

Intention to Change Jobs

In each survey, wage and salary workers were asked: "Taking everything into account, how likely is it that you will make a genuine effort to find a new job with another employer within the next year?" The answers reveal a slight shift towards greater willingness to seek a different employer. In 1969, 70 percent of wage and salary workers said that it was "not at all likely" that they would try to find a new job; in 1973, the figure was 72 percent; but by 1977, it had fallen significantly to 66 percent. Therefore, as a behavior-oriented indicator of increasing worker discontent, willingness to change employers discloses a shift between 1973 and 1977 that is not incompatible with the decline in job satisfaction suggested by other measures. The magnitude of the shift is not great, but it should be remembered that between 1973 and 1977 the availability of alternative employment declined significantly, and job change became an increasingly impractical medium for expressing discontent.

Table 2. Overall job satisfaction index by demographic and occupational groups, 1969, 1973, and 1977[1]

Characteristics	1969 Number of respondents	1969 Mean job satisfaction	1973 Number of respondents[2]	1973 Mean job satisfaction	1977 Number of respondents[2]	1977 Mean job satisfaction
Sex:						
Men	993	7	1,291	0	1,359	-26
Women, sole wage earners	176	-16	182	-1	235	-21
Women with other wage earners in household	362	-8	616	-5	691	-21
Age:						
Under 21	97	-40	173	-42	203	-41
21–29	333	-21	568	-26	594	-49
30–44	489	5	634	11	759	-20
45–54	340	12	422	11	389	-4
55–64	210	19	248	17	271	-2
65 or older	55	23	41	63	45	11
Race:						
White	1,354	5	1,853	3	2,019	-21
Black	157	-34	166	-32	167	-59
Education:						
8 years or less	240	0	234	-1	173	-17
Some high school	269	-7	294	-10	315	-39
High school diploma	554	-1	805	-6	863	-26
Some college	253	-2	436	-8	515	-24
College degree	111	14	162	18	193	-28
Graduate education	102	23	153	35	201	2
Employment status:						
Self-employed	205	25	184	39	287	15
Wage and salary	1,326	-3	1,270	-7	1,998	-30
Occupation:						
Professional and technical	225	20	311	26	365	0
Managers, administrators, and proprietors	206	27	315	18	317	-6
Salesworkers	80	4	105	10	112	-3
Clerical workers	244	-6	344	-10	370	-19
Craftworkers	224	9	277	7	309	-14
Operatives	294	-11	361	-38	389	-67
Laborers, nonfarm	45	-25	73	-36	79	-58
Farmers and farm managers	43	28	44	31	41	18
Farm laborers and supervisors	22	-55	8	1	11	0
Service workers	146	-35	241	-6	292	-27

[1] The overall job satisfaction index is an equally weighted combination of the general satisfaction and the specific satisfactions values transformed to a mean of zero and standard deviation of 87 in 1969. Negative figures indicate deviations below the 1969 mean. Because significance indicators are not provided, the reader should note that some subpopulations are very small and have unstable means
[2] Number of respondents in 1973 and 1977 was weighted to provide comparability with 1969 data.

Life Satisfaction

The index of overall life satisfaction contains two equally weighted components. The first, general life satisfaction, is measured by two questions: (1) "Taking all things together, how would you say things are these days? Would you say you're very happy, pretty happy, or not too happy these days?" and (2) "In general, how satisfying do you find the ways you're spending your life these days? Would you call it completely satisfying, pretty satisfying, or not very satisfying?" In the second component, satisfaction is assessed through eight scales representing specific moods or affective states that can characterize a person's life (for example, interesting versus boring, full versus empty, and hopeful versus discouraging). Life satisfaction declined between 1969 and 1977, although the change occurred between 1973 and 1977. The data from the first component (general life satisfaction) display this pattern significantly, with the response "very happy" declining from 38 percent in 1973 to 27 percent in 1977 and "completely satisfying" from 23 percent to 15 percent. The data on the second component (specific moods and affects) are available only for 1973 and 1977; they evidence an unmistakable and significant decline between these 2 years, with responses in the most positive category dropping by an average of 8 percentage points.

WORK-RELATED PROBLEMS

All workers were asked about aspects of their employment they considered to be problems; those who mentioned a specific problem were asked to judge its severity. Table 3 shows the percent reporting one problem or more in each of 12 problem areas commonly mentioned. Problem severity is represented by the proportion reporting the problem as "sizable" or "great."

From 1969 to 1977, problem frequency varied by direction and degree of change, but problem severity declined consistently by small amounts. Inadequate family income as a problem was mentioned significantly less frequently in 1973 and 1977 than in 1969 (although no change since 1973); however, in 1977, it maintained the highest rated severity. Problems relating to the desire for additional fringe benefits were frequently mentioned and were rated relatively high in severity. The proportion reporting problems related to occupational handicaps remained constant over the 8-year period, but the severity of such problems in 1977 remained nonsignificantly below that reported in 1969. The results on trends in the desire for additional fringe benefits and trends in safety and health were anomalous because of survey method changes in 1977.

The frequency of work-related problems can be considered in more detail if account is taken of certain data that are available for 1977 but not necessarily from the prior surveys. (See table 4.) The problems related to earnings, income, and fringe benefits generally had higher rates of occurrence than other problem areas. The relatively frequent mention of problems concerning work content, specifically workers reporting they had skills they would like to use but could not and those "overeducated" for their jobs suggests a prevalent concern about misfit between job requirements and self-appraised capabilities. Unsteady employment and layoff or job loss were relatively uncommon problems, although only employed people were interviewed. In four areas for which such questions were asked,

Table 3. Frequency and severity of selected work-related problems, 1969, 1973, and 1977

Problem	Percent reporting problem			Percent regarding the problem as "sizable" or "great"		
	1969	1973	1977	1969	1973	1977
Inadequacy of family income for meeting monthly expenses	26	21	21	63	55	57
Desire for additional fringe benefits, all workers	39	40	[1]46	43	39	[1]40
Wage and salary workers receiving at least one benefit[2]	45	45	[1]55	43	39	[1]40
Exposure to one or more safety and health hazards	38	42	[1]78	46	40	[1]32
Work-related illness or injury during last 3 years	13	14	15	56	48	44
Occupational handicap(s)	9	9	10	39	30	29
Inconvenient or excessive hours	30	39	34	38	34	36
Age discrimination	5	4	6	[3]35	[3]35	[3]34
Sex discrimination, all workers	3	5	5	[3]44	[3]37	[3]33
Women only[2]	8	14	12	[3]44	[3]37	[3]33
Race or national origin discrimination, all workers	3	3	6	[3]53	[3]52	[3]51
Blacks only[2]	17	15	16	[3]62	[3]68	[3]37
Unsteady employment	11	9	9	36	26	27
Transportation problems	35	40	34	40	37	33
Unpleasant work environment	33	40	37	38	36	37

[1]The 1969 and 1973 data are not comparable to those from 1977.
[2]The percentage is based on all workers in this subsample.
[3]$N < 100$ in 1969 or weighted $N < 140$ in 1973 or 1977.

lack of control over conditions very often was seen as a problem, not the conditions themselves. For example, lack of control over days worked (77 percent) was a problem more frequently than was working on days that did not suit the worker (12 percent), and lack of control over own job assignment (54 percent) was a more frequent problem than not being able to use one's skills in present job assignment (36 percent). Also, 42 percent said it would be difficult to find a job similar to the one they have, but only 15 percent said they were likely to lose their job in the next year.

Earnings, Income, and Fringe Benefits

The three surveys reveal only limited changes in levels and adequacy of income. Adjusted for inflation, levels of family income increased somewhat between 1969 and 1973 and then decreased between 1973 and 1977. Similarly adjusted figures for job earnings showed little change between 1969 and 1973, but declined between 1973 and 1977. As judged by workers, inadequacy of family income for meeting monthly expenses declined significantly between 1969 and

Table 4. Frequency of work-related problems in 1977

Problem	Number of respondents[1]	Percent reporting problem
Earnings, income, and fringe benefits:		
Desire for improvement of present fringe benefits (including wage and salary workers receiving at least one benefit)	1,829	58.1
Desire for additional fringe benefits (includes wage and salaried workers receiving at least one benefit)	1,943	54.5
Earns less than deserved compared to others doing similar work	2,199	39.0
Inadequacy of family income for meeting monthly expenses	2,261	20.8
Safety and health hazards:		
Exposed to one or more safety and health hazard	2,289	78.0
Not informed about dangerous or unhealthy conditions (includes wage and salary workers only)	1,947	15.7
Work-related illness or injury during last 3 years	2,289	15.6
Occupational handicap(s)	2,291	10.0
Work schedule:		
Difficult to get work days changed	2,264	76.6
Difficult to get work hours changed	2,251	71.5
Inconvenient or excessive hours	2,258	33.6
Difficult to take time off for personal matters	2,251	26.0
Hours do not suit	2,267	19.3
Employer determines overtime and worker cannot refuse (includes wage and salary workers who work some overtime)	1,506	15.9
Days do not suit	2,261	12.0
Work content:		
Difficult to get duties changed	2,274	54.0
Feeling that time drags at work	2,290	39.6
Skills underutilized in present job	2,290	35.6
"Overeducated" for job	2,236	32.2
Conscience violated by required job duties	2,215	28.2
Substandard quality of product or service provided	2,179	12.8
Low value of present job skills 5 years hence	2,268	11.8
Job mobility and security:		
Shortage of jobs in worker's line of work (including only those not reporting a shortage of workers with their skills)	1,405	54.1
Stake in present job too great to change jobs	2,241	47.8
Difficult to find another job with similar pay	2,254	41.9
Likely to lose job in next year	2,219	14.6
Unsteady employment	2,276	9.4
Laid off in last year	2,268	5.1
Other problems:		
Inadequate time for leisure activities	2,259	55.2
Transportation problems	2,284	37.7
Unpleasant work environment	1,666	37.1
Interference between work and family life (includes only workers with spouse or children 17 years or younger in household)	1,622	34.7
Interference between work and leisure	2,258	32.8
Child care cost problems (includes only workers who used a child care arrangement)	215	20.0
Problems with work schedules caused by child care arrangements (includes only workers who used a child care arrangement)	276	14.5

[1]Number of respondents weighted to provide comparability with earlier surveys. (See appendix.)

1973, with no change thereafter. Inadequacy of family income for living comfortably remained virtually constant over the 8-year span.

Between 1969 and 1977, there was a modest but significant gain in the proportion of wage and salary workers reporting the availability of various fringe benefits. For example, between 1969 and 1977 the proportion with paid vacations rose from 74 percent to 81 percent, those with a retirement program other than social security rose from 61 percent to 67 percent, and medical contingency insurance rose from 72 percent to 78 percent. The gain was especially noticeable for two benefits offered to women only—maternity leave with full reemployment rights, and maternity leave with pay. The proportion receiving these benefits increased a significant 15 percentage points between 1969 and 1977.

These findings regarding economic benefits available to wage and salary workers reveal two different trends between 1969 and 1977. There was no gain over time in direct monetary returns, but fairly steady gains in fringe benefits. Such findings indicate that workers may have been exchanging additional pay for more fringe benefits.

The 1977 interview schedule included a question about the tradeoff between pay and other job returns. Workers were asked whether they would prefer a 10-percent pay raise or some other improvement in their conditions of employment (such as more interesting work, more comfortable working conditions, better fringe benefits, a shorter workweek, or greater job security). About one-half of the respondents indicated they favored more fringe benefits over additional earnings. Wage and salary workers were frequently willing to trade increments in pay for three economic benefits: better

retirement benefits (54 percent preferred an improvement in such benefits over a pay increase), more paid vacation days (48 percent), and better medical insurance benefits (47 percent). It is likely that increases in the total economic package over the last 8 years have been in the form of more fringe benefits rather than additional earnings.

The 1977 survey permits a detailed examination of how workers evaluate 18 fringe benefits. Table 5 presents five items of information on each benefit: the percent of workers to whom it is available, the percent receiving the benefit who describe it as most important, the percent who describe it as least important, and the percent saying they would like to see the benefit improved. The fifth item concerns fringe benefits that workers do not receive but would like to; for each such benefit, the column records the percent of all mentions (not of all persons) that refer to this benefit.

The data reveal considerable concern by workers over their current fringe benefits. More than half of the workers wanted improvement in some of their fringe benefits. Of these, large percentages desired improvements in widely available benefits: 51 percent in the case of medical contingency insurance, 42 percent for retirement programs, and 28 percent for paid vacation. More than a third of those with dental benefits wished them to be improved, and 22 percent of all mentions of desired additional benefits referred to a dental program. Additional data indicate that workers expressed less satisfaction with fringe benefits than with numerous other features of their conditions of employment. Also, fringe benefits were the only workplace improvements, among several suggested, for which large numbers of workers were willing to sacrifice a pay increase.

Table 5. Wage and salary workers' evaluation of fringe benefits

Benefit	Availability of benefit		Most Important benefits		Least Important benefits		Want benefits Improved		Want to receive benefit[1]
	Number	Percent	Number[2]	Percent	Number[2]	Percent	Number[2]	Percent	Percent
Paid vacation	1,956	80.8	1,550	47.0	1,534	6.6	899	28.1	3.1
Medical, surgical, or hospital insurance that covers any illness or injury that might occur to you while off the job	1,962	78.1	1,506	83.9	1,504	2.3	921	51.4	9.7
Maternity leave with full re-employment rights[3]	707	74.5	513	12.7	509	33.4	266	3.8	[4]1.7
A retirement program	1,949	67.4	1,288	50.3	1,286	7.9	764	42.3	8.1
Life insurance that would cover a death occuring for reasons not connected with your job	1,942	64.1	1,218	41.2	1,220	9.4	730	14.1	4.3
Sick leave with full pay	1,940	62.8	1,193	59.1	1,190	5.1	665	18.6	7.9
A training program that you can take to improve your skills	1,963	49.0	941	18.3	936	13.8	526	10.3	2.0
Thrift or savings plan	1,913	39.8	757	13.1	761	19.1	450	3.6	1.5
Free or discounted merchandise	1,992	34.3	669	10.5	660	33.3	382	5.8	0.0
Dental benefits	1,934	29.4	569	35.5	568	12.1	353	36.3	22.3
Maternity leave with pay[3]	691	29.4	197	10.7	197	47.2	78	6.4	(4)
Eyeglass or eye care benefits	1,911	21.8	416	25.5	415	21.0	264	15.9	12.2
Profit sharing	1,939	19.8	378	33.1	377	13.3	220	16.8	3.9
Stock options	1,912	17.6	333	16.2	332	27.4	181	4.4	1.8
Work clothing allowance	1,969	16.8	330	18.5	322	33.2	169	15.4	3.4
Free or discounted meals	1,982	16.3	313	14.7	308	40.3	157	9.6	1.6
Legal aid service	1,885	10.3	193	13.5	191	18.3	104	6.7	2.0
Child care arrangements for working parents .	1,943	2.2	42	9.5	42	38.1	18	0.0	1.6

[1]The base number for this column (N = 2278) is the (total) number of benefits mentioned by all workers in response to the question: "Are there any fringe benefits you are not getting that you'd like to be getting?" Percentages add to less than 100 percent because some benefits mentioned by workers do not appear on this list.

[2]Includes only workers who report the benefit as available and, in the case of desired improvement of fringe benefits, only those who want at least one benefit improved.

[3]Only women were asked about this benefit.

[4]The category for this item is nonspecific maternity leave.

Prevalence of Safety and Health Hazards

In all three surveys, workers were asked if, within the previous 3 years, they had experienced any illnesses or injuries that they thought had been caused or made more severe by any job held during that period. The frequency of such reported illnesses or injuries changed little from 1969 to 1977; nonetheless, workers in 1977 rated such illnesses or injuries as somewhat less severe and were less likely to report missing more than 2 weeks of work as a consequence.

Although a casual examination of the data seems to indicate dramatic changes in the frequency of various safety and health hazards, these changes, in part, represent only a change in measurement methods. In both 1969 and 1973, workers were asked an open-end question about safety and health hazards: "Does your job at any time expose you to what you feel are physical dangers or unhealthy conditions?" The 1977 survey, however, asked the worker to report exposure to each of 13 specific hazards (plus a residual category for any other hazards). The open-end and close-end procedures produce substantially different estimates of the prevalence of safety hazards, with the close-end approach suggesting a much higher rate of occurrence.

The 1977 survey collected specific information on frequency and severity of 13 presumably hazardous conditions on the job. The four hazards most frequently reported were air pollution (cited by 40 percent of the workers), fire or shock (30 percent), noise (30 percent), and dangerous chemicals (29 percent). However, these hazards are not all regarded as particularly severe by the workers exposed to them. Noise was among the highest ranked hazards (40 percent of the workers exposed described it as a "sizable" or "great" problem), and air pollution ranked in the middle (32 percent); fire or shock and dangerous chemicals were regarded as less severe (21 percent and 18 percent, respectively).

The 1977 survey also generated an additional finding that underscores the salience to workers of issues involving safety and health. The 1977 interview schedule included questions concerning how much say workers should have about work-related decisions, such as safety equipment and practices, how the work is done, the wages and salaries paid, the particular days and hours of work, and hiring or layoffs. The respondents singled out safety equipment and practices as the area in which workers should have the greatest say. In fact, 76 percent of respondents believed that workers should have "complete say" or "a lot of say" regarding safety decisions. No other category of decision produced a figure over 41 percent.

Decision	Percent responding "complete say" or "lot of say"
Safety equipment and practices......................................	76
How work is done	41
Wages and salaries..............	30
Days and hours of work.....	19
Hiring or layoffs	16

Working Hours

The 40-hour week persisted as the prevalent workweek. However, the surveys reveal a distinct and significant decline between 1969 and 1977 in the proportion working exactly 40 hours per week on their main job (from 39 to 30 percent) and an increase in the proportion working more than 40 hours (from 39 to 42 percent) or less than 40 hours (from 22 to 28 percent). Using a broader range of hours, for example, 35 to 44 hours as a "normal" workweek, there is still a significant decline in the proportion working such a "normal" workweek (from 57 to 51 percent). These changes do not reflect sex differences in work-hour preferences or in labor force composition. The same pattern of changes applied to both men and women—declines in the proportions working exactly 40 hours per week with compensating changes of similar magnitude and directions.

Another important dimension of working hours concerns the extent to which workers have control over their work schedules. In all three surveys, workers were asked how much control they felt they had over whether or not they worked overtime. Between 1969 and 1977, there was a small but significant increase in the percent reporting control of their overtime hours. More workers in the third survey were in the top two categories of overtime control (mostly up to the worker, and both worker and employer have a say but worker can refuse without penalty), up significantly from 36 percent in 1969 to 52 percent in 1977. The proportion reporting that it was up to their employers and that they could not refuse overtime without penalty remained constant between 1969 and 1977 at about 16 percent.

The percent reporting some kind of problem concerning ". . . the hours you work, your work schedule, or overtime" rose slightly between 1969 and 1977 (nonsignificantly from 30 to 34 percent), but the nature of these problems changed. Of the total number of problems mentioned, inadequate control by workers over hours (excluding the issue of overtime) rose from 4 percent of the problems in 1969 to 16 percent in 1977. Such evidence points to a sizable consti-

tuency of workers who would be receptive to flexitime and other experiments in which workers could help determine their own work schedules.

Beyond the issue of trends, the 1977 data indicate that workers took off very little time for personal activities during a regular workday. Among full-time workers, 60 percent spent no more than 30 minutes a day on meal breaks. Nor did workers take off much time during an average workday on regular coffee breaks or scheduled rest breaks. Almost 40 percent of the full-time workers received no such time off, and more than 70 percent received less than half an hour. Workers also were asked how much additional time they spent on activities such as talking to friends, doing personal business, or just relaxing. Among full-time workers, 45 percent reported no time off at all, and two-thirds reported less than half an hour. By comparison, among part-time workers (those who worked 20 to 34 hours a week) the use of time during an average workday for personal activities was even more restricted: almost a third of all part-time workers (compared with 8 percent of all full-time workers) reported no time off for meal breaks; and almost half (compared with 39 percent of all full-time workers) reported no time off for coffee or rest breaks. By their own accounts, part-time workers spent virtually all of their time at work on the tasks for which they are paid.

Discrimination

The data on different types of job discrimination are as interesting for the trends they do not show as for those they do. All workers in the three surveys were asked whether they felt discriminated against on their jobs because of age. There was no significant change in overall age discrimination. Young workers reported nonsignificant decreases during the period (from 24 to 15 percent for those under age 21). Workers age 55 and over reported no change in age discrimination between 1969 and 1973 but reported a significant increase between 1973 and 1977 (from 4 to 10 percent). The proportion of women reporting sex discrimination at work increased significantly from 8 to 14 percent between 1969 and 1973, but in 1977, the figure dropped to 12 percent. Among black workers, reports of job discrimination based on race or national origin held relatively constant at 15 to 17 percent between 1969 and 1977.

Utilization of Skills

Evidence from the surveys suggests a decline in the extent to which jobs provide the opportunity for full use of skills. This decline applies to future as well as current opportunities. With respect to the future, the interviewed workers were asked, "How useful and valuable will your present job skills be 5 years from now?" In 1973, 68 percent reported their skills would be "very useful and valuable;" the proportion dropped to 62 percent in 1977.

The decline relating to use of available skills on the worker's present job was even more substantial. In 1969, 27 percent of those interviewed claimed that they had some skills from their experience and training that they would like to use but could not on their present jobs. By 1977, this measure of underutilization of skills had risen significantly to 36 percent, with all of the change occurring between 1973 and 1977. One plausible source of underutilization of skills is "overeducation." Workers who feel that their levels of formal education exceed those required by their jobs seem likely

to possess skills that cannot be used on their present jobs. "Overeducation" (or underutilization of education) might, thus, be expected to increase in tandem with underutilization of skills. This prediction, however, is not confirmed by the 1969 and 1977 data. Data from these 2 years show no increase whatsoever in the proportion of workers with more education than their jobs required. Consequently, the increase in perceived underutilization of skills may have originated outside of formal education.

Such findings should not be taken to mean that workers felt that their jobs made few demands on their skills. Some of the 1977 data indicate that most workers reported that their jobs utilized a fair measure of their skills. For example, 69 percent of all workers "strongly agree" or "agree" that their jobs required "a high level of skill" and 78 percent said they were using their "skills and abilities." Moreover, most workers reported that their jobs helped them acquire new skills. Thus, 62 percent of all workers "strongly agree" or "agree" that their jobs required them to be "creative" and 83 percent said their jobs required them to "keep learning new things." Nevertheless, the trend data on skill utilization do suggest that these percentages may be on the decline.

Job Mobility and Security

The 1977 survey investigated job security in greater detail than did the earlier surveys. In 1977, job insecurity appeared among the less frequent and less serious problems. Nine percent of all workers reported their employment as irregular or unsteady: and among those, 27 percent described the problem as "sizable" or "great." Five percent had experienced a layoff in the preceding year, and among those, 31 percent characterized the problem as "sizable" or "great." Moreover, 15 percent reported that they were likely to lose their present jobs during the next couple of years.

The 1977 survey included two measures of locking-in that appeared also in at least one of the earlier surveys. (Locking-in is the extent to which workers feel constrained in seeking alternative employment.) In all three surveys, wage and salary workers were asked: "About how easy would it be for you to find another job with another employer with approximately the same income and fringe benefits you now have?" In 1969, 40 percent thought it would be very easy to find a similar job. In 1973, the proportion dropped significantly to 27 percent, and by 1977, had dropped significantly again to 20 percent. In 1973 and 1977, workers were asked: "Is there a shortage of workers in this (geographical) area who have your experience, training, and skills?" Almost half (48 percent) perceived a shortage in 1973, but only 37 percent did so in 1977. Also, in 1977, of those not reporting a worker shortage, 54 percent reported a shortage of available jobs for people with their experience, training, and skills. These data demonstrate that between 1969 and 1977 workers became increasingly locked-in to their jobs, a change that undoubtedly reflects the economic climate and unemployment rates.

ATTITUDES TOWARD LABOR UNIONS

Trend data on union issues are not available because the questions asked in 1977 differed from those in the previous surveys. Workers in the 1977 sample expressed fairly positive attitudes toward labor unions. On the subject of union goals, workers were asked what things they thought unions in this country were trying to do. Among union members, 66 percent mentioned only positive things (such as improving wages or benefits, improving job security) and 15 percent mentioned only negative things (such as self-aggrandizement). Among the nonmembers, the corresponding proportions were 45 percent and 28 percent.

Union members gave their unions higher marks for handling traditional functions than for less traditional functions. A majority reported that their unions did a "somewhat" or "very" good job in securing better working conditions, such as better wages (76 percent for white-collar workers, 75 percent for blue-collar workers), better fringe benefits (69 percent and 71 percent), improved safety and health on the job (74 and 71 percent), and improved job security (76 and 74 percent). Members also rated their unions high on handling grievances and on other indicators of responsiveness. Members were less positive about their unions' handling of nontraditional issues such as helping to make jobs more interesting, getting workers a say in how their employers run the business or organizations, and getting workers a say in how they do their own jobs. However, members also expressed the view that their unions should put greater effort into the traditional than into the less traditional union functions. Overall, union members expressed satisfaction with their unions—77 percent of the white-collar workers and 71 percent of the blue-collar workers reported that they were "somewhat" or "very" satisfied.

Workers not belonging to a union nor covered by a union contract were asked how they would vote if there were an election for representation by a union or an employee association; 29 percent of the white-collar workers and 39 percent of the blue-collar workers reported that they would vote in favor of such representation.

SOME INTERPRETATIONS OF TRENDS

The survey results show that American workers experienced declines between 1969 and 1977 in job satisfaction, intentions to stay on with their present jobs and employers, and overall life satisfaction. The changes were greater during the 1973–77 period than during the 1969–73 period.

There are three possible explanations for the declining job satisfaction: (1) perhaps the composition of the labor force is changing in ways that give added weight to those segments that are characteristically low in job satisfaction; (2) perhaps the objective qualities of jobs and conditions of employment are deteriorating; or (3) perhaps workers are raising their expectations regarding their jobs.

The segments of the labor force that are increasing include women with other wage earners in the household, workers with educational attainments beyond high school, workers who live in the South, workers who are not members of unions, workers under age 30, and workers in service occupations. If these also are demographic classes with characteristically low job satisfaction, the composition argument has some support, but that is not clearly the case. The first four groups characteristically have job satisfaction levels at or above the national means. The last two groups are characteristically below the national means in job satisfaction measures, but the period of their greatest increase in numbers in our surveys, 1969 to 1973, does not match the period of greatest decline in job satisfaction, 1973 to 1977.

Further, table 5 shows that the decline in job satisfaction involved virtually all groups.

Given the limited available measures, the argument relating to objective deterioration of jobs and employment conditions gains little support from the data. Such changes in objective factors that did occur between 1969 and 1977 were not great, and in any case, indicate more gains than losses in the objective qualities of jobs and employment conditions: increased availability of fringe benefits; diminished severity of work-related illnesses and injuries; more control by the worker over overtime hours. Between 1973 and 1977, the slight decline in earnings may have contributed to the decrease in satisfaction with financial rewards over that period, but it does not address the decrement in satisfaction with other domains. Moreover, over the same period, the slight decline in family income was not matched by a corresponding decline in the adequacy of family income. The decrease in availability of alternative employment opportunities, or locking-in, could have accounted for some reduction in job satisfaction, but did not; locking-in increased considerably more between 1969 and 1973 than between 1973 and 1977.

There remains, by the process of elimination, the argument concerning rising expectations. Unfortunately, the survey interviews included few measures of workers' expectations, so this argument cannot be sufficiently tested. Nonetheless, data on three indicators of the discrepancy between workers' expectations and the realities of their work experiences (namely, level of educational attainment, degree to which worker is "overeducated" for present job, and underutilization of skills) give essentially negative results. Neither of the measures involving education exhibits the expected pattern of stability between 1969 and 1973, followed by an increase in unmet expectations between 1973 and 1977. The measure of underutilization does meet this first test, yet fails when used as a control variable: the decline in job satisfaction between 1973 and 1977. The measure of under-utilization does meet this first test, expectations argument may gain greater

empirical support in the future, when tested using more and better measures.

In any case, the search for single, simple, and universally relevant explanations for changes in job satisfaction, and other measures of worker well-being is likely to be fruitless. The explanatory factors may be complex, and may well be quite different for the various sub-populations that make up the American labor force.

Finishing time:_____

FOOTNOTES

[1]Data from the 1969 and 1973 surveys appear in Neal Q. Herrick and Robert P. Quinn, "The working conditions survey as a source of social indicators," *Monthly Labor Review,* April 1971, pp. 15-24, and Robert P. Quinn, Thomas W. Mangione, Martha S. Baldi de Mandilovitch, "Evaluating working conditions in America," *Monthly Labor Review,* November 1973, pp. 32-40.

[2]The theoretical and empirical bases for development of the measures of job satisfaction, along with their statistical significance appear in Robert P. Quinn and Linda J. Shepard, *The 1972-73 Quality of Employment Survey* (Ann Arbor, Mich., Survey Research Center, 1974), pp. 50-69.

[a]Job Satisfaction: Is There a Trend? Manpower Research Monograph 30 (U.S. Department of Labor, 1974).

SKIM READING COMPREHENSION CHECK: "American Workers Evaluate the Quality of Their Jobs"

1. The authors' *assertion* is that:

   a. _____ U.S. workers are becoming more satisfied with their jobs and less inclined to want to leave them.

   b. _____ U.S. workers are becoming less satisfied with their jobs; however, they are less inclined to want to leave them.

   c. _____ U.S. workers are becoming less satisfied with their jobs and more inclined to want to leave them.

2. The authors *supported* their assertion by reviewing:

   a. _____ a questionnaire survey.

   b. _____ telephone interviews.

   c. _____ a battery of tests.

3. Which of the following was *not* used as an indicator of workers well-being?

   a. _____ Job satisfaction.

   b. _____ Leisure satisfaction.

   c. _____ Life satisfaction.

4. The decline in job satisfaction is present among:

   a. _____ the higher skilled workers only.

   b. _____ the lower skilled workers only.

   c. _____ all occupational classes.

5. In the 1977 survey, fringe benefits were:

   a. _____ a considerable concern to workers.

b. _____ the most important concern of workers.

c. _____ of little importance to
workers.

6. The most frequently reported
severely hazardous conditions of
a job were:

a. _____ dangerous chemicals.

b. _____ noises.

c. _____ fires.

7. With respect to the degree to
which jobs provide an opportunity for full use of skills, there
has been:

a. _____ an increase since 1969.

b. _____ a decrease since 1969.

c. _____ no change.

8. In 1977, workers felt:

a. _____ neither more nor less
locked-in to jobs than in
the past.

b. _____ less locked-in to jobs
than in the past.

c. _____ more locked-in to jobs
than in the past.

9. In general, workers attitudes
towards unions are:

a. _____ favorable.

b. _____ unfavorable.

c. _____ indifferent.

10. Employers who read this article
and agree with the authors' assertion will probably:

a. _____ take a hard-nosed
approach to their em-
ployees.

b. _____ try to make working
conditions better.

c. _____ write a letter of protest
to the authors.

Check your answers with the Answer Key.

INSTRUCTIONS FOR RAPID READING: "Women in Management: An Endangered Species?"

Read this article as fast as possible while trying to maintain a
comprehension score of at least 70 percent. Time yourself. When you
finish the article, write down your reading time in the space provided at
the end of the article. Answer the comprehension questions following
the article, then check your answers with the Answer Key. Determine
your reading rate from the Words Per Minute: Rapid Reading Chart,
then record your reading rate and comprehension score on your Rapid
Reading Progress Chart.

Rapid Reading

Women in Management: An Endangered Species?

John F. Veiga

Doors to the upper levels of the corporate hierarchy recently have begun to open for women, and most of the time, women themselves have opened these doors. But if the typical career strategies of women in management are indicative of how they pursue career advancement, only a few more doors will be opened in the years to come.

Recent studies have suggested that the number of women in upper level management positions is beginning to increase. Currently about 2 percent of all women in business are in management positions.[1] The increase can be attributed in part to affirmative action legislation and to more positive social attitudes toward women pursuing traditionally male careers. However, even with all the pressures for change, the relative impact on the corporate hierarchy will be minimal in the years to come. To increase the impact, women will have to take a closer look at their career strategies and values, and they will have to decide whether or not they are willing to play the corporate success game.

The conclusions of this article, based on a cross-sectional study of more than 500 women who hold positions up to the level of vice-president, could have far-reaching implications for women in, or aspiring to, management. The women studied (coming from 60 firms, including several on the *Fortune* 500 list, and representing 25 industries) attended career development workshops held during the past four years. In the majority of cases, they were nominated by their firms to attend because of their management potential. The participants averaged 35 years of age; half of them were

married; almost all had attended college; and they were earning an average income in excess of $16,000. The information received from them was compared to data obtained from men (with similar backgrounds, same average age, and same level of responsibility) who had attended other career development workshops.

In a study of individual career strategies and values, participants were asked to write down their career advice to young persons. Their responses remained anonymous. Here are some examples:

Person A: "Don't be a sex symbol or apple polish the boss—do it by merit, being the best worker with the most cooperative attitude."

Person B: "Don't be afraid to play politics."

Person C: "Continuously develop new skills so as to prepare yourself for advancement."

Person D: "Be the well wrapped package.with brains as opposed to the brown paper bag with brains—be noticed."

Person E: "Work hard, aim high, learn something new each day, let the sky be your limit."

Few people have difficulty in attributing the advice given by Persons A and D as coming from women. The sex of the remaining persons is not so obvious: B and C were men, and E was a woman. Generally, only about 10 percent of the advice could be readily identified. However, it was possible, upon closer examination, to distinguish some major differences in career perspectives between men and women.

The purpose of the exercise was to get individuals to recognize the limitations of giving or receiving career advice. When the responses were read aloud, it was easy for the participants to see how varied and naive such advice would be. For example, one woman wrote: "Work for a male boss first." A newly promoted man wrote: "If you want to become an executive, look like one." When some of the participants volunteered to elaborate further on their advice, it was evident that these were not frivolous responses but seemed to represent an integral part of the individual's career strategy and values.

By categorizing the advice, two distinct perspectives emerged. For the majority of the 500 men, the common theme expressed was a plan-ahead strategy. Often they stressed a need for planning not only career goals but also the methods of attainment. It was clear that many of the men felt the need to give opportunity a hand. In contrast, women commonly emphasized the value of proving one's ability by doing a good job. The majority expressed advice reminiscent of Horatio Alger, which can best be summarized as a "work hard and some day you will be rewarded for your effort" strategy.

In a related finding, a researcher of factors contributing to women's success in business found that women are culturally conditioned to feel uncomfortable when making demands in their own interest. Such hesitancy, she theorizes, was probably learned at an early age. For example, at a dance, young girls stand "all dolled up against a wall, waiting to be chosen."[2] Such waiting-to-be-picked behavior appears to have carried over into women's career strategies.

It seems that women are taking a myopic view of their careers, almost a short-run perspective of taking care of today and letting the future take care of itself. One woman epitomized this attitude when she said she had no need for specific career plans. "My company knows what is best for me," she said. On the other hand, the men generally were more career wise and questioned the management myth, prevalent until the late 1940s, that good managers, like cream, rise to the top.

Men become more career wise because of their access to what has been described as the "old-boy" network. One executive put this phenomenon simply: "If you are going to play the game, you have to know the rules." Unfortunately, women do not have this access, and there are too few women in management to act as role models and to advise aspiring young women. Myra Strober and Francine Gordon, in *Bringing Women into Management,* point out that "because most of today's women have been socialized to believe that management, like fatherhood, is for men, women who aspire to managerial careers need frequent reinforcement of their aspirations."[3] Unfortunately, such reinforcement might be long in coming if women in management are unable to break what appears to be a self-perpetuating cycle of passive acceptance in career strategy.

MOST WOMEN ARE UNWILLING TO PLAY THE GAME

One remedy for breaking the passive acceptance cycle might be to teach women how to play the game. To some degree assertiveness training has taken this direction. Certainly a nonassertive woman who follows a waiting-to-be-picked strategy will lessen her chance of reaching top management. However, making a woman more assertive and career wise when she is unwilling to play the game is not enough. Basic career motives need to be understood.

Unlike women, most men are expected to play the game. American businessmen often have been characterized as archetypical strivers. In reality, only about one in ten managers can be characterized as possessing the upward or unlimited success orientation.[4] Curt Tausky and Robert Dubin found that many men either are unwilling to play the game necessary to reach the top or do not aspire to top positions. Using the Career Orientations Anchorage Scale (COAS), Tausky and Dubin identified three managerial career orientations: upward, ambivalent, and downward. Male managers with these career orientations were found to possess the following characteristics:

Upward: Value high upward movement; career satisfaction is a function of proximity to the peak.

Ambivalent: Have an uncrystallized career perspective; dissatisfied without advancement but unwilling to actively pursue success.

Downward: Have a limited success perspective; after achieving adequate career rewards, express little interest in further advancement. Career satisfaction is a function of how far they have come in their careers.

Results of several studies which have validated the COAS all have indicated similar career orientation distributions for men in middle management. Male workshop participants included in this study showed virtually no significant differences from the typical pattern. However, when representative women were administered the COAS, some dramatic differences were found. Results are shown in Table 1.

These findings suggest that even fewer women than men (6 percent versus 10 percent) are strivers. Because the sample was an atypical group of women picked for their management potential, a higher incidence of upward orientation could have been expected. A reduction of more than half in the downward category (20 percent versus 47 percent) resulted in almost a doubling of the

number of women (74 percent versus 43 percent) in the ambivalent category. The fact that most of the women were in this category suggests they have uncrystallized career perspectives, which is consistent with their shortsighted career strategies. It also suggests that most women value advancement but are unwilling to play the game necessary to achieve success. However, these results may be overinflated. Women have been subjected to pressures from the women's movement as well as their organizations' affirmative action efforts. Perhaps some career ambivalence is merely a side effect of these awareness-raising efforts?

TABLE 1
MANAGERIAL CAREER ORIENTATION BY SEX

Orientation	Women[a] Percentage	Men[b] Percentage
Upward	6	10
Ambivalent	74	43
Downward	20	47

[a]N = 194.
[b]Tausky and Dubin, p. 729 (N = 308).
NOTE: $X^2 = 47.97$, df = 2, p < .001.

As might be expected, most studies show a connection between age and career orientation. By 45 years of age, 73 percent of all males have a downward perspective, in part because these managers have recognized their career limitations and accepted the inescapable fact that only a few will reach the top. In contrast, there is no difference in the career orientation between women over 45 and under 45 years of age. This finding lends credence to the hypothesis that women are being affected by awareness-raising pressures. While only 18 percent of the males over age 45 are experiencing ambivalence, almost four times as many women (70 percent) at this stage in life continue to experience ambivalence.

In a 1976 study,[5] twice as many younger women were found to be highly disillusioned with their present management positions (69 percent) as compared to older women (31 percent). Therefore, despite what might be expected, older women are more likely experiencing career ambivalence because of organizational and societal pressures and not because of unhappiness with present positions. However, since a younger person, male or female, often experiences career ambivalence, it is impossible to determine to what extent the higher level of ambivalence found in women over 45 is a result of awareness-raising pressures and how much might be attributed to the acculturation process found in our society today. Yet, it is possible to conclude that women over 45 are experiencing greater career anxiety than they probably should.

CHOICE ANXIETY IS A MAJOR PROBLEM

Consistent with the higher incidence of career ambivalence, women also have greater difficulty in making career choices. About 79 percent of the women attempting to develop a career plan express difficulty, as compared to 60 percent of the men. In addition, women express different career adaptation problems than men. Milton E. Hahn identifies four adaptation problems normally encountered when making career decisions: choice anxiety, lack of skill, lack of assurance, and lack of information.[6] Workshop participants were asked to identify problems that they anticipated in accomplishing their career plans. The results, shown in Table 2, were categorized by problem type.

Given the high incidence of ambivalence found in women, it was not too surprising to find almost half with the problem of choice anxiety. Comments such as these were typical: "I have such overriding personal obstacles at the moment that I can't really be as interested as I should be in a career plan," "I'm not sure which way I want to go," and "I just don't know what I really want." Even though their problems varied, many of these women seemed to be expressing anxiety over trying to make decisions they were unaccustomed to making. One woman said: "I'm just not accustomed to planning my life the way I want it. I've always accepted things the way they were." Often their expression of choice anxiety sounded like a lack of assurance as well. Hence, even though 20 percent of the problems were classified as a lack of assurance, realistically it was a much greater problem than the table suggests. Surprisingly, lack of skill was rarely mentioned by women even though a great deal of emphasis has been placed on business training for women, primarily because of their lack of business school degrees.

TABLE 2
MANAGERIAL CAREER ADAPTATION PROBLEMS ENCOUNTERED, BY SEX

Problem	Women (N = 400) Percentage	Men (N = 300) Percentage
Choice anxiety	48.5	23.3
Lack of skill	4.0	33.0
Lack of assurance	20.2	12.3
Lack of information	27.3	31.3

NOTE: The sample size is a result of the number of managers who indicated some problems in achieving their career goals. Out of 506 women, 400 (79 percent) reported problems. Out of 500 men, 300 (60 percent) reported problems.

In contrast, the men expressed lack of information and/or skill as their major problems. Statements such as these were common: "I really don't have the educational background to do what I'd really like to do," "I'm not sure what future opportunities are available to me in my present company." The men tended to obscure any choice anxiety or lack of assurance by rationalizing that lack of skill or information was the major obstacle. Those over age 40 tended to fall into the skill trap. They regarded their careers as continuous investments in skill development and often were unwilling to consider any career options requiring them to start over. On the other hand, women seemed to have the greatest difficulty in deciding where they should invest themselves and whether or not investment was really worth it.

ARE WOMEN IN MANAGEMENT AN ENDANGERED SPECIES?

Throughout this article, an attempt was made to avoid any value judgments about which career strategy is best. However, women must become more career wise if they are to survive in the corporate environs. That does not mean that all women should strive for the top. Each one needs to decide where she wants to go, and if the price is worth it.

We all have a choice. We can approach the future as pawns and accept whatever life offers us, or we can recognize our ability to influence our future and take some responsibility for what happens. The outcomes, which vary greatly, often benefit both organization and individual. One woman said: "I've finally dis-

covered that I have wasted a lot of time and energy trying to get a promotion which I thought I wanted. Now that I've decided that goal is not important, to hell with working overtime! I'm going to start taking tennis lessons this weekend." A talented Ph.D. found that by taking an active interest in the direction of her career and by actively pursuing outside opportunities, she won a significant promotion with a major insurance company.

In summary, most of the evidence suggests that it will not be easy for women to assume their rightful place in the corporate hierarchy. While it is clear that, to effect a change, women will have to modify their career strategies, it is unfair to place all the burden for change on them. A great deal still needs to be done to alter the sex-role stereotyping found in business today. Equal pay for equal work has been accepted, but the notion that women and men are interchangeable in management has not.

While there is too much evidence of forward motion to conclude that women in management are an endangered species, it should be recognized that the same pressures that produce change also can be counterproductive. For every woman who achieves a top management position, several others, especially those over age 45, will suffer increased career anxieties and uncertainties. However, along the way women may help modify the corporate environment so that playing the game may become obsolete; or perhaps a new game will emerge.

Finishing time:_____

FOOTNOTES

[1]Garda Bowman, N. Beatrice Worthy, and Stephen Greyer, "Are Women Executives People?" *Harvard Business Review* 43 (July-August 1965): 14.

[2]Margaret Hennig quoted in "Women in Banking: Transition to Management," *Carnegie Quarterly* 24 (Spring 1976): 7.

[3]Francine Gordon and Myra Strober, *Bringing Women into Management* (New York: McGraw-Hill, 1975), p. 79.

[4]Curt Tausky and Robert Dubin, "Career Anchorage: Managerial Mobility Motivation," *American Sociological Review* 30 (October 1965): 725-35.

[5]John F. Veiga and John N. Yanouzas, "What Women in Management Want: The Ideal vs. the Real" *Academy of Management Journal* 19 (March 1976): 137-43.

[6]Milton E. Hahn, *Planning Ahead After Forty* (Los Angeles: Western Psychological Services, 1973), pp. 2-3.

RAPID READING COMPREHENSION CHECK: "Women in Management: An Endangered Species?"

1. What is the writer's *assertion* or *theory*?

   a. _____ In the future, there will be as many doors open to women for management positions as there are now.

   b. _____ In the future, more and more doors will be open to women for management positions.

   c. _____ In the future, fewer doors will be open to women for management positions.

2. One way this theory is *supported* is with research dealing with:

   a. _____ an in-depth analysis of the careers of women in management positions.

   b. _____ futuristic management research.

   c. _____ a comparison of men's and women's career advice to young persons.

3. The major perspective of the women studied is that:

   a. _____ you can get ahead if you prove your ability to do a good job.

   b. _____ you can get ahead by planning.

   c. _____ you can get ahead by keeping a low profile.

4. The authors of "Bringing Women Into Management" *support* the writer's *theory* because they stress:

   a. _____ the continued impact of affirmative action legislation.

   b. _____ that women have been conditioned to believe that management is for men.

   c. _____ the increased positive social attitudes toward women in management roles.

5. The researchers who used the career orientation anchorage scale *support* the writer's *theory* because they found that:

   a. _____ more women than men are strivers.

   b. _____ few women were in the ambivalent category and thus have their career strategies planned.

   c. _____ many women were in the ambivalent category and thus have short-sighted career strategies.

6. With respect to making a career choice, men experience:

   a. _____ more difficulty than women.

   b. _____ less difficulty than women.

   c. _____ about the same level of difficulty as women.

7. Men expressed a concern for

lacking the skills necessary for a job:

a. _____ more than women.

b. _____ less than women.

c. _____ as often as women.

8. The author's major *support* for his theory comes from examining:

a. _____ attitudes in general.

b. _____ career motives.

c. _____ feminist groups.

9. Women who accept the writer's *theory* will probably:

a. _____ look more closely at their career strategies and values.

b. _____ give up on seeking management positions.

c. _____ enroll in an assertiveness training program.

10. The writer probably:

a. _____ disapproves of women in managerial positions.

b. _____ feels women should not take their careers too seriously.

c. _____ feels that qualified women should be placed in managerial positions.

Check your answers with the Answer Key.

INSTRUCTIONS FOR RAPID READING: "The Frightened Consumer?"

Read this article as quickly as possible while trying to maintain a comprehension score of at least 70 percent. Time yourself. When you finish the article, write down your reading time in the space provided at the end of the article. Answer the comprehension questions following the article, then check your answers in the Answer Key. Determine your reading rate from the Words Per Minute: Rapid Reading Chart, then record your reading rate and comprehension score on your Rapid Reading Chart.

Rapid Reading

The Frightened Consumer?

Walter P. Gorman

In recent years, newspapers, books, magazines, and television have advised American consumers that certain food and cosmetic additives are possibly harmful.[1,2,3] Consumer reaction to these food and cosmetic additive warnings has decided implications for the retailer's mix. Manufacturers now confronted with the additive decision may select to omit certain additives and advertise natural products or continue to use suspected additives and benefit from longer product storage life and possibly better product taste and eye appeal.

Very few available studies have attempted to measure consumer awareness of and reactions to food and cosmetic additive safety. Accordingly, in April and May 1973, a sample of 350 supermarket customer respondents patronizing Northwest Tennessee supermarkets (Martin and surrounding cities) were interviewed to gauge consumer response to food and cosmetic safety. All supermarkets in Martin and certain supermarkets in Trenton, Paris, Milan, and Lexington were interview sites. Student interviewers selected respondents at each site by securing cooperation from the first shopper exiting the store after each completed interview. Interviewers operated on different days of the week and at different hours to assure a more representative sample. Under these circumstances, while the sample is not a true random sample, it should be representative of supermarket shoppers and adequate for the exploratory purposes of this study.

FINDINGS

Six questions about food and cosmetic safety were asked respondents. Out of the 350 respondents, 41 percent stated that they had discontinued buying at least one supermarket product within the past three years because they learned that the product contained harmful ingredients. When asked specifically what they had discontinued, 29 percent stated deodorants with hexachlorophene; 20 percent indicated diet foods with cyclamates; and 6 percent specified fish because of possible mercury contamination. Others mentioned personal allergies to cosmetics and soaps.

Supermarket customers were also asked which products they used "less of" because that product may have contained harmful ingredients. Again, products containing hexachlorophene and cyclamates were indicated repeatedly; but 23 respondents specifically noted tuna. Many other meat products were mentioned. Apparently, while many shoppers were not willing to give up specific meat products entirely, they were influenced to cut down on their consumption of suspected items.

Respondents, when asked from what source they first learned about a harmful food substance, aggregately reported 261 communications. Over half of these messages, 54.5 percent were television messages; 20.7 percent were newspaper; 9.6 percent were magazine; 9.6 were from "other people"; and 5.7 percent were from other sources. Figure 1 compares the sources.

Interviewers also asked respondents to express their attitudes toward each of eight allegedly harmful ingredients. Table 1 indicates their responses.

Most shoppers evaluated most additives as not being harmful if consumed in small quantities. Mercury in fish, hexachlorophene, fattening hormones in meats, and sodium cyclamates were estimated as being more harmful than the other four substances. It is noteworthy that substances receiving no more than 25 percent of the vote as being harmful (except for food coloring), received at least 25 percent "don't know" responses. Sodium nitrate, for example, carcenogenic [*sic*] when blended with certain other substances, was judged not harmful by almost one third of the respondents, while 37.4 percent indicated that they did not know about its safety.[4] Mercury received the most negative response; food coloring, in contrast, was adjudged not harmful by almost 50 percent of the sample. About half of those sampled did not know about the safety of BHT and BTH, which are banned in Sweden and Australia.[5]

FIGURE 1

A Comparison of First Sources of Information About Food Additive Danger (In Percent of Total Messages Reported)

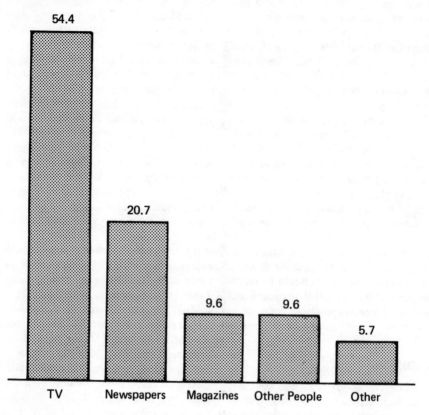

TABLE 1

Suppermarket Customers' Evaluation of Food and Cosmetic Substances Suspected of Being Harmful to Humans (Percentage Distribution of Sample's Response)

		Evaluation		
		Not Harmful in Small		
Substance	Not Harmful	Quantities	Harmful	Don't Know
Sodium Cyclamate	20.9	36.9	27.4	14.9
Hexachlorophene	24.0	24.3	33.4	18.3
BHT + BTH	28.3	18.6	05.4	47.7
Sodium Nitrate	31.4	24.0	07.4	37.4
Monosodium Glutamate	29.4	19.1	10.0	41.4
Food Coloring	48.3	18.6	16.3	16.9
Fattening Hormones (Meat)	19.4	17.4	31.4	31.7
Mercury	07.4	10.9	75.7	06.0

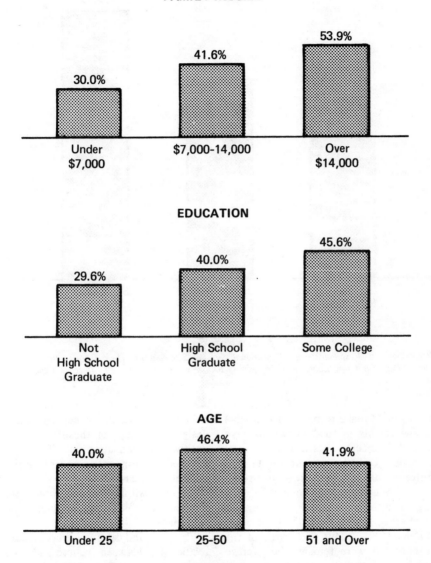

FIGURE 2

Percentages of Respondents by Income, Education, and Age Groups Who Discontinued Using Suspected Supermarket Products

The respondents were requested to select one of three statements that best expressed their feelings about food safety. Approximately 22 percent se-lected: "I believe the products with the above ingredients are generally safe in the quantities consumed by humans;" while 60 percent selected: "I believe the

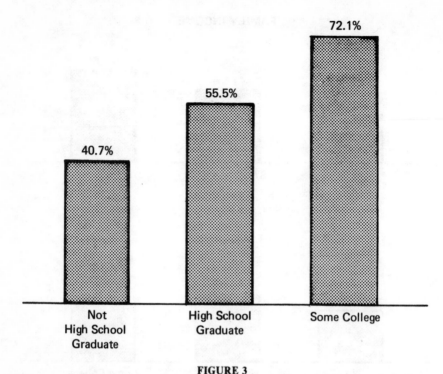

FIGURE 3

Percentages of Respondents by Educational Groups Selecting as Their Choice the Statement Demanding Mandatory Labeling of Ingredients Known to Have Caused Ill Effects in Experimental Animals

FTC should make it mandatory to label all ingredients in food known to have caused harmful effects in experimental animals." Only 18 percent selected: "I believe that all suspected products should be taken off the shelves."

In additional questions consumers were asked to determine their socioeconomic status. About two thirds of the respondents were female; the average age was 35; and the average education was approximately 12 years (high school graduate). Of respondents answering the questions about income, 35 percent were in families with under $7,000 income; 45 percent had family income of between $7,000 and $14,000; and 25 percent were in families with an earning capacity of over $14,000.

Figure 2 charts the percentages within designated groups of those responding positively to the question: "Have you stopped buying or using any supermarket products (food, deodorant, or cosmetics) within the last three years because you learned that the ingredients were harmful?"

Figure 2 indicates a direct positive relationship between income and food-safety sensitivity. Perhaps shoppers with higher incomes can afford to be more selective. The higher the income group, the greater the percentage of respondents within that group selecting the choice of mandatory labeling of possibly harmful ingredients. Education showed a strong relationship with discontinuance of suspected foods. Accordingly, the percentage selecting the statement demanding labeling of suspicious ingredients was also higher in the more educated groups (see Figure 3). The middle-age group, rather than the younger or the older group, showed a greater percentage of positive responses to the discontinuance of use question.

A SUPPLEMENTARY STUDY

The same procedures and forms of the first study were used to select and question a smaller sample of one hundred shoppers in May 1974. Respondents from two Martin and one Union City supermarkets were represented in the subsequent study.

A larger proportion, 49 percent, reported discontinuing a product because it was learned that the ingredients were harmful. Again, deodorants with hexachlorophene, fish (particularly tuna), and artificially sweetened foods were most mentioned as items discontinued. Again, over 25 percent of the respondents reported mercury in fish (80 percent) fattening hormones in meat, hexachlorophene, and sodium cyclamates as "harmful." In the second sample, 19 percent reported sodium nitrate "harmful" as opposed to just 7.4 percent in the first sample, and only 27 percent as opposed to 37.4 percent put sodium nitrate in the "don't know" category. Again, about 60 percent (62 percent) selected the statement requiring labeling for substances with doubtful additives. Slightly over 50 percent (51 percent) again mentioned television as the first source of information about additive dangers; but a greater proportion (15 percent) mentioned "other people" in the later sampling. Again, greater interest in food safety was associated with higher education and income.

The second sampling largely substantiated the earlier study, but it indicated a slightly increased awareness of food safety. This is contrary to a statement of Denty Cheatham, a Nashville attorney, Head of Tennessee Consumer Alliance, who expressed in March 1974, that consumer interest had shifted from safety aspects to concern with high prices.[6]

CONCLUSIONS

Dramatic information on television and in newspapers has increased shoppers' awareness of additive dangers, but apparently many consumers are not very frightened since less than half discontinued buying or using suspected products. Shoppers were particularly aware of dangers from mercury, hexachlorophene, fattening hormones in meat, and sodium cyclamate. The fattening hormone D.E.S. has been outlawed in animal feed since the first sample interviews were completed. Wealthier and more educated shoppers are apparently more sensitive to possible additive dangers and appear to support the idea of mandatory labeling rather than inaction or removal of the suspected item from the market. Middle-aged shoppers may be slightly more sensitive to additive dangers than the younger and older shoppers.

Sensitivity to additive dangers may increase in the future, even in the face of distracting inflation, as new threats are uncovered and exposed through the mass media. There may be increasing opportunities to feature goods free from known chemical additives at market-plus prices. Supermarket operators in high-income areas may have greater success with such pure foods because of the indicated correlation of safety sensitivity with income and education. Certainly, in this age of "consumerism," there is a need for more research measuring consumer reaction to food and cosmetic danger publicity. This exploratory study indicates at least a noticeable consumer response to additive dangers and suggests hypotheses about response as related to income, education, and age. Response may also vary between races, social classes, life cycles, geographical locations, occupations, and other socio-economic factors. Millions of dollars have already been lost because of ballooning publicity about a nonessential ingredient. The "additive decision" is made by too many firms today with too little information on possible consumer reaction.

Finishing time:_____

FOOTNOTES

[1]Tom Alexander, "The Hysteria About Food Additives," *Fortune* (March 1972), p. 63.

[2]Joan Z. Majtenyi, "Food Additives—Food for Thought," *Chemistry*, 47, No. 5 (May 1974), 6–9.

[3]Beatrice Trum Hunter, *Consumer Beware* (New York: Simon and Schuster, 1971), 17ff.

[4]Joan Z. Majtenyi, "Food Additives—Food for Thought," p. 7.

[5]Beatrice Trum Hunter, *Consumer Beware*, p. 93.

[6]Nancy Varley, "Consumer Group Rebuilds," *The Tennessean*, Tuesday, March 26, 1974, p. 20.

RAPID READING COMPREHENSION CHECK: "The Frightened Consumer?"

Directions: Answer the questions below. Base your answers on the information included in the reading.

1. The author's *assertion* is that the consumer:

   a. _____ is frightened.

   b. _____ is not frightened.

   c. _____ may be frightened.

2. The author *supports* his assertion by:

   a. _____ interviewing super-market customers.

   b. _____ reporting research completed by scholars.

   c. _____ sending questionnaires to consumers through the mail.

3. According to the author, studies on consumer awareness of and reactions to foods and cosmetics are:

   a. _____ widely available.

   b. _____ scarce.

   c. _____ unavailable.

4. The people who gathered the data for this study were:

   a. _____ students.

   b. _____ businessmen.

   c. _____ professors.

5. Which statement, according to this article, is true?

   a. _____ The lower your income, the higher your sensitivity to food safety.

   b. _____ There is no relationship between income level and food-safety sensitivity.

   c. _____ The higher your income, the higher your sensitivity to food safety.

6. Which group registered the greatest number of positive responses to the "discontinuance of use" question?

a. _____ The younger group.

b. _____ The middle-age group.

c. _____ The older group.

7. When the second sampling (study) is compared with the first, one finds:

a. _____ a slight increased awareness of food safety.

b. _____ a slight decreased awareness of food safety.

c. _____ the same level of awareness of food safety.

8. The author concluded from this study that consumers are:

a. _____ very frightened.

b. _____ not frightened at all.

c. _____ somewhat frightened.

9. In the future, the author expects the dangers of food additives to:

a. _____ increase.

b. _____ decrease.

c. _____ stay the same.

10. An *expected outcome* of this study is that:

a. _____ business firms will seek no information on consumer reaction to their "additive decisions."

b. _____ those participating in the study will become less sensitive to "additive decisions."

c. _____ business firms will seek more information on consumer reaction to their "additive decisions."

Check your answers with the Answer Key.

7
Data Pattern I: Informational

INTRODUCTION

When you walk into a large place of business, you often find a directory. The directory clearly provides you with the necessary data that tells you *what* departments are a part of the business and *where* they can be found. For example, when you walk into a bank, you find where different departments, such as loans, savings, retirement plans, and checking, are located.

Articles written in the data patterns can be likened to a place of business with its various departments. Authors select a major topic and provide you with data about it. The writers' "departments" are the various subtopics. For example, one author recently wrote about "Bills That Made It In Congress's Rush" (major topic). The various subtopics were "Banking Reform," "Tuition Aid," "Airline Deregulation," "Full Employment," "Pregnancy Benefits," and "Waterway Use." For each subtopic, the writer offered one or two main ideas.

How are the data patterns different from the problem-solution and persuasive patterns? The difference lies primarily in the writer's motivation or purpose for writing the article. Writers choose to use the problem-solution or persuasive patterns when they hope to move the reader to some action. For example, when you studied the persuasive patterns, some actions, either stated or implied, included improving your image by selecting an appropriate briefcase, being more aware of food additives, and looking more closely at your career values and strategies. When you studied the problem-solution pattern, some actions, either stated or implied, included attaining construction loans from insurance companies, consulting advisers before implementing the open office concept, and lobbying to forestall consumer legislation. However, when writers choose to use one of the data patterns, their motivation is basically to inform the reader (no action suggested) or to instruct the reader. The only action is to follow the advice or instructions.

We will investigate two types of data patterns. One is the common *informational article* that readers find in most business magazines or feature columns in newspapers. For example, in the October 23, 1978, issue of the *U.S. News and World Report,* an article appeared entitled "What You Can and Cannot Do If You Run A Business" (major topic). The subtopics of this article were: "Credit Rights," "Anesthesiologists," "Stockbrokers," "Fringe Benefits," "Employers," "Sales of Toys," "Stock Options," and "Banks". The reader's main task in analyzing articles such as this is to determine each subtopic. In this article, the task was simple because the subtopics were easily identified by their bold-face type. Unfortunately, in many articles the subtopics are not identified in this way. When this happens, readers may have to slow down their rate enough so as not to miss precisely where the author had moved on to a new subtopic.

The diagram shown in Figure 3 illustrates how important main ideas and details are related to the various components (subtopics) of the informational type of data pattern.

The second type of data pattern is the *instructional article.* This, like the informational article, starts with a major topic. The subtopics

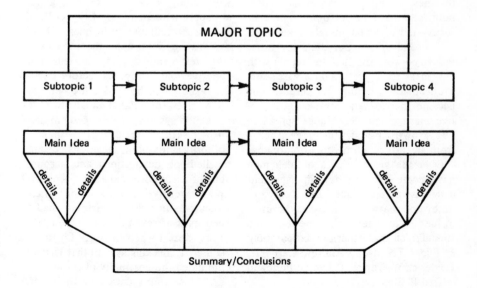

Figure 3 Relationship of Main Ideas to Data: Informational Pattern

usually are the steps one must follow to learn how to do things such as: completing a project, saving money, or losing weight. Often, the steps one must follow appear in bold-face type.

In this chapter, the informational type of data pattern will be further developed. Chapter 8 will discuss the instructional type of data pattern.

INSTRUCTIONS FOR ANALYZED READING: "The Masterminds of Management"

After you read this article and the analysis that follows it, you will have a clear idea of the approach that authors use when their writing is organized by the informational data pattern.

Analyzed Reading

The Masterminds of Management
Paula Smith

Corporate management did not spring from theorists in ivory towers. It was created out of necessity. By the mid-nineteenth century, the enterprises put together by the early tycoons had grown so big and posed so many new problems that new methods of control and communication had to be found. The railroads—more capital hungry, expensive to run and spread out than any other industry—were the first to grapple with new ideas for operating on a vast scale. From that beginning, as corporations became increasingly complex, innovative management techniques spread to one growth industry after another—from steel to chemicals to automobiles.

Over the years, scores of idea men have come up with new management concepts and techniques. But five major innovators have proven to be the most influential in determining the form and function of the American corporation: J. Edgar Thomson, Andrew Carnegie, Frederick W. Taylor, Pierre du Pont and Alfred P. Sloan.

J. Edgar Thomson, who became the first president of the Pennsylvania Railroad, developed the world's biggest and first truly modern business organization. When Thomson took over the newly formed Pennsy in 1852, a theory of large-scale administration had been worked out by Daniel McCallum, general superintendent of the Erie Railroad. Taking McCallum's principles, Thomson was the first to apply them in a major way—testing and developing them into a cohesive management structure during the two decades he guided the Pennsy.

Thomson formulated an advanced information system for management decision-making. He defined lines of authority and communications, created detailed job descriptions and accountability for employees at all levels and set up an extensive record-keeping system. Executives in every department had to keep track of revenues and expenses in great detail—providing, Thomson claimed, a checking system that virtually eliminated the possibility of fraud.

All this minute data gave the central office a precise picture of the railroad's strengths and weaknesses. Statistics such as train mileage, the number of passengers and the amount of time a locomotive spent in service or repair each day were collected at the lowest level, combined at the divisional level and presented to the general superintendent—who could then see which divisions and which services were profitable and efficient and which needed to be restructured or eliminated. This in turn allowed management to better determine the most profitable use of resources—whether, for instance, to make a repair or postpone it, whether to raise or lower rates. So effective was the system that the Pennsy came to be known as the "standard railroad of the world."

Thomson's techniques were carried into other fields by men who would also build huge organizations. Theodore Vail, for one, used the methods he had learned operating the U.S. Post Office's railroad mail service to create the world's most efficient and biggest privately owned communications system — American Telephone & Telegraph Co.

Thomson's most notable disciple, however, was Andrew Carnegie, former superintendent of the Pennsy's Western division. Carnegie transferred Thomson's accounting and information system to manufacturing—and added ideas of his own. Starting out in the iron and steel industry in the 1860s when it was an assortment of small producers, Carnegie built a company so large and so efficient that his competitors were forced to imitate his methods. Carnegie was obsessed with costs. At Carnegie Steel Corp., not only was every bit of material kept track of, small slivers that accumulated in the rolling of steel were collected and recycled, and the blast-furnace flue-cinder, which other steelmakers threw away, was saved to be reused as fuel.

Carnegie systematized cost analysis by setting up a detailed unit system for tracking the company's labor and material costs; the cost data were then applied in making marketing, investment and personnel decisions. Knowing his costs so precisely enabled Carnegie to price his products precisely—and undersell his competitors. His fanaticism about costs also led him to constantly seek more efficient and technologically advanced machinery, and Carnegie plowed back profits into new equipment on a scale that no one in manufacturing had ever done before. He was even known to tear down half-built new furnaces and start over if somebody came up with an idea for better cost efficiency.

Carnegie was also one of the earliest chief executives to use profit-sharing as an incentive—if in his own tightfisted way. He kept management salaries at a minimum, with a top annual salary of about $5,000 at a time the railroads were paying $100,000. Instead, he offered his managers partnership shares. But he held down the book value of the company by not allowing the capitalization to reflect true assets so that the partners' shares would not rise in value. Believing that one day their shares would be worth a great deal of money—which they were—the partners felt they could not afford to leave Carnegie.

While Carnegie started industry on a new way of thinking about production and costs in the overall manufacturing operation, it was Frederick W. Taylor who first systematically sought ways to get the most out of every man and machine on the factory floor. By the last decades of the nineteenth century, mass-production techniques were spreading, and methods for controlling and administering the factory floor were badly needed. Building on a number of ideas already known, Taylor, an engineer, formulated his concept of "scientific management," aimed at reorganizing the production line for maximum efficiency.

Taylor started developing his theories in the 1880s with time-and-motion experiments at Midvale Steel Works and Bethlehem Steel Co. Armed with a stopwatch, he tried to determine how much time and physical movement it took for workers to perform their tasks. From this knowledge, he felt that a high degree of standardization could be achieved, which would lower labor costs and increase profits. Each job was broken into as many elementary movements as possible. By observing the most skilled workmen at their jobs, the best and quickest methods were selected. Each movement was timed and recorded, and additional time was added to cover such things as unavoidable delays, a new worker's lack of familiarity with the job and rest periods. A file of these elementary movements and times could then be built for use in other jobs or types of work. Taylor conducted experiments on everything from lighting to the less tangible aspects of the working environment, such as social hierarchies in the plant and the suitability of workers to their jobs.

Needless to say, labor was not enchanted with Taylor's experiments and interpreted them as ways to push workers harder for bigger profits. Workers also balked at Taylor's incentive wage system, which penalized substandard performance. But Taylor, who always denied charges that his ideas were "inhuman," believed that maximum efficiency and output was not possible unless workers were reasonably content in their jobs.

Scientific management was promoted and publicized by Louis D. Brandeis. A lawyer for customers of Eastern railroads, Brandeis used Taylor's theories as an argument against proposed increases in freight rates. Taylor's ideas were further popularized in the press, and in 1911 more than 300 educators, consultants and businessmen gathered at Dartmouth College for the world's first Scientific Management Conference. That same year Taylor published his major treatise, *The Principles of Scientific Management.* Through the work of his many followers, Taylor's methods became standard practice throughout industry and the foundation for modern industrial psychology and personnel management.

Pierre du Pont knew the work of both Carnegie and Taylor. He had hired Taylor as a consultant when he was in the steel business. Du Pont, though, was particularly concerned about higher-echelon management problems. While Carnegie and Taylor worked out ideas at the factory level, it was with du Pont that modern top management came into being.

When du Pont took over the family firm, E.I. du Pont de Nemours & Co., already a century old, most industrial companies were still run from a central office that was basically a one-man show. Du Pont revolutionized the general office, setting up the procedures for forecasting, long-range planning, budgeting and allocating resources that executives today take for granted. Charles A. Coffin was building a general office along the same lines at General Electric, but du Pont's creation was more systematic. And while some students of management consider John D. Rockefeller the founder of top management, the committee system he had established at Standard Oil some thirty years before was eventually scrapped and replaced almost entirely with the du Pont system.

Du Pont built functional departments for manufacturing, sales, purchasing, capital expenditures planning and traffic. On top of the departments he set up a tightly centralized general office to control sales, purchasing, manufacturing, personnel and so forth for the entire organization. The company's governing body was the executive committee, composed of the president and the heads of the major departments.

To enable the executive committee to allocate resources, du Pont set up a system to provide it with information about departmental capital expenditures—data on costs, anticipated rate of return on proposed spending, and so forth. Departmental expenditure requests were also checked by purchasing, engineering and traffic specialists. Plant managers and department heads were allowed to authorize smaller capital expenditures, but a senior executive reviewed the big ones.

Besides being judged on their likely rate of return, capital spending proposals were evaluated as part of the company's long-term growth plans. That, in turn, was based on estimates of market demand, for which du Pont developed advanced forecasting techniques. The executive committee also coordinated the flow of materials through the corporate empire, attempting to control inventory at all stages, the physical movement of goods and the fluctuating demands for working capital.

But this functional, highly centralized structure broke down after World War I, when du Pont diversified into paints, dyes, chemicals and fibers. The complexities created by diversification, coupled with a severe postwar recession, brought about an inventory crisis, and du Pont suffered big losses. In a major administrative reorganization, the central office that du Pont had created was altered to become the banker and resource allocator for decentralized divisions. In effect, the company separated top management and the allocation of resources from the day-to-day operations of the divisions.

Controlled decentralization, though, really came into its own at General Motors Corp. The du Pont family had a $25 million investment in GM and Pierre du Pont became president in 1920. What he found was a company trembling on the edge of collapse, a corporate shambles. Its founder and former president William Durant, a collector of automobile and parts manufacturing companies and one of the greatest business promoters the country has ever known, had not set up any central financial or policy control. The division presidents set prices independently of each other, had complete authority over inventories and income, and very often made their own financial arrangements with banks. Durant put little stock in data and seldom bothered to tell anyone, even his executive committee, what he was up to.

One of Durant's top managers was Alfred Pritchard Sloan Jr., who headed a group of supply companies that Durant had acquired. Sloan had evolved a detailed plan for reorganizing the company. But it was ignored by Durant, and Sloan was on the verge of quitting when du Pont stepped in. Du Pont recognized and endorsed the management concepts set down in Sloan's now-famous 1920 Organization Study. Together, du Pont and Sloan, who succeeded him as president and chief executive in 1923, instituted a formula for "decentralized operations with centralized policy control." Similar to the one that was simultaneously emerging at du Pont, Sloan's system became the model for most industrial corporations.

Essentially the system enabled top management to control the various parts of the business in a rational way. Each division was basically an individual operating company, with its own manufacturing, sales, purchasing departments and so on. But it would have to operate according to guidelines—on everything from basic organization to reporting procedures—established by top management. Under the system, the divisions were required to come up with very detailed figures on costs, sales, purchases, profits and the like so that top management could authorize production levels. And while the divisions had the responsibility of developing their own operating plans and proposals, it was ultimately headquarters that made the big decisions on how the company's resources would be deployed.

Sloan's devotion to controls, measurements and forecasts, and an organizational mechanism that made them work, was responsible for much of GM's success. It was Sloan who recognized at the right moment, after World War I, that Americans' taste in automobiles was changing. In the early 1920s, he saw, as Henry Ford did not, that consumers were no longer being adequately served by a single car that would provide reliable transportation at the lowest cost. They wanted variety—a car for every taste and every purse—with style, not engineering, as the dominant consideration. By 1926-27, GM was offering a line of cars that covered the price and range from Chevrolet to Cadillac. Needless to say, GM's flexible marketing strategy would prove to be correct.

ANALYZED READING ANALYSIS: "The Masterminds of Management"

In this article, author Paula Smith has some historical information to present to her readers; consequently, she chose to use the informational type of data pattern to advance her topic. The main points of the article are presented below. Notice how she began with her major topic ("The Masterminds of Management") and then proceeded to comment on various aspects of the major topic (Thomson, Carnegie, Taylor, du Pont, and Sloan). Her primary purpose was to identify the major concepts and techniques each mastermind has contributed to the field of management.

Also notice how the ideas are associated with the different subtopic components of the informational data patterns.

Pattern Components (Subtopics)	Main Ideas and Details (Mastermind Contributions)
J. Edgar Thomson	First modern business organization; a decision-making and checking system.
Andrew Carnegie	Cost analysis system; profit sharing.
Frederick Taylor	Scientific management; time-and-motion studies; incentive wage system

| Pierre du Pont | Developed functional departments in central office; advanced forecasting techniques; controlled decentralization. |
| Alfred Sloan, Jr. | Refined du Pont's decentralized approach; flexible marketing strategy. |

INSTRUCTIONS FOR UNTIMED READING: "The Trauma Of a Systems Change"

In this article, the authors take their major topic, trauma, and subdivide it into five stages. Your task is to identify the stages and the basic point the authors make about each stage. Read the article and answer the questions that follow it. Then check your answers in the Answer Key.

Untimed Reading

The Trauma Of a Systems Change

Russell A. Johnston and Guy J. De Genaro

A dramatic change in an organization's way of doing business can be a traumatic experience for administrative managers. Reactions may range from mild depression and feet-dragging to absolute rejection of the new system. In some cases, the executive may even leave the organization.

During our work with business, industry, and government in setting up Management by Objectives (MBO) programs, we observed that this is one of the major systems changes that can bring about severe executive trauma.

Typically, an administrator perceives his or her job as a set of duties and responsibilities, with job performance measured in terms of the effectiveness and efficiency with which those duties are carried out. However, with the introduction of an MBO program, the individual is forced to define exactly what the goals and objectives of the job are, while the how of achieving those objectives is left to his or her discretion.

Job performance of the individual is measured, not just in terms of efficient function-filling, but by the progress made towards achieving those set goals. The emphasis shifts from functions to objectives.

In conducting numerous MBO training programs, we have noted a certain similarity between the typical executive's reaction to change and that of a terminally ill patient to the news that he is dying, as outlined in Dr. Elisabeth Kübler-Ross' well-known study on the psychology of death.

FIVE STAGES

It was Kübler-Ross' observation that a person with a terminal illness generally reacts by progressing through five distinct stages:[1]

(1) *denial;* (2) *anger;* (3) *bargaining;* (4) *depression;* (5) *acceptance.*

In each of the stages, the patient gradually adjusts only to move to the next stage. Just as this psychological process occurs with the terminally ill patient,

---

[1]Elisabeth Kübler-Ross, *On Death and Dying* (New York; MacMillan, 1969).

there may be a vaguely similar response by a manager facing a dramatic company-wide systems change, such as the introduction of a MBO program.

The average administrative manager may be quite comfortable in a given role in the management system. He or she may be happy plodding along year after year with minor increases in output, and little or no increases in personal effectiveness and efficiency. The sudden prospect of having to go through the changes of developing objectives, writing action plans and trying to meet those objectives and deadlines can be a truly traumatic experience for the executive.

For example, here's what often happens when the previously secure executive is told that his organization is adopting an MBO program. First, there is the Denial Stage. Kübler-Ross describes it this way:

Denial is the first reaction of a person who is made aware of terminal illness. This is a temporary state of shock and disbelief. The patient cannot accept the fact he has a severe illness, and that he will eventually die of it.

Confronted with what is perceived to be a drastic, threatening change in his or her organization life, the executive's first reaction may be to tell him or herself that MBO will not work in their particular organization. After all, his or her managerial efforts may lie in the creative arena and "everyone knows objectives cannot be written for creative efforts." Or, if the administrator has a staff function, the reaction may be that "everyone knows measurable objectives cannot be written for a staff operation." Managers may go through vehement reactions, denying that objectives can be applied to their jobs, much less their company.

In phase two of the Denial Stage, the manager may express these feelings to his or her boss. In the confrontation with the boss, the manager usually finds out that MBO is going to be put into effect and that he or she might as well move forward on this fact. This will bring on the Anger Stage. According to Kübler-Ross:

Anger is the next stage in a dying patient's reaction. The patient slashes out at the world, asking, why me? It did not happen to anyone else; others are alive and healthy and here am I waiting to die. He is mad at the world and at himself. Family and loved ones may also react with anger of their own, which tends to fuel the patient's hostile behavior.

At this point, the manager passes through two phases of the Anger Stage. Phase one may involve belittling the organization, the boss, and fighting with his or her spouse. The executive may decide simply not to put this MBO nonsense into effect in his or her department. It cannot be done; he or she will not do it and will go tell the boss just that!

Phase two of the Anger Stage occurs when the administrative manager discusses his complete frustration over the MBO plan with his boss. In a fit of anger, the administrator may make rash statements to his boss, but he learns that if he is to remain a part of the system, he will have to put MBO into effect in his unit. Next comes the Bargaining Stage:

Anger is often followed by a stage in which the patient may ask God to spare him. "Give me this one chance, and I will be a good boy from here on." Patients may try negotiating with anyone just to gain additional time.

After the traumatic session with the boss in the Anger Stage, the manager usually moves through two phases of the Bargaining Stage in which he tries to negotiate the impact of MBO on him and his organization.

In phase one he fantasizes. Perhaps he can get the boss to measure performance on some sort of "happiness index," one that would reflect only good feelings at the end of the year—whether the objectives are accomplished or not. He believes that anything would be better than having to submit to precise measurements of nebulous outputs. Perhaps the objectives should not be too measurable, for if they are one might get into trouble, especially if they are not met at the end of the year.

After a period of thoughts such as these, the manager goes to phase two of the Bargaining Stage. He now makes every effort to convince his boss that MBO will not work in his organization but that he will try it if he is given additional staff members, new resources, a larger budget, and if he is provided with additional services. Then, and only then, he might be willing to try. However, the boss will usually tell him that MBO will be put through on a measured-criteria basis without additional resources.

DEPRESSION

The Depression Stage is next:

Pain, the hardships of surgery and hospitalization will often lead to severe depression. Agonizing, wakeful nights occur as the patient feels sorry about what has happened to him and that he is going to die. Financial and emotional burdens lead to a stage of deep depression.

His fantasies shattered and his bargaining frustrated, the manager now falls into a state of depression. In phase one of the Depression Stage he may sit in his office, dejectedly, contemplating the possibility of leaving the organization as soon as he can. He will not stay in a company where people will not listen to him. Such depression may carry over into the executive's home life as he struggles to prepare himself psychologically for leaving the organization—or coming around to the idea of MBO.

In phase two of the Depression Stage, the downcast executive may go back to his boss again to say that he just does not know how he is going to manage with the new chores that are being thrown his way.

This is a crucial point in the MBO response pattern. Much depends on the sensitivity of the boss, the manager's personal investment in the organization, his financial resources, the economic situation, and alternative job opportunities. In a few cases, the manager leaves the organization—retires or quits. Sometimes he retires in place—not accepting MBO and not leaving—merely hanging on until he is fired. Fortunately the manager usually recognizes reality and proceeds to the Acceptance Stage:

Finally the patient accepts the fact that he is going to die. He begins to make plans, feverishly attacking chores such as wills, burial plot locations and all else that goes with the perceived realities of leaving the earth. This is not to be confused with a feeling of happiness or serenity, but simply an acknowledgement that the reality of death is near.

Confronted with the inevitable and the need to relieve his frustrations, the manager slowly accepts the idea that there is no escape; that he might as well prepare for the advent of MBO. Just as the terminally ill patient might proceed to prepare wills, grave plots and so forth, the MBO "patient" proceeds to lead his staff and himself to learn more about MBO.

Managers, in trying to go through the tedious processes of setting objectives may cycle back through the stages. Acceptance leads to the accumulation of increased knowledge about the subject and results in new and complex requirements that may be brought to bear on the manager. Such frustrations may cycle the administrative manager back to his earlier stage of denying that MBO can be applied to his organization. This reaction may lead to another round of depression. But finally, the executive will move forward to again proceed with the process.

Managers have been observed to go through the cycle several times before their first set of objectives were actually put into operation. One of the redeeming features is that it seems to take an individual less and less time to cycle through the stages.

The fact remains that MBO is not a concept that is easily accepted by managers. The analysis of the trauma many managers go through in adjusting to change in terms of Elisabeth Kübler-Ross' study of the psychology of death is, of course, an intentional exaggeration. Nevertheless, the anguish many executives undergo in coping with a new management program is real.

MBO, for example, is a new way of thinking for many administrative managers and it cannot be adhered to in a "business as usual" manner. The change is discomforting and frustrating to many people. For the top executive responsible for putting through a company-wide management by objectives program, means that extreme patience will be needed. Any attempt to force such a change on others, before they have had a chance to sort it out, is likely to result in failure.

UNTIMED READING COMPREHENSION CHECK: "The Trauma Of a Systems Change"

Subtopic (Stage)	Idea (Characteristic of Stage)
1.	
2.	
3.	
4.	
5.	

Check your answers with the Answer Key.

INSTRUCTIONS FOR PACED READING: "Improving Employee Motivation in Today's Business Environment"

The pacing rate for this article is 500 words per minute. This means that you should finish reading the article in 8 minutes, or a total of 480 seconds. Ask someone to tell you when the time has expired. This article contains approximately 4,000 words. After reading the article, write down your answers to the test that follows.

Paced Reading

Improving Employee Motivation in Today's Business Environment

Kenneth A. Kovach

In today's complex business world with rapidly changing technology, crumbling traditions, and growing pressures from labor unions, stockholders, consumer groups, and militant minority groups (both within and outside the organization), employee motivation has become both more difficult and more important than ever before.

People today are subjected to a much more varied and must less stable set of influences than in the past. Local traditions and conventional wisdom are no longer the chief determinants of most people's ideas. Although man's basic nature has not changed, the information available to him for shaping his ideas about himself and his job has increased explosively. As his ideas have become less predictable, so has his behavior.

Ever since 1972 when workers at the General Motors plant in Lordstown, Ohio, walked off their jobs for twenty-two days to protest the monotony of their work, American concern with worker discontent has grown.

In developing material for his book, *Working,* Studs Terkel interviewed 133 workers from a wide range of jobs. When asked to condense in a few words the meaning of these interviews, his response was "loneliness and boredom." "The price our nation is paying from manifestations of worker alienation is staggering: under production, poor quality, sabotage, turnover, absenteeism, and alcoholism are but a few of them."[1]

Keeping employees motivated so as to accomplish company objectives in the face of growing obstacles is one of the major keys to business success.

Over the past several years a great deal of research has been conducted by both "managerial" and "behavioral" scientists on the subject of motivation. A wide range of theories and differing viewpoints have [*sic*] evolved. The purpose of this article is to compare some of the more significant theories and viewpoints on motivation and to suggest some practical steps which, if followed, should improve motivation in any organization today.

DEFINITIONS AND THEORIES OF MOTIVATION

Disagreements and conflicting definitions frequently appear in the literature on the subject of motivation. Many writers, however, conclude that the various theories on motivation are not really incompatible, but deal with different aspects of the entire motivation process.

Motivation theories can generally be classified as either *process theories* or *content theories.*[2]

Process Theories

Motivation in the more traditional sense refers to the process of stimulating people to action to accomplish desired goals. In other words, motivation is a function which a manager performs in order to get his subordinates to achieve job objectives. Process theories of motivation generally are based on the assumption that behavior which leads to rewards tends to be repeated, while behavior which does not lead to rewards will not be repeated. These theories consider pay as the major motivating factor. Expectancy Theory and Equity Theory are among the significant types of process theories.

Expectancy Theory assumes that people have certain built-in beliefs (reenforced by management attitudes) regarding their expected roles within an organization and that their behavior must conform to these roles if they are to be rewarded.

Equity Theory assumes that each individual is most concerned with his own situation (for example, income) in relation to that of his peers, and that he will tend to limit production to that of his peers.

Content Theories

Instead of viewing motivations as a management process, it can also be looked at from the standpoint of the individual who is motivated. People act differently and unpredictably because of different environmental experiences. These differences in turn cause each person to view the work situation in a manner not quite like his fellow employees. Content theories of motivation focus on individual motives which are considered in relation to their job performance.

The Achievement Motivation Theory deals with individuals who derive satisfaction from resolving difficult problems, influencing others, making decisions, and achieving results. This theory tends to explain the motivation of higher level executives.

Need Hierarchy and Self Actualization Theories assume that each individual has a hierarchy of needs, and that as more basic needs—such as food, shelter, and security—are fulfilled, he becomes more concerned with higher level needs such as self-actualization.

The Two-Factor Theory divides motivation into "intrinsic" or job content factors and "extrinsic" or hygienic factors.[3] Under this theory, the hygienic factors such as wages and working conditions do not actually motivate; they merely minimize dissatisfaction. On the other hand, intrinsic factors such as "full appreciation for work performed" contribute to real job satisfaction and serve as real motivators.

Process versus Content Theories: Two Sides of the Same Coin

Dwight Eisenhower is credited with saying that "leadership is the ability to get a person to do what you want him to do, when you want it done, in a way you want it done, because he wants to do it."[4] (Process Theory) Rensis Likert calls motivation the core of management and concludes that "the nature of human motivation shows that every human being earnestly seeks a secure, friendly, and supportive relationship which gives him a sense of worth in face-to-face groups which are most important to him . . . a superior should strive to treat individuals with dignity and a recognition for their personal worth."[5] (Content Theory)

WHAT PEOPLE WANT FROM THEIR WORK

To some people, their jobs—while pleasant or at least not distasteful—are nevertheless merely a means to the securing of sufficient funds with which to purchase necessities or luxuries for themselves and their families. To others, work—while not an end in itself—is in a very real sense a way of life. To those persons, the complex relationships of the job situation—social as well as economic—are quite as satisfying as the outside social contacts of the person who engages in work solely as a means of earning a living.

TABLE 1
WHAT PEOPLE WANT FROM THEIR WORK

Employee Ranking		Supervisor Ranking
1	Full appreciation of work done	8
2	Feeling of being in on things	10
3	Sympathetic help on personal problems	9
4	Job security	2
5	Good wages	1
6	Interesting work	5
7	Promotion and growth in the organization	3
8	Personal loyalty to employees	6
9	Good working conditions	4
10	Tactful disciplining	7

Numerous surveys have been conducted to determine what employees want from their jobs. One of the most widely known surveys was published in *Foreman Facts* by the Labor Relations Institute of New York in 1946.

The ranking of items is not necessarily the important thing to observe, since conditions have changed since 1946 when the survey was taken. The significant point is the wide variance between what workers consider to be important in their jobs and what their supervisors think workers believe to be important. Research indicates that a wide gap still exists between what workers want from their jobs and what management thinks they want.

WAGES AND MOTIVATION

Traditionally, wages have been considered to be the primary motivating force behind employee action. Wages, however, operate like a price mechanism to distribute the labor supply among employers, but do not affect job performance in any lasting or significant way.

Money can motivate or influence action only when the increment is large enough relative to existing income.[6] Most salary increases, bonuses, profit sharing plans, and many commission and incentive pay plans, do not provide an increment that is large enough to motivate any action other than the purely passive action of staying in the organization.

Employees tend to expect pay increases as something they are entitled to, rather than something they must earn. When the time at which the increase is expected is still remote, the prospect of the increase serves to motivate continued membership in the organization, provided the expected increase is considered to be equitable.

If the increase does not occur on schedule, that fact will generate disappointment and feelings that the system is unjust. If the delay is prolonged, the employee may search for another job or he may be motivated to complain, not necessarily about money alone, but about all the petty annoyances he is ordinarily willing to tolerate. He probably will even reduce his work performance.

When the size of the increase becomes known and it is less than the worker expected, he may feel that he has been deceived. Although his expectations may have been unrealistic, it is likely that the individual will become cynical and mistrustful of the organization.

If the increase is about equal to what he expected, he will simply see the company as having purchased his continued membership at a fair price. He will also be reassured that the system is fair;

however, *such reassurances only satisfy, they do not motivate.*

If the increase exceeds his expectations, he may increase his productivity to some degree or he may feel that he is being compensated for work already performed.[7]

There can be some serious problems associated with the rapid growth of income, when the job for which the income is paid is not sufficiently satisfying to the individual. There is a tendency for some workers in repetitive, unchallenging jobs to demand wage increases that bear little relationship to the contribution of their work to profits or to the growth of their productivity. They tend to demand whatever the traffic will bear and support militant union leaders who will press management for the largest possible wage settlement. These workers can hardly be said to be motivated by their incomes in the sense of deliberately producing at a higher-than-usual rate.

Such situations suggest that the monetary drives of some may really be psychologically motivated; that is, money may be a sort of "revenge" against management, a way of hitting back at an adversary where it presumably will hurt most. The tendency of these individuals to see management as an adversary has less to do with feelings of inadequate pay than with feelings of alienation. Present day management is doing little to change this situation.

HUMAN GOALS

Man is diversely motivated. Each individual's heredity, environment, and experience shape his attitudes, his motives, his behavior, and his goals in life. The basic needs of man are classified as: physiological needs, safety needs, social needs and egoistic needs.[8] Although these needs are found in all people, each person places a different hierarchy of importance on them, and this hierarchy is constantly changing. This explains why each employee acts differently and views the work situation in a manner not quite like his fellow employees.

Although psychologists are not all in complete agreement, there are several generalizations regarding human behavior on which most reach accord.[9] They are:

- An individual strives to satisfy his needs. The twelve most important factors affecting job satisfaction are: security, interesting work, opportunity for advancement, recognition, working conditions, wages, supervision, social aspects, opportunities to learn or use ideas, hours, ease of job, and fringe benefits.

- Individuals differ greatly in the importance they attach to various need satisfactions. Their attitudes also change with time and circumstances, and are heavily influenced by the attitudes of their colleagues and superiors.

- Needs may be unconscious or they may be expressed as aspirations or goals. Motivation is weakest when the individual perceives a goal as either unattainable or too easily attainable. Motivation is strongest when the goal is perceived as a challenge or an achievement.

- Individuals are receptive to changing their ways of doing things only when they personally recognize the inadequacies of the present method or when they are given an opportunity to participate in the development of the new method.

- Individuals resist change when they perceive it as a threat to any of the twelve motivation factors just listed.

- Individuals tend to accept evidence of their performance more willingly and use it more constructively when it is presented in a manner that they regard as objective; that is, without personal bias.

- Beyond a certain point, pressure for improved performance accomplishes nothing, and may, if continued, reduce performance.

ORGANIZATIONAL GOALS

Man created the organization as a device through which to satisfy needs which he could not satisfy himself. Organizations were thus created to serve man and not vice versa. Once established, however, they become entities with goals of their own. Their goals consist of growth, efficiency, productivity, profits and survival. As organizations grow, there is usually a separation between their ownership (stockholders) and control. The stewardship for operating business organizations has been entrusted to a group of "professional managers." Because of the interdependency of individuals both within and outside of the organization, these managers are in a position of great power and influence.

Managers today, as never before, have to maintain balance between satisfaction of human needs and the accomplishment of organization goals. The following are just a few of the changing conditions which management must adapt to while trying to maintain this balance: ever-changing human needs, changing organizational goals, the population increase, rapid transportation, improved communications, mass education, automation, development of more bureaucracies, urbanization, more government controls, increase in non-skilled workers, technological unemployment, higher wages, more leisure time, standardization, and increases in the number of administrative personnel.

To the extent that an individual accepts organizational objectives as being desirable, fulfilling them becomes one of his needs. He must understand and accept the objectives of the organization and his job if he is to work productively.[10]

CURRENT TREND—JOB ENRICHMENT

Basically, job enrichment means letting workers plan and control more of their work, even to the point of encroaching on management decision making. More and more companies think it may be a way to overcome absenteeism, high turnover, and lagging worker productivity, as well as a way to challenge workers, especially the restless younger ones.

For example, American Telephone and Telegraph encourages subsidiaries to grant repairmen greater autonomy and make each of them responsible for maintaining the telephones in entire neighborhoods. Chrysler Corporation involves workers in departmental decisions. In some cases workmen are allowed to run their own departments when foremen are on vacation. General Electric gives machine operators at its Lynn, Massachusetts, plant a greater role in scheduling work and devising work rules.[11]

Job enrichment is, however, a controversial concept. Even though it seems to be working at some places, at others it has collapsed. Among big city, blue collar workers it has fallen on especially tough times.

Frederick Herzberg, who is widely regarded as the founding father of job enrichment, believes that workers become motivated when their jobs are seasoned with "motivators" such as recognition, a sense of achievement, and personal growth. Once these conditions are met, this "motivation-hygiene theory" implies that employees will become far more industrious.

Look at the rewards we are offering our people today: higher wages, medical benefits, vacations, pensions, profit sharing, bowling and baseball teams. *Not one can be enjoyed on the job.*

Critics argue that enrichment efforts are based on a faulty view of human nature. Charles L. Hulin observes that "the assumption behind job enrichment is that everyone can be made to think that his job is his life. That simply isn't always the case."[12]

MOTIVATION UNDER DIFFERENT POLITICAL/ECONOMIC SYSTEMS

Motivation appears to be a worldwide problem.

A. S. Tannenbaum conducted a study in which he visited factories in Italy, Israel, Yugoslavia, Austria, and the United States to compare worker attitudes under various political/economic systems.[13]

Although under communism the alienated worker is supposed to become the happy producer, Tannenbaum found that workers in Marxist Yugoslavia are no happier or more motivated than their American counterparts.

An analysis of American participation indicated that worker participation in plants does make a difference, "but not entirely," as Marxists would expect. Yugoslav workers participate in more decision making than do American workers, but their attitudes toward the plant are no more favorable, and communication is no more open.

Supervisors are not necessarily more interested in and responsive to ideas of their subordinates in plants where there is a formal worker-participation-plan than where there is not such a plan. Tannenbaum found that attitudes were worse in Italy, under the "autocratic version of the way to run a business."

STEPS TOWARD IMPROVING MOTIVATION

What management needs most is not so much a revolutionary technique for motivating employees but a new way of thinking about it. Once managers realize that the rules for motivation have changed, they can begin making progress toward discovering new and better ways of motivating workers.

Although each work situation is different, steps that managers in any organization could and should take in order to make motivation more effective are the following:

1. Give individual freedom but maintain control. Authority and responsibility should be delegated to the level which is closest to the problem situation. Allowing subordinates to make decisions (particularly those decisions which they are more qualified to make) fosters a feeling of confidence.[14] It gives the subordinate a feeling of independence and individual expression. It gives him a chance to learn and an opportunity to make a contribution which he can call his own. Controls can be set up which will enable the manager to take corrective action in case things go wrong. Individual freedom is basic to any motivation system.

2. Create an atmosphere conducive to growth. Management should not be expected to play the role of mother, father, minister, and psychiatrist to its workers. It should, however, create an atmosphere which affords each employee the opportunity to develop and utilize voluntarily his capacities, his knowledge, his skill, and his ingenuity in ways which contribute to the success of the enterprise.[15] It is this type of atmosphere in which management derives the greatest benefits from its human resources.

All new ideas begin in a nonconforming mind that questions conventional ideas. All improvements originate in a critical mind that mistrusts the popular image.

Robert N. McMurry states that great progress can be made if top management can be led to see that: (1) their points of view are not the only ones; (2) most issues are not absolutely black or white but do have some grey areas; (3) they personally do not enjoy a monopoly on the truth; (4) because someone espouses a system of values which differs from theirs, he is not necessarily ignorant, stupid, or disloyal.[16]

The average human being learns under proper conditions not only to accept but to seek responsibility. The average person has the capacity to exercise a high degree of imagination, ingenuity and creativity under proper conditions.

The intellectual potentialities of the average individual are only partially used. The authoritarian leader inhibits the intellectual growth of his subordinates. Management should create situations where group goals coincide with individual needs to the greatest extent possible. As a result, the individual, organization, customers and society will gain.

3. Foster good communication within the organization. Most individuals work for a business which is their only source of income, security, social status, and self-respect. Through feedback, they want to know what their supervisor thinks of them.[17]

Sometimes, the supervisor says one thing but conveys another through gesture, intonation, and expression — hence his subordinates complain that they don't really know where they stand. This is precisely where the potentialities for motivation are strong. The employee is eager to have the organization confirm his own estimate of his capabilities, and where his supervisor can be regarded as a valid spokesman for the company, good communication of attitudes is vitally important.[18]

4. Preserve competence. Competence, after all, is a relative rather than an absolute quality. It is a matter of being able to do what is expected of one. Until recently, most men were never really free of fundamental pressures of job security and income, and accordingly kept up their skills.

Today, income is a less crucial problem and people tend to become concerned with such esoteric motivators as dignity, recognition, and a sense of fulfillment in their work. David McClelland states that money is not the incentive to effort that it used to be, but is rather the measure of its success.[19] The tendency is to demand more of one's job and less of one's self and the result is sometimes a gradual decline in output. Most jobs should not be designed in ways that minimize the exercise of intelligence.[20] With the exception of relatively few people, it is much wiser to design difficulty, variety, and challenge into most jobs. If employees become less competent, an attempt can be made to train them to meet the standards set through the use of refresher courses, retraining and encouragement. Management must try to keep the problem of competence in perspective and avoid being overly pessimistic about conclusions of human capabilities.

5. Change the organization structure. In a large organization, a position could be created for a full-time analyst of, or worrier about, motivation. He should be a member of every planning committee and every major decision-making conference. He should know as much as it is possible for one person to know about what is going on in the organization. However, his only responsibility, or at least his chief responsibility, should be to assure that the motivational impact of all management decisions is weighed before actions are decided upon.[21]

An organization that is left to its own devices will seek to run smoothly and this is all too easily accomplished by stressing what is superficial, by ignoring what is difficult, and by discouraging dissent. The organization whose members accept its ways passively, is likely to conclude its ways are right. But the main purpose of an organization is to achieve results, not to exist merely to create harmony.[22]

CONCLUSION

To fully capitalize upon our existing knowledge and insights into the nature of motivation and its effect upon human performance, the manager's attitudes must be changed radically. The basic motivational deficiency in many businesses today is the lack of sufficient decision-making authority and responsibility in jobs held by people who are best qualified to make decisions.

There is no actual shortage of decision-making power; it is simply and unnecessarily monopolized by management, and especially by higher organizational levels. This is due to the traditional concept that relatively few people are capable of making effective decisions or willing to accept responsibility. Such attitudes cause managers to define their

principal tasks as: deciding what should be done by other people, and then making sure that they do it. This type of thinking is already antiquated and will become increasingly out of tune with reality in the future.

In order to effectively motivate the people whose work they direct, managers are going to have to learn to be a "bit of a behavioral scientist" themselves. At least, they will need to know how to use the findings of behavioral scientists in practical, discriminating ways.

It is doubtful whether scientists will ever learn enough about man to reduce the practical problems of management to a simple system that can be applied without a great deal of judgment. However, that really does not matter. We already know enough to improve substantially both the individual's contributions to the organization, and his satisfaction in belonging to it.

Robert Townsend, past president of Avis-Rent-A-Car put it this way:

Get to know your people. What they do well, what they enjoy doing, what their weaknesses and strengths are, and what they want and need from their job. And then try to create an organization around your people, not jam your people into those organization-chart rectangles. The only excuse for organization is to maximize the chance that each one, working with others, will get for growth in his job.[23]

You can't motivate people. That door is locked from the inside. You can create a climate in which most of your people will motivate themselves to help the company to reach its objectives. Like it or not, the only practical act is to adopt Theory Y assumptions and get going.

FOOTNOTES

[1]"No 'heigh-ho' it's off to work we go," *Business Week,* 13 April 1974, pp. 10–13.

[2]John B. Miner, *The Management Process-Theory, Research and Practice* (New York: The Macmillan Company, 1973), pp. 297–322.

[3]Frederick W. Herzberg et. al., *The Motivation to Work* (New York: John Wiley & Sons, 2nd. ed. 1959), pp. 12–35.

[4]Bradford B. Boyd, *Management Minded Supervision* (New York: McGraw-Hill Book Co., 1968), p. 113.

[5]Rensis Likert, "Motivation: The Core of Management," *American Management Association Personnel Series,* No. 155, New York, 1953, p. 21.

[6]Edmund Faltermayer, "Who Will Do the Dirty Work Tomorrow?", *Fortune,* January 1974, pp. 132-38. Faltermayer believes that in the case of "menial jobs," the only way to motivate people is *"more money."*

[7]Saul W. Gellerman, *Management by Motivation* (New York: Vail-Ballou Press, Inc., 1968), pp. 187-196.

[8]A. H. Maslow, *Motivation and Personality* (New York: Harper & Brothers, 1954), pp. 20-35.

[9]William G. Scott, *Human Relations in Management* (Homewood, Ill.: Richard D. Irwin, Inc., 1962), pp. 43-68.

[10]William H. Newman, Charles E. Summer, and E. Kirby Warren, *The Process of Management* (Englewood Cliffs, N.J.; Prentice-Hall, Inc., 2d. ed., 1967), p. 197.

[11]"Job Enrichment: Sometimes it Works," *Wall Street Journal,* 13 December 1971, p. 3.

[12]Charles L. Hulin, *New Perspectives in Job Enrichment* (New York: Van Nostrand Reinhold, 1971), p. 4.

[13]Arnold S. Tannenbaum, "Rank, Clout and Worker Satisfaction: Pecking Order-Capitalist and Communist Style," *Psychology Today,* September 1975, pp. 40-51.

[14]Gerald C. Davidson and G. Terence Wilson, "Behavior Therapy: A Road to Self-Control," *Psychology Today,* October 1975, pp. 54-60. The authors suggest that workers should be allowed to choose their own goals: "As long as the boss sets the goals, workers will feel manipulated."

[15]Robert Kreitner, "PM—A New Method of Behavior Change," *Business Horizons,* December 1975, pp. 79-85. Positive Management (PM) stresses learning instead of motivation, Kreitner's thesis is that managers should be trained in "proper attitudes" and that productivity increases will follow.

[16]Robert N. McMurry, "Conflicts in Human Values," *Harvard Business Review,* May-June 1963, pp. 130-45.

[17]Rick Minicucci, "Motivating Employees in a Down Economy," *Administrative Management,* June 1975, p. 20. Minicucci believes that the key to motivation is "rapport between management and employees."

[18]"Personal Problem Roundtable: Motivating the Worker," *Administrative Management,* December 1975, pp. 26-30. This article stresses the importance of communication in motivating workers.

[19]David McClelland, *The Achieving Society* (Princeton, N.J.: Van Nostrand Co., Inc., 1961), p. 62.

[20]"Those Boring Jobs—Not All That Dull," *U.S. News & World Report,* 1 December 1975, pp. 64-65.

[21]Joan Zaffarano, "Managements Leading Edge: Future Trends—Human Resources Matrixing—Motivation Control," *Administrative Management,* January 1976, pp. 31-42.

[22]George A. Steiner, *Business and Society,* (New York: Random House, Inc. 1971), p. 225.

[23]Robert Townsend, *Up the Organization,* (London, England: Coronet Books, Hodder-Fawcett, Ltd., 1971), p. 130.

PACED READING COMPREHENSION CHECK: "Improving Employee Motivation in Today's Business Environment"

1. According to the author, what is one reason that it is difficult to keep employees motivated?

   a. _____ Their minds are on outside interests.

   b. _____ They are subjected to more varied and less stable influences.

   c. _____ They have been improperly trained for the job.

2. The author's major purpose is to:

   a. _____ present and compare major motivation theories and provide steps to improve employee motivation.

   b. _____ present his own theory of motivation and defend it.

   c. _____ present a history of motivation theory.

3. An essential component of the process theories is:

   a. _____ extrinsic rewards.

   b. _____ punishment.

   c. _____ intrinsic rewards.

4. An essential component of the content theories is:

   a. _____ extrinsic rewards.

   b. _____ punishment.

   c. _____ intrinsic reward.

5. According to the author, the sig-

nificance of the survey "What People Want From Their Work" is:

a. _____ the employee rankings one-to-ten.

b. _____ the supervisor rankings one-to-ten.

c. _____ the variance in the employee ranking vs. supervisor ranking.

6. As a motivator, money generally:

a. _____ has a positive and lasting effect on job performance.

b. _____ does not motivate much worker action.

c. _____ is considered most important to employees.

7. With respect to the basic needs hierarchy of importance, people:

a. _____ vary in their placement of them.

b. _____ are generally similar in their placement of them.

c. _____ are reluctant to rank them at all.

8. Job enrichment effects have had a:

a. _____ general lack of success.

b. _____ large success rate.

c. _____ mixture of success and lack of success.

9. Motivation is a problem:

a. _____ primarily in the United States.

b. _____ everywhere.

c. _____ primarily in Europe.

10. An important concept to remember when trying to improve motivation is that:

a. _____ the average individual only partially uses his intellectual potentialities.

b. _____ you are the boss and know more than your employees.

c. _____ pay workers enough and they will be happy.

Check your answers with the Answer Key.

INSTRUCTIONS FOR PACED READING: "Dads on Duty"

The pacing rate for this article is 500 words per minute. This means that you should finish reading the article in 4 minutes, or a total of 240 seconds. Ask someone to tell you when the time has expired. This article contains approximately 2,000 words. After reading the article, write down your answers to the test that follows.

Paced Reading

Dads on Duty

Eric Morgenthaler

STOCKHOLM—Jonny Bjarskog heats a jar of baby food on the gas stove, peels a banana and mashes it with a fork, squeezes three drops of vitamins into a spoon and starts to feed Lena, his wailing baby daughter.

Thus, the blond-haired young Swede passes another morning at his newest job: being a father. Full-time. Paid.

Jonny Bjarskog, who has just turned 30, is taking advantage of one of Sweden's newest responses to the push for sexual equality: paternity leave. And in many regards, what he is doing may well be the way of the future.

Since last August, Jonny has stayed home with the baby, who was born last March 29. That enabled her mother—Jonny's girlfriend, Karin Marcus, with whom he has lived for almost four years—to return at the start of the fall school term to her job as a music teacher.

Jonny gets the same benefits that Karin would get, were she staying home—including 90% of his salary, drawn from a state insurance program financed 85% from a social-security tax on employers and 15% from the national budget. His employer, a Swedish record distributor, is required by law to hold his job open until he returns, as he expects to do soon.

IT'S HARD WORK

Now, after several months of changing diapers, fixing meals and keeping house, Jonny cheerfully reports, "I like it very much—I think it's nice to be home." But he admits that the baby took some getting used to, mainly because "you have

to put your own wishes second." And he advises that housework is "not as easy as you think."

Those are facts that more young Swedish men are learning first-hand. This country has started a major effort to involve fathers more actively in the rearing of their children. It's doing so basically by extending to fathers most of the child-care benefits, such as time off at nearly full pay, that it extends to mothers. The cost of the insurance benefits granted to both fathers and mothers last year totaled the equivalent of $525.6 million, the government estimates, and an increase to $584.2 million is forecast for this year.

Although paternity leave, which was introduced in 1974, is one of the most visible programs involved in the insurance plan, there are others. One, for instance, allows parents of preschoolers to work shortened weeks at little loss in pay (they can take off the equivalent of three full months of working time). Another gives parents time off to care for sick children. And it's all accompanied by a big publicity campaign. One poster, for instance, shows a Goliath-sized weight lifter happily cuddling a baby.

UNDERLYING FORCES

The paternity push is partly the result of the women's movement, the influx of working women into the labor force and the belief that a mother has as much right to a career as a father. But it also involves the feeling—among many men, as well as women—that fathers really should be more involved in raising their children: It's good for children, these people say, and it's good for fathers.

"If a man wants children, he ought to take more than economic responsibility for them," says Berit Rollen, who's with the National Labor Market Board, a government agency that deals with social and labor problems. She supports the idea—backed by the Social Democratic Party, which was voted out of power in the last election—that fathers should be *required* to take a certain share of the leave-time available to new parents.

"In the long run, it will give women more of a foothold in the labor market," she says. "They won't be regarded as unstable labor. If employers have to expect that both young men and women have to stay at home for a few months, it will be a shared risk."

That sort of idea won't get official backing until at least next fall, when Sweden is slated to hold general elections that could return the Social Democrats to office. But even without such official prompting, the number of men involved in the program is increasing.

RISING PERCENTAGES

According to Sweden's Ministry for Social Affairs, about 10% to 12% of eligible fathers—or about 6,000 a year— now take paternity leave, up from 2% in 1974. The average leave for a father lasts 42 days, up from 28 days in 1974 and out of 210 working days available to both parents.

The paternity programs are helped along by Sweden's tax system, which features some of the world's highest tax rates. The 10% drop in pretax income that an at-home parent experiences often is negligible after tax. (Moreover, some companies make up the 10%, so there isn't any loss.) And the tax system encourages two-career families; at many income levels, Swedes can take home more from two small salaries than one large one.

Whatever the reasons, Sweden is much further along in the paternity-leave effort than most other Western nations are. In the U.S., for instance, there has been some talk about the idea, but almost no serious action. In Britain, paternity leave is gaining a toehold, although on a company-by-company, rather than a national basis. A study of 400 U.K. companies last year by the British Institute of Management found that 3% of them gave paid paternity leave and 5% gave unpaid leave. And most of the programs are modest; the British Broadcasting Corp., for instance, gives a total of only two days of paid paternity leave.

However, if Sweden's programs succeed, they probably will be copied in some fashion by other countries because the programs spring from problems and trends common to many advanced societies.

"If women are to have a reasonable chance in professional life, obviously both parents have to share in responsibility towards children and the home," says Martin Wilkins, a 37-year-old Swedish diplomat, who took paternity leave after each of his two children was born. However, he adds, "I think that's a hard readjustment for some men to make."

Mr. Wilkins's own experience shows how hard it can be. In late 1977, both he and his wife—who is a first secretary in the Foreign Office—decided to work shortened weeks in order to stay home with their children, now aged two and four. Mr. Wilkins was to take Mondays off. But his effort lasted only a few months.

One problem was that Mr. Wilkins found disputes between preschoolers more trying than the disputes between nations he is more used to dealing with. "I didn't have the patience," he says.

Also, there were problems at work. Although he was supposed to be working only 80% of his regular time, the ministry hadn't arranged for someone else to handle 20% of his work—"so I had the same amount of work to be done, but in four days instead of five," he says. That required night work, which, ironically, reduced the time that he spent with his family.

Mr. Wilkins now is back working full-time, although his wife still takes off a day or so a week to be with the children. (She made a "more serious effort" than he to hand over part of her work to others, Mr. Wilkins says, and she also is "more successful than I in making family life compatible with a career.") Mr. Wilkins says the whole experience convinced him "that it's hard work to reach anything similar to equality."

MANAGERIAL PROBLEMS

Others would agree. Part of the problem is that most of the men taking advantage of the parental programs are, like Mr. Wilkins, well-educated and well-paid—and thus likely to hold responsible positions. When they are gone from work, it's difficult to fill the gap. "It seems there is this tacit understanding that it's perfectly okay to be on 80% if you deliver 100%," says Kjell Holm, who runs the Foreign Ministry's foreign-press office.

From January to August of last year, Mr. Holm worked 80% of his regular time—taking off Monday and Friday afternoons to be with his children, ages 10 and seven. He says he "enjoyed it very much" and found the experience "rewarding." But, he adds, "It simply didn't work."

"I am the boss in this operation, and in my opinion, it is rather ridiculous that

that fact should have any importance at all," Mr. Holm says. "But the pressure on the rest of the people was too much, and I decided to forget about all this and go back to 100%." As a result, his wife further trimmed her working hours, to 60% from 80%.

The problem isn't as great with women, because fewer of them are in management. More than 70% of Swedish women work, but most are part-timers. However, that's a vicious circle—one reason women are part-timers is that they have to be home with the kids—and some experts think that programs like paternity leave will help break the cycle.

Moreover, paternity leave isn't terribly popular in many Swedish board rooms. Although employers are required to give leave to men who request it, many do it grudgingly. "A lot of people who think of their careers won't take off," says 34-year-old Leif Malmring, as his six-month-old son, Nicolas, grabs for his beard; Mr. Malmring is on paternity leave from the Central Statistical Board.

Corporate resistance isn't the only source of restraint. Many grandparents don't approve of their sons' taking off to play nursemaid, and a lot of mothers also prefer traditional family roles. And a father on paternity leave still is considered an oddity in many social quarters—particularly among blue-collar workers. "Changing attitudes is a very slow job," says Margaretha Beckerus, who is on the government-sponsored Committee on Equality of Men and Women.

The Swedes are trying to change attitudes on many fronts. In many of the schools, for example, boys must take homemaking courses and girls take woodworking—requirements intended to alter traditional perceptions of sex roles. The country also is trying to recruit more men into traditionally female jobs—such as being nurses or preschool teachers—and to move more women into men's jobs.

But the results of those efforts have been mixed. "We have done a lot to make a difference, but nothing has really happened," says Ingegerd Odmark, who is with the National Board of Education. "Maybe in 10 years we can pick the fruits of what we have done."

NOTE OF CAUTION

As sexual frontiers recede, even many liberal-minded Swedes are saying there is a limit to how far changes should be pushed. "I think it's very important that the children learn they are male and female," says Anders Rottorp, father of a two-year-old girl and four-year-old boy. "They must learn who they are. Otherwise, they will be very unhappy."

Mr. Rottorp, however, favors most of what's being done here, and he typifies the sort of approach that many young Swedes are taking. Two afternoons a week, he leaves his job with the Swedish Employers Federation at 2 o'clock instead of 5 to pick up his children at nursery school. He calls it a "splendid" arrangement—"even though I may have to work a little more other days to compensate." (Mrs. Rottorp—a political analyst in government—does the same on two other days, and a grandmother picks up the children the fifth afternoon.)

"I think it's very important to have these weekday contacts," Mr. Rottorp says, "because you see a lot of how the children change and grow and talk in new ways. It's very subtle, it's very hard to describe. We don't do many exciting things—just kind of be together. But it's different being together on a weekday than it is on Saturday and Sunday."

As for the children, he says, "They think it's normal. They don't react to it. They've always been used to the fact that I was home as much as my wife."

PACED READING COMPREHENSION CHECK: "Dads on Duty"

1. How many of Sweden's fathers take advantage of paternity leaves?

   a. _____ 5 - 7 percent.

   b. _____ 10 - 12 percent.

   c. _____ 15 - 17 percent.

2. Sweden's fathers are able to take paternity leaves because:

   a. _____ they demand it.

   b. _____ it is a social custom.

   c. _____ the law allows it.

3. Paternity leaves were introduced in:

   a. _____ 1974.

   b. _____ 1980.

   c. _____ 1965.

4. One reason Sweden has paternity leaves for fathers is:

   a. _____ the feeling among men and women that fathers should be involved in raising their children.

   b. _____ the recognition from grandparents that such a plan is necessary.

   c. _____ the tremendous support from business and industry.

5. According to Berit Rollen,

required paternity leaves for fathers will lead to women being perceived as:

a. _____ more efficient at their jobs.

b. _____ more stable in the labor market.

c. _____ more confident at their jobs.

6. The average paternity leave for a father is about:

a. _____ three weeks.

b. _____ one month.

c. _____ one-and-one-half months.

7. Generally, men taking paternity leaves are:

a. _____ well paid.

b. _____ blue-collar workers.

c. _____ school teachers.

8. One reason men have more difficulty than women in rear-ranging their time schedules at work is that men are:

a. _____ less flexible than women.

b. _____ less organized than women.

c. _____ more apt to be in managerial positions.

9. In general, Sweden's employers:

a. _____ resist the idea of paternity leave for fathers.

b. _____ support the idea of paternity leave for fathers.

c. _____ are indifferent about the idea of paternity leave for fathers.

10. Efforts to change attitudes on equal rights have met with:

a. _____ little success.

b. _____ great success.

c. _____ mixed success.

Check your answers with the Answer Key.

INSTRUCTIONS FOR SKIM READING: "Taking the Profit Out of Arson"

Using the skimming techniques you learned in chapter 2, skim the following article in order to find five ways of stamping out arson. Time yourself to find your skimming rate; you should take no longer than 2 minutes and 15 seconds to finish the article. Complete the exercise following the article, then check your answers in the Answer Key. (Remember, a score of 50 percent or higher is acceptable when skimming.) Determine your skimming rate from the Words Per Minute: Skimming Chart, then record your skimming rate and comprehension score on your Skim Reading Progress Chart.

Skim Reading

Taking the Profit Out of Arson

The Editors, Commerce America

A major effort to stamp out the nation's most expensive crime—arson—is presently under way on several fronts in this country in an effort to reverse the spread of "fires for profit" and other forms of arson. Firefighters across the continent generally agree that taking the profit out of arson will, in one insurance executive's words, take the sting out of it.

That sting costs American business a bundle every year and produces for the U.S. the sad reputation as the worst of all industrialized nations from the standpoint of destruction and death from fire.

Commerce's National Fire Prevention and Control Administration (NFPCA) through its National Academy for Fire Prevention and Control are undertaking to organize and promote an anti-arson campaign. At the same time, a number of communities are carrying on campaigns of their own that are showing results.

The American Insurance Association is in the process of setting up a computerized fire loss claims data bank to be operated by its Property Claims Services. This will be a subscription data service to begin operation when companies writing 75 to 80 percent of the property insurance volume indicate their support.

Wilfred J. Perry, Assistant Vice President of the Association, says that thus far companies writing 53 percent of the property insurance volume have indicated their support, and that the required percentage should be obtained soon. He believes the system should be in full operation by July 1, 1978.

The data bank will provide an index of all insured fire losses of more than $500, and will give insurers access to information about recorded claims that bear similarities to a current claim. By providing a central source of fire loss histories, it is expected to help expose major arson and property fraud rings which now move undetected from city to city, as well as persons who purchase additional insurance for the purpose of filing duplicate claims.

A NFPCA grant of $69,375 has been made to Lincoln Land Community College of Springfield, Ill., to develop a model fire-arson investigation training program. The completed program will be turned over to the National Fire Academy to be implemented. The course will be used nationwide as a standardized education and training program for fire and arson investigators.

"With this course," says David M. McCormack, National Fire Academy superintendent, "we expect to be able to train fire personnel in investigation and detection so as to have more arson cases culminate in arrest and conviction."

One problem is to have arson classified as a Part 1 crime in the FBI's Uniform Crime Reports. Arson specialists stress the paradox of a system of crime classification in which the theft of a bicycle or of a handful of change from a parking meter is a Part 1 crime while arson, which often results in death and may cost more than $3 billion a year in fire losses, still limps along in the Part 2 category of crimes.

Classification of arson as a Part 1 crime, the arson fighters say, would place this brutal crime in the spotlight where it belongs, take it out of the neglect category, and assure that it gets the funds needed to dampen its increase.

However, a change in the classification of arson confronts a major problem. The International Association of Chiefs of Police, Inc., at its meeting in Miami Beach last fall, voted against a change.

A spokesman for the organization says the reason is primarily a reporting problem. The spokesman explained that one of the criteria for reporting a crime to the FBI is that it can be reported reliably. However, he pointed out that in many jurisdictions the responsibility for reporting and investigation, in the case of arson, is not clear. The fire departments in many jurisdictions have the responsibility, he said, but fire departments usually are not in the crime reporting business. Thus the problem of reporting arson falls between musical chairs.

Another problem, the spokeman said, is that where arson is committed, other crimes, such as burglary, often are committed also. Where a series of crimes are committed, he said, only the most important is reported. Thus, if arson is accompanied by burglary, only the burglary is reported. The question then would be whether arson should be rated as more important than burglary.

Howard D. Tipton, NFPCA Administrator, thinks a basic problem is a widespread reluctance to change the present reporting system. He says he is hopeful that those opposed to making arson a Part 1 crime can be persuaded to change their minds.

Another goal of the arson fighters, the achievement of which is in the future, is the development of better and less expensive equipment for determining whether a fire was arson and if so what "accelerator" was used to get it going. At present, a hydrocarbon detector can be used to ascertain whether gasoline was used to start a fire. But this is expensive equipment, which the smaller fire departments cannot afford. Something cheaper and better awaits the availability of funds for the necessary research.

Plans, when funds are available, call for a management study program to identify what is needed and a program to develop better technology. The management study would involve the formation of a model task force to combat arson and produce ideas as to how communities could work together effectively. Technology developed for the space program is said to be available for adaptation to arson investigation.

Tipton says the first problem in dealing with arson is the lack of accurate information as to how big a problem it actually is. The best estimate, he explains, is that arson accounts for 20 to 30 percent of the national fire loss, while city fire chiefs believe that arson accounts for probably 50 percent of all building fires.

"We have a different problem with arson than with a lot of other crimes," Tipton remarks. "Arson can be used to cover up crime."

It is generally recognized that a basic difficulty in detecting arson is that the fire often burns up the evidence. This places a special emphasis on the development of better means for determining whether arson has been committed, and for spotting arsonists.

Tipton emphasizes the importance of the American Insurance Association data bank, since it will make possible the development of a pattern of insurance frauds.

"We are also asking insurance companies," he says, "to do a better job of looking at properties before they insure them, and the fire departments to do a better job of investigating fires after they happen. . . ."

Tipton points up the necessity of better training for persons seeking to reduce the arson tide, and for developing in prosecutors a better awareness of the problem.

Better and cheaper instruments for ascertaining whether a fire has been set deliberately, he observes, can often furnish leads to the person who set it. For example, if gasoline was used to start a fire, it might be possible to develop leads as to who was buying gasoline in a portable container nearby and whether the person was in the habit of buying gasoline in such quantities.

"We could develop profiles of known or suspected arsonists," Tipton says.

He observes that there are behavioral patterns in arson that may lead to evidence of deliberate fires—the teenager who may set a fire out of revenge or for kicks, the wife who may burn the house down to get even with her husband, the nursing home inmate who may start a fire out of boredom or in the hope of getting relocated.

"Arson," Tipton comments, "is the quickest parking lot maker in the world. Besides the tremendous property losses from arson, in the neighborhood of 1,000 persons die each year.

"We are doing more and more," he says, "to combat the problem as we have more funds. We will ask for additional funds to support a bigger program."

Victor U. Palumbo, Arson Program Manager for the National Academy for Fire Prevention and Control, points to the recent fire-arson investigation seminar held at George Mason University in Fairfax, Virginia, as an example of workshops to be conducted throughout the country.

This seminar dealt with such advanced concepts as management of an arson squad, and with auto and electric fires as well as building fires.

Emphasizing that many prosecutors need to be educated in handling arson cases, Palumbo says the National College of District Attorneys will be asked to stage an arson seminar in their round of discussions later this year.

The arson task force concept, he explains, should exclude the police and fire departments, the insurance industry, and the prosecutor. "Those four groups are mandatory on the local level for an effective task force," he says. "Without the participation of the prosecutor you will go nowhere."

The NFPCA course for training fire personnel in running down arson cases and preparing evidence will be ready, he says, in April 1978.

"In the next two or three years," Palumbo predicts, "you will see an increase in arson cases because they will be detected. Eventually, they will level off. People will think twice about starting a fire if they know they will be investigated, and this will eliminate a lot of fraud fires."

Palumbo says that arson is flourishing because of the need for better trained fire personnel in the area of detection and the low conviction rate due to improper investigative techniques.

"The only way we can lick this thing," says John Wrend, of the American Mutual Insurance Alliance's Property Loss Research Bureau in Chicago, "is to get all agencies dealing with arson under central guidance. You must have direction from the state attorney's office."

One problem, Wrend says, is the slum landlord, who buys up a dilapidated property, brings it up to minimum underwriting standards, and obtains insurance on it. Then there is a fire and the landlord collects the insurance. Sometimes, Wrend comments, the landlord doesn't have to set the fire or hire someone to start it, as vandals will do it for him.

The largest increase in fraud fires, Wrend says, occurs at times of economic downturn. Fires are set, he adds, merely to make money, to liquidate debts, to eliminate competition, to get rid of obsolete inventory, to get out from under a losing business, or because the owner is in declining health.

"If you take the profit out of arson," he says, "you will take the sting out of arson."

Finishing time: _____

SKIM READING COMPREHENSION CHECK: "Taking the Profit Out of Arson"

Directions: Read the statements below. Check the five that the authors mentioned as ways of solving the arson problem.

a. ____ Promote an anti-arson campaign.

b. ____ Reason with slum landlords.

c. ____ Institute a claims data bank.

d. ____ Develop better equipment to detect arson.

e. ____ Conduct an arson seminar on every college campus.

f. ____ Improve the quality of building materials.

g. ____ Classify arson as a Part 1 crime.

h. ____ Stop insuring old buildings.

i. ____ Stop publicizing fires in the media.

j. ____ Develop arson task forces.

Check your answers with the Answer Key.

INSTRUCTIONS FOR SKIM READING: "Solar Energy: A $10 Billion Industry By the Year 2000?"

Read the four questions on the next page and then skim the following article to find the answers to them. Time yourself; you should take no longer than two minutes and 30 seconds to finish the article.

Check your answers in the Answer Key. (Remember: a score of 50 percent or higher is acceptable when skimming.) Determine your skimming rate from the Words Per Minute: Skimming Chart, then record your skimming rate and comprehension score on your Skim Reading Progress Chart.

Questions

1. In which major city would solar energy be unable to compete with electricity at a cost of twenty dollars per square foot?
Answer:

2. Given the major city closest to where you live, how many years will it take you to attain "positive savings" with solar energy when it is in competition with oil?
Answer:

3. Given the major city closest to where you live, how many years will it take you to "payback" with solar energy when it is in competition with oil?
Answer:

4. What are the advantages to solar energy?
Answer:

Skim Reading

Solar Energy: A $10 Billion Industry By the Year 2000?

The Editors, Commerce America

Solar energy could be a $10 billion industry providing 7 percent of the nation's energy requirements by the year 2000. That means the sun would heat 17 million or 15 percent of the nation's buildings by that time saving the equivalent of five million barrels of oil a day, according to Paul D. Maycock, Coordinator of Solar Energy Planning and Program Implementation for the Energy Research and Development Administration (ERDA).

While this may make only a minor dent in the nation's tremendous energy bill, it promises to make a major dent in the energy bills of homeowners and businesses using solar-produced heat and hot water.

Maycock says there is a good chance that advancing technology will make it possible by 1980 to construct solar collector systems for $10 a square foot, in 1980 dollars, as contrasted with the present cost of $20 or more a square foot in current dollars. If this hope materializes, and if Congress meanwhile should provide a tax incentive to encourage solar construction, the process of installing home solar systems would greatly accelerate.

The 1974 Solar Heating and Cooling Demonstration Act gave the Department of Housing and Urban Development (HUD), the responsibility for demonstrating the practicality of solar heat for homes, while ERDA was given responsibility for commercial and other projects.

Commerce's National Bureau of Standards is supporting HUD and ERDA in these programs by: defining the technical performance data to be collected during the residential and commercial demonstration programs; developing intermediate standards for domestic solar hot water and space heating systems that can be used in conjunction with HUD's Minimum Property Standards; and developing performance criteria for commercial buildings.

An economic analysis of solar water and space heating, recently prepared for ERDA by the Mitre Corp., shows that such systems, installed at a cost of $20 per square foot of collector, are competitive now against electric systems throughout most of the United States, and that if the system's cost were reduced to $15 per square foot, the solar systems would become competitive against oil and electric heat pump heating in many cities.

On this basis, a solar collector system of 10 by 35 feet, for example, would cost $7,000 at $20 per square foot or $5,250 at $15 per square foot.

The analysts selected 13 cities which are representative of the variations in climate and fuel costs across the United States. To calculate relative costs, solar heating and hot water systems were compared to conventional systems using natural gas, fuel oil, electricity or electric heat pumps. Solar cooling systems, which to date are much more expensive, were not considered.

Only new residential single family construction was considered, although the analysis would apply to retrofit applications where 8.5 percent financing was available and no additional costs were incurred as a result of the retrofitting. The terms of payment were assumed to be the same as those on the home mortgage, which in the case in question would be 8.5 percent over 30 years. No additional down payment was assumed to be required.

Assumptions as to the building were that it was a residence for a family of four, 1,500 square feet, brick veneer, asphalt roof, storm windows, 12 inches of attic insulation figured with a 15-mile-per-hour wind factor. The house was assumed to be relatively well insulated. For the purpose of estimating the tax savings due to additional interest paid in financing the solar system, a combined federal and state income tax of 30 percent was assumed. Since current trends have favored not charging property tax on the added value of the solar system, no incremental property tax was assumed for the system.

Annual operating and maintenance costs for the first year were assumed to be 2 percent of the initial cost. This would increase at the same rate as general inflation, which was assumed to be 6 percent a year. Fuel prices were assumed to escalate at a rate of 10 percent a year.

The analysis also assumes that a solar system would be economic if positive savings occurred in five years or payback occurred in 15 years or less.

This set of assumptions, of course, was adopted only because it was believed to reflect realistic situations. But those using the assumptions point out that they are merely illustrative and are not absolute for all time.

Based on a cost of $20 per square foot for solar collectors installed, under these standards the solar system would be competitive for hot water and heat against electricity in 12 of the 13 cities. The cities were: Atlanta; Bismarck, N.D.; Boston; Charleston, S.C.; Columbia, Mo.; Dallas-Ft. Worth; Grand Junction, Colo.; Los Angeles; Madison, Wis.; Miami, New York, and Washington, D.C. Only in Seattle, where electricity costs less than a penny a kilowatt hour, would solar not be competitive.

Based on a cost of $15 per square foot for solar collectors, the solar systems would be competitive for hot water and heating against the electric heat pump in five of the cities: Bismarck, Grand Junction, Los Angeles, Madison, and New York. They would be competitive for hot water and heating against oil in six of the cities: Atlanta, Bismarck, Charleston, Grand Junction, Los Angeles, and Miami.

Finally, if the cost should be reduced to $10 per square foot in 1980 dollars, solar hot water and heat would be competitive against electricity and the heat pump everywhere except Seattle, against oil in all 13 cities, and against gas in nine of the cities, in fact, against all except Bismarck, Charleston, Columbia, and Madison.

In figuring positive savings and payback, the analysis used the following standards:

Positive savings are defined as the year in which the solar system first becomes profitable; that is, the year that the annual conventional fuel bill without solar exceeds the annual fuel bill with solar plus the annual cost of the solar system.

The annual cost for the solar system would include maintenance, interest on the mortgage relating to the solar system, and the annual amortization of the mortgage, less the income tax saving resulting from deduction of interest on the mortgage.

Payback is defined as the year in which the compounded net savings equals the remaining principal on the mortgage for the solar system. Net savings are computed on the basis of the fuel cost of the conventional backup system.

Based on a cost of $20 per square foot for solar collectors, installed, this would work out in the following way in competition with electricity for 12 of the 13 cities in the analysis, omitting only Seattle:

One year to positive savings: Charleston, Grand Junction, Los Angeles, Miami, and New York; three years: Atlanta, Boston, Columbia, Dallas-Ft. Worth and Madison; four years: Bismarck and Washington.

Years to payback: Miami, 9; Los Angeles, 10; Charleston, 11; Grand Junction and New York, 12; Dallas-Ft. Worth, 13; and Atlanta, Bismarck, Boston, Columbia, Madison and Washington, 14.

In Competition with Heat Pump

Years to positive savings: Grand Junction, 6; Bismarck and Los Angeles, 7; and Miami, 8.

Years to payback: Grand Junction, 17; Bismarck and Los Angeles, 19; and Miami, 20.

In Competition with Oil

Years to positive savings: Grand Junction, 6; Bismarck, Charleston, Los Angeles and Miami, 7.

Years to payback: Grand Junction, 17;

Bismarck, 18; and Charleston, Los Angeles and Miami, 19.

Based on a cost of $10 per square foot, in 1980 dollars, for solar collectors installed, only one year is required to achieve positive savings in competition with electricity for solar hot water and heat in all cities except Seattle. The years to payback range from 4 for Miami to 9 for Atlanta, Boston, and Washington.

In Competition with Heat Pump

Years to positive savings: Bismarck, Charleston, Grand Junction, Los Angeles, Madison, Miami, and New York, 1; Atlanta, Boston 2; Columbia, Dallas-Ft. Worth, and Washington, 3.

Years to payback: Miami, 9; Grand Junction and Los Angeles, 10; Bismarck and Madison, 11; Charleston and New York, 12; Atlanta, Boston and Columbia, 13; Dallas-Ft. Worth and Washington, 14.

In Competition with Oil

Years to positive savings: Atlanta, Bismarck, Charleston, Grand Junction, Los Angeles, and Miami, 1; Columbia, Dallas-Ft. Worth, and Madison, 2; Boston, New York, Seattle, and Washington, 3.

Years to payback: Miami, 9; Grand Junction and Los Angeles, 10; Atlanta, Bismarck, and Charleston, 11; Dallas-Ft. Worth, 12; Columbia, Madison, Seattle and Washington, 13; and Boston and New York, 14.

In Competition with Gas

Years to positive savings: New York, 2; Dallas-Ft. Worth, 3; Boston, Los Angeles and Miami, 4; Grand Junction and Washington, 5; Charleston, 6; and Bismarck and Madison, 7.

Years to payback: New York and Dallas-Ft. Worth, 13; Boston, 14; Los Angeles, Miami and Washington, 15;

Grand Junction, 16; Charleston, 17; Madison, 18; and Bismarck, 19.

From these figures, it will be seen that, based on the assumptions in the analysis, solar energy for heat and hot water on the basis of $10 per square foot in 1980 dollars for collectors is in competition even with gas in six of the nation's large cities.

HUD has authorized grants totaling nearly $5 million to more than 150 builders and other project sponsors to install solar heating and cooling equipment in more than 1,550 housing units scattered throughout the country. Additional grants are to be made.

The purpose of the projects is to help people become acquainted with solar energy in homes. The experience gained from the projects is expected to be useful in developing information on systems and market practices that will encourage the further use of solar energy equipment and reduce the nation's dependence on fossil fuels.

Grants are awarded to applicants on the basis of a number of factors, including the type of solar system to be used, the status of the housing project, and the usefulness of the project to HUD's demonstration program. Solar equipment is provided for heating and hot water, and to some degree for cooling, and is installed in both single family and multi-family projects.

Awards are made only to builders and developers who market the homes after they are completed. Funding is not considered for pre-sold units or for individuals for their private homes. Likewise, grants are made to builders who will use the projects as sales models, to public housing authorities for testing alternate ways of reducing operating costs, and to community groups active in housing.

Applications are expected to have already arranged financing, secured land and escalated and completed the basic engineering design for their solar system.

More than a dozen federal agencies, including ERDA and the National Science Foundation (NSF), have authorized multiple millions of dollars for well over 200 solar projects involving a wide variety of facilities ranging from fire houses and shopping centers to hospitals. Solar energy is now providing, or will in the future, a large percentage of the heating and cooling for many of these projects. It is part of an escalating trend in which solar projects are mushrooming in all parts of the country.

The extraordinary reach of American inventiveness is shown in the range of solar projects that are emerging. Nine sites have been proposed for the world's first solar electric power plant, scheduled for completion in 1980. The plant will produce 10,000 kilowatts of electric power under optimum, full-sunlight conditions, approximately the power required by a city of 10,000.

Solar projects are under way to pump irrigation water from deep wells in New Mexico and Arizona to determine the technical feasibility of solar energy for this purpose. More fanciful ventures are in the offing, such as greenhouses that double as solar energy collectors, so that a person may grow vegetables and bananas year-round while cutting down on his fuel bill.

Solar energy has two unique advantages: it is inexhaustible and free.

Finishing time:_____

INSTRUCTIONS FOR RAPID READING: "TM"

Read this article as fast as possible while trying to maintain a comprehension score of at least 70 percent. Time yourself. When you finish the article, write down your reading time in the space provided at the end of the article. Answer the comprehension questions following the article, then check your answers with the Answer Key. Determine your reading rate from the Words Per Minute: Rapid Reading Chart, then record your reading rate and comprehension score on your Rapid Reading Progress Chart.

Rapid Reading

TM

The Editors, Commerce America

Business, industry and government are looking increasingly to a new management technique called Transcendental Meditation (TM) as a means for increasing productivity and some significant results are already being reported. At the moment, Blue Cross-Blue Shield, General Motors, AT&T, Connecticut General Corporation, and the U.S. Army are but a few of the organizations investigating this technique.

In the past six years, the number of Americans practicing the TM technique has increased from 50,000 to more than one million. During the same period, more than 200 scientific studies have validated the benefits of the TM program to health, physical and mental performance, productivity and general well-being.

Courses in the program are available from the American Foundation for the Science of Creative Intelligence (AFSCI), a nonprofit, educational organization. As its vice president for government programs, Stephen F. Beck, explains: "We have technologies today for just about everything, for putting men on the moon, for printing microcircuits, for agriculture and for a myriad of society's functions. What has been missing until now is a technology for developing the full potential of the human mind. It has been said that the greatest underdeveloped resource in the world today is human intelligence. More than 50 years ago, William James concluded that man is using about 5 percent of his mental potential; the optimists among contemporary researchers give figures that range up to 10 percent. So at best, 90 percent of human potential is undeveloped.

"A factory or other industrial activity at only 10 percent of its capacity would be considered very unproductive and action would be taken to change its operation. But when we are told that our personnel are performing with such limited use of resources, we don't know what to do. The TM program provides an answer," he points out.

The rapid rate of technological development and the accelerating pace of life generate a tremendous amount of stress and tension in society. The frequent elicitation of the "flight or fight response" without a specific need is an example of how stress can activate the system in such a way as to produce negative effects. Hypertension, ulcers, and a variety of other diseases have all been related to stressful occupations. Research has shown that life expectancy is reduced by prolonged exposure to highly stressful environments. A decline in executive productivity due to stress overloads is difficult to measure but many industrial psychologists think the economic loss to business is significant.

Stress and tension are two by-products of advanced technology that seem to place a limit upon how much activity and responsibility a person can successfully handle. It has been estimated that the average individual today is confronted with more sensory input in a month than a person one hundred years ago experienced in a lifetime. The tremendous increase in the amount of information, sometimes called the "information explosion," and the fast pace of change place increasing demands upon today's manager. Proponents of the Transcendental Meditation program state that, if the negative effects of stress can be reduced, then a manager will be more adept at keeping pace with change and will be more capable of making a positive contribution to progress.

John Burns, a Washington, D.C. management consultant, says "Whatever management system an organization uses, it will be more effective if the people using it are operating with more of their intellectual and creative abilities. There are many good systems designed to eliminate organizational problems, but it is the creativity of the manager and his ability to use a system that is the critical factor. Friction and stress and lack of achievement of organizational goals are directly traceable to stress, tension, and poor performance in the individual. To increase the rate of progress requires that the negative effects of stress and tension be minimized. At the same time more of the individual's creative and intellectual potential must be unlocked. The TM technique accomplishes both of these objectives."

The Transcendental Meditation technique is defined as a "simple, natural and effortless procedure that allows the mind to experience a more relaxed and refined style of functioning." As the mind settles down during the TM technique, studies have shown that the body experiences a profound relaxation which appears to have a beneficial effect on the entire nervous system. Numerous scientific studies have shown that people using the technique have faster reaction time, better eye-hand coordination, increased resistance to infection, less hypertension, improved memory and increased learning ability.

TM teachers insist the technique is completely effortless, both to learn and to practice. One frequent injunction: trying is prohibited because any effort injected into the process will only interfere with its naturalness, like trying to fall asleep. The TM technique is practiced twice a day, once in the morning to dissolve any fatigue or stress that may remain after the night's sleep, and to gain energy for the day's activities, and again in the afternoon to eliminate the stressful effects of the day's work and to increase energy for enjoying the evening's activities.

During the TM technique a person rests deeply but is not in a trance. In fact, the individual is more alert than at any other time of the day. The technique involves no suggestion and is completely unlike hypnosis. No changes in lifestyle, diet, or philosophy are required to practice the technique.

Managers using the Transcendental Meditation technique state that it provides a level of rest that dissolves the accumulated tension and stress that sleep is unable to release. "The decline in energy experienced at the end of a long day has two components," says Bob Kory, AFSCI vice president for expansion. "One is the physical aspect of fatigue, the other is the mental component, stress."

Scientific research indicates that during the practice of the TM technique the individual gains a deeper state of rest than in deep sleep. Physiologist R. K. Wallace reports that oxygen consumption, a measure of metabolic activity, drops 16-18 percent during the practice of the TM technique as compared with only an 8-11 percent drop during the deepest part of sleep. This deep level of rest allows accumulated stress and fatigue which may have built up over months and years to be systematically eliminated. As a result, the individual has increased energy and experiences less strain and stress while taking on more activity at work and at home. Many people report that they need less sleep as a result of practicing the technique. This is a boon to the executive whose time has become increasingly precious.

Along with deep rest the Transcendental Meditation technique also seems to increase the orderliness of brain functioning. Studies with the electroencephalograph or EEG (a device for measuring the brain's electrical activity) have shown that the normally random and disorganized activity of the different areas of the brain tends to become more orderly and synchronous during the TM technique.

While early research on the TM program has emphasized the physiological and psychological effects of the program, more recent studies have looked into its impact on the performance of individuals in organizational settings. A carefully controlled study was designed by Professor David R. Frew, Director of the Graduate School of Business at Gannon College, Erie, Pennsylvania, to measure the effects of the TM program on productivity and job satisfaction. Over 600 meditators and non-meditators, in a cross section of occupations, participated in the studies.

Dr. Frew found that while a vast majority of meditators report an increase in physical energy, a propensity for getting work done, and heightened creativity, the result could be a desire to accomplish personal goals at the expense of corporate goals. Thus, Dr. Frew's research question was "What is the effect of the TM technique on the primary work organization of the meditator? Does it make him a better, more productive worker, or does it present a very basic ideological conflict?"

The research subjects were asked to rate themselves over a period of time on dimensions of productivity such as job satisfaction, performance, turnover, aspiration level, and quality of interpersonal relationships. Each subject was also cross-rated by his supervisor. The results of his study show that:

- Meditators show increases in job satisfaction, a decreased desire to change jobs, better performance, and better relationships with supervisors and co-workers.

- The farther up the organizational ladder the executives are and the more democratic the organization, the greater the impact of the TM technique upon productivity.

The study concludes that if the TM technique relieves stress at an equal rate for all people, then the people who experience the greatest benefit must be the people undergoing the greatest stress— in short, managers.

Roy Morter, Director of Personnel at GM's Lordstown, Ohio, Assembly Plant, states: "In the 12 months that the study ran, there have been no days lost due to personal illness among those using the TM technique. The usual rate is about 5 percent, so we feel that the program shows much promise in terms of cost benefits. It appears that for management personnel, the TM technique definitely points to the direction of greater energy, increased clarity, better organizational ability, as well as improved health," he said.

When asked if the TM program might produce less ambitious managers less likely to succeed in a highly competitive setting, Morter said, "On the contrary, a significant number of those who took the AFSCI management course have been offered promotions or have been promoted."

Other results of the study were seen in more than half of the subjects' giving up or decreasing their use of alcohol and cigarettes. Over a third of the individuals in the program feel that they now require less sleep and one half of the group said that they fall asleep faster. A majority of those who took part in the program state that they have increased self-confidence in their decision-making and 53 percent reported that their organizational ability has improved as a result of the program.

Regarding his personal involvement in the TM program, Morter said, "I am personally sold. I can get through 12 and 14 hour days, and try to bring about some constructive changes in the way we are doing things, and still manage to keep cool during the day and have energy for enjoying life at home. I feel confident that we will see a continued expansion of TM activity at GM."

E. R. Polk, chairman of the PA Medical Corporation, near Nashville, Tennessee, reports more than half of his administrative staff practices the TM program. As a result, Polk says, "I have noticed that employees, after beginning the TM program, interact more harmoniously among themselves. This is especially true of the interaction between workers and supervisors."

With regard to actual plant operations, Polk continues, "A case of dramatic improvement has been seen in the area of absenteeism. Our average percentage of absenteeism has been 15 percent daily, but among the TM practitioners, it has been less than 1 percent. This improvement alone has enabled the company to show greater profit and productivity."

Gordon T. Beaham III, President of Faultless Starch/Bon Ami Company, reports that "Out of 24 executives and staff in our executive office, 16 have begun the TM program. I feel that the overall atmosphere of the office has improved as a result of this large number of TM meditators. The TM technique reduces stress, improves interpersonal relationships and develops creativity. Communications in the office seem better and more open. I might add that we have encouraged the TM program here in order to keep our health insurance rates from rising as they did rather precipitously a year ago. We expect the TM program to pay for itself in saved premiums in future years."

Stanley Eisenberg, president of a Brooklyn-based dairy company called Sunnydale Farms, began the TM program three years ago. Last year he offered TM courses to some of his employees. After six months he concludes: "I think it's the best investment we've made in our personnel. It has helped them become more productive, more levelheaded and better able to cope with pressure. If you compare the cost-benefit of the TM program to all the other fringe benefits we offer our employees, the TM program is by far the best investment for the company and the most helpful for the individuals who work here."

In a recent Defense Department research paper, Edward E. Winchester looked at the effects of the TM technique and analyzed its application to management systems and problem solving. He finds that the two primary components of decision-making are the intellectual faculty and the creative or intuitive abilities. The quality and quantity of problem solving output is directly related to the available input of creative and analytic thinking. Using the tools of financial analysis, he suggests the existence of an "awareness baseline" with which a manager confronts problems. If a sufficient quantity of intellect or intuition is not available to the manager, then the number of problems the executive manager can successfully deal with will be limited.

Winchester points out that studies have shown that the TM technique not only increases balance of mental abilities, but that it actually increases the energy available for both analytic and creative thinking, thus raising the "awareness baseline" to a point at which problems of increasing number and complexity can be solved.

Several other government departments and agencies are also considering the potential of the TM program for improving the performance of their personnel. Joseph N. Coffee, Associate Director of the General Management Training Center at the Civil Service Commission, who has conducted an evaluation of the Transcendental Meditation program says, "I was rather skeptical of what I would get out of the course. I had difficulty seeing how it could accomplish all that is claimed. Also I doubted whether or not I would be willing to put in the time to meditate, especially in the morning. However I found the experience very rewarding and I had no problem learning to meditate. Now I look forward to meditating, even in the morning. Before TM, I would come home from work quite drained and unwilling or unable to do much of anything constructive. Now, I come home, meditate for 20 minutes and then undertake all kinds of constructive activities. In essence the TM technique seems to revitalize me at that particular time of day. As I have been able to overcome lack of sleep and increase my energy, I seem to be able to concentrate more. Most noticeable is my ability to increase my concentration in the evening."

Dr. Louis Werner, Assistant Director, Division of Geothermal Energy at the Energy Research and Development Administration, says he has "found the long-term value of the TM technique to have a significant effect on the decision-making process. Answers to complex problems now come spontaneously to mind with little effort. In light of the fact that the benefits of the technique are cumulative, I look forward to increasing performance in this area."

Whether or not the TM technique is the missing technology that will enable American business to reduce personnel problems and dramatically increase productivity remains to be seen. But while the number of companies offering the TM program to their employees is as yet limited, the number is growing rapidly, and those already using it claim an impressive list of benefits both to the company and the individual employee.

Additional information is available from the AFSCI Management Training Institute, 2127 Leroy Place NW., Washington, D.C. 20008.

Finishing time:_____

RAPID READING COMPREHENSION CHECK: "TM"

1. The research reported in this article is:

    a. _____ generally favorable.

    b. _____ generally unfavorable.

    c. _____ balanced; both favorable and unfavorable.

2. TM programs in companies are:

    a. _____ limited.

    b. _____ widespread.

    c. _____ limited, but growing.

3. According to Stephen F. Beck, the world's greatest underdeveloped resource is:

    a. _____ creativity.

    b. _____ human intelligence.

    c. _____ interpersonal relations.

4. TM appears to be successful in reducing people's:

    a. _____ stress.

    b. _____ job frustrations.

    c. _____ boredom.

5. According to TM teachers, the technique is:

    a. _____ demanding.

    b. _____ expensive.

    c. _____ effortless.

6. When compared with sleep, TM usually results in:

a. _____ the same amount of rest.

b. _____ less rest.

c. _____ more rest.

7. Recent studies of TM have focused on the individual's:

a. _____ physiology.

b. _____ psychological reactions.

c. _____ performance in organizational settings.

8. Benefits of the TM technique mentioned were:

a. _____ increased sexual activity and enjoyment.

b. _____ decrease in the use of cigarettes and alcohol.

c. _____ fewer automobile accidents resulting in lowered insurance rates.

9. One major reason some companies endorse the TM approach is that their employees are:

a. _____ happier.

b. _____ complaining less.

c. _____ more productive.

10. The TM technique is usually practiced:

a. _____ once a day.

b. _____ twice a day.

c. _____ three times a day.

Check your answers with the Answer Key.

INSTRUCTIONS FOR RAPID READING: "The Unreasonable Manager"

Read this article as quickly as possible while trying to maintain a good comprehension score of at least 70 percent. Time yourself. When you finish the article, write down your reading time in the space provided at the end of the article. Answer the comprehension questions following the article, then check your answers with the Answer Key. Determine your reading rate from the Words Per Minute: Rapid Reading Chart, then record your reading rate and comprehension score on your Rapid Reading Progress Chart.

Rapid Reading

The Unreasonable Manager

David B. Norris, C.M.C.

Most management authorities say the management function consists of:

- Planning
- Organizing
- Staffing
- Directing
- Controlling

It is my experience that three essential ingredients are missing from this definition of management. These essential ingredients are:

- Dreaming

- Teaching
- Being unreasonable

DREAMING

One cannot initiate plans without a mental image (dream) of the desired accomplishments. The most valuable manager can look at the real world today and envision how it ought to be tomorrow. Constructive dreaming is a rare quality. The capable manager is one whose imagination and dreams can open the possibilities of the development of an organization next month, next year and far into the future. Once the desired picture of the future is established, and made known, then others can go to work to help make that dream become reality.

THE REASONABLE MANAGER

The reasonable manager is balanced and adjusted. This manager adapts to the organization, the surroundings and the realities of this environment. A reasonable manager responds and reacts to day to day changes and problems. Convictions are not strong; plans are not crisp; plans change frequently as they are buffeted by stray forces within the environment. This person is only a reactor to a series of events. Over 50% of all managers fit in this category. They are really reactors and caretakers, not managers, even though that is what they are called.

THE CRISIS MANAGED COMPANY

Over 50 percent of all companies are crisis managed. It takes a crisis to get management's attention. There is usually not enough management capacity to both take care of today and also to think in terms of the future where management should be concentrating. The crisis managed company can be a most interesting place to work. Phones ring; decisions are made right and left; crises and panics are handled and resolved. Each night one can feel one has really worked as a manager—think of all the events handled today!

MANAGEMENT BY ANTICIPATION

The well managed company manages by anticipation. It solves problems before they occur. The well managed company can be dull. Problems are foreseen and are resolved before they become today's crises. The president may make only two or three or less significant decisions a month. The high adrenalin type personality will get little personal satisfaction from operating in this calm, cool, well managed environment. This manager must be a self-starter, working in the future, rather than a fire horse needing the gong of a crisis to get going.

THE UNREASONABLE MANAGER

Those relatively few managers who are really effective are those managers who look at the environment, analyze present conditions, dream about what could be better, and then formulate plans to achieve those dreams. They change the environment rather than simply respond and adjust to it. The effective manager is unreasonable whenever something would cause diversion or block his organization from achieving its dreams and goals.

Unreasonable managers get results. Unreasonable managers impose their strong will and direct the organization to meet these dreams. They have standards of excellence which will not be compromised. They force the world to change and mold to them—not vice versa. The techniques of management may be autocratic or participative. They certainly will not be laissez-faire. It is far easier to work under a rough, tough, autocratic manager who knows what he wants and knows what he is doing than it is to work with a nice, warm, humanistic manager who is confused. It is the job of the manager to get results. To do this, each manager must earn and maintain the respect of his subordinates. A manager does not necessarily have to be liked, but he must be followed and respected.

MANAGING SELF

To manage others, a manager must first manage himself. Usually managers have followers other than themselves. They are both managers and leaders. Some managers are managers without being leaders. A credit manager in a one person credit office is such a manager. By definition, a person is a leader only so long as there are followers. The leaders can only go as far as their followers are capable of carrying out their directions. If leaders have no sense of timing, or do not understand the process by which human beings change, it is quite likely their followers will stray. These managers are not leaders because they have no followers.

PLANNING/ORGANIZING

Management scientists distinguish between planning and organizing. I believe they are different parts of the same thing. Planning/organizing is the process of deciding now, what to do in the future, who is going to perform the tasks and when they are going to do them. This should be done on paper. This is thinking in the future.

STAFFING

Next to dreaming perhaps the single most important function a manager performs is selecting a staff. Insurmountable problems frequently disappear with the change of one person. Organizations sometimes change more rapidly than key people can change. It is the rare person who can be a good start-up manager, work his way through the one-person entrepreneur phase, encourage and control the transition to team management and into management by specification and anticipation.

Some years ago I had a college professor who had three principles of management:

1. In case of doubt, fire the SOB.

2. If it does not fit, get a bigger hammer.

3. Greed is good!

As a naive young man, these principles upset and bothered me. Now I know he was close to the truth.

The Bible also expresses the thought, "You cannot make a silk purse out of a sow's ear." If a manager does not have the right people, nothing else can help.

TEACHING

One of the vital functions of management, thus far neglected in the theory of management, is the requirement that each manager must teach and teach and teach. A manager's job is to develop his subordinates and work himself out of his present job. The measure of a good manager at the department head level is that any absence would not be noticed or felt for two or three months. A manager who wants to be on a fast track for promotion has to have a replacement trained. Yes, it is job security to be the absolutely essential manager in a given situation without a replacement trained and ready. These are also the threads binding the manager to the job. The non-replaceable manager is not eligible for promotion under these circumstances. He cannot advance because there is no replacement.

Security minded people try to make themselves essential. They keep things to themselves and surround themselves with lesser people. But this is not a good security technique. Real security lies in one's abilities, experience and track record. This gives one the security of reputation, an attitude allowing the manager to move into other areas of the same company or to transfer to another company requiring these special talents.

DIRECTING

The autocratic manager orders people to do things. The participative manager says, "What do you think?" After discussion the participative manager then says, "This is what we will do." The laissez-faire manager says, "Do what you think best" and then walks away.

The subordinates of an autocratic manager will adapt to his style if he is reasonably consistant. The participative manager gets the most help from his subordinates. While the laissez-faire manager is not really a manager at all.

CONTROLLING

Well over 50 percent of a manager's time is, or should be, spent on the function of control. Controlling is the function of comparing plans to results. If one has no plans, then he is comparing what happened to some vague, ill defined standard of performance.

When a manager compares performance to plans, and does not like the results, then a decision must be made as to whether the plans or the performance were wrong. Then the manager should re-plan and re-staff (assign someone else); or re-direct and recontrol to obtain fresh results.

ACHIEVING RESULTS

The normal state of the universe has a high degree of confusion within it. Things are not normally neat, clean and orderly. It takes direction, energy and discipline to manage a smooth running, effective organization. The effective managers are bright and lazy. These people achieve results by organizing and multiplying the thinking and energy of all those about them. They are lazy and do not do everything themselves.

The top manager must keep all functions in balance in relatively equal strengths. It does no good to have a popular, new product and not have the production facilities to produce it in time, in quality and at a reasonable cost.

To multiply this effectiveness, they should manage by specification, recording procedures in simple language. The manager and team should have the philosophy of managing by anticipation. Problems should be solved in advance, before they become crises.

EFFECTIVE VERSUS EFFICIENT

The god of industrial engineers and many managers is *efficiency*. That is a false god. The really valuable manager is *effective*. This individual does the right thing at the right time. He may be quite inefficient. Being first, pioneering, taking a new and different direction is usually done quite inefficiently at first. As soon as a manager does something efficiently, he probably should not be doing it all. It should be delegated.

CONCLUSION

The most effective managers:
- Dream constructively.
- Plan and organize to make the dreams come true.
- Staff with the best people.
- Direct them, preferably with a participative style.
- Teach, teach, teach their staff, particularly the backup, while working themselves out of the current positions into new challenges.

- Constantly follow up and check performance against plans and expectations.
- Re-plan, re-organize, re-staff and re-direct as necessary to achieve the dreams.
- Are unreasonable when people want to lower standards, excuse substandard performance, go in a different direction without sufficient reason, etc.
- Are effective rather than efficient.

- Do not confuse effort with results.

Unreasonable managers bend events, circumstances and people to their personal wills. If they do not like something in the environment, they change it. They demand that certain results be achieved and that people do what is required. They establish the standards and make everyone else adhere to them. They are the truly effective managers in business and industry.

Finishing time:_____

RAPID READING COMPREHENSION CHECK: "The Unreasonable Manager"

1. How does the author feel about the unreasonable manager?

   a. _____ Negative

   b. _____ Positive

   c. _____ Neutral

2. The reasonable manager lacks:

   a. _____ strong convictions.

   b. _____ the ability to adapt.

   c. _____ the ability to react to day-to-day problems.

3. As compared to the crisis managed company, those companies managed by anticipation are:

   a. _____ dull.

   b. _____ exciting.

   c. _____ confusing.

4. Managers are unreasonable when they are:

   a. _____ frustrated.

   b. _____ blocked from achieving goals.

   c. _____ asked to be accountable.

5. The unreasonable manager is almost never:

   a. _____ autocratic.

   b. _____ participative.

   c. _____ laissez-faire.

6. According to the author, reasonable managers are really:

   a. _____ followers.

   b. _____ leaders.

   c. _____ reactors.

7. One distinguishing characteristic of the unreasonable manager is that he is a:

   a. _____ dreamer.

   b. _____ screamer.

   c. _____ company person.

8. One key to promotion is to have a:

   a. _____ group of incompetents surrounding you.

b. _____ good relationship with your staff.

c. _____ trained replacement.

9. Once a manager becomes efficient at doing something, it should be:

a. _____ delegated to somebody else.

b. _____ recognized by his or her supervisor.

c. _____ his or her continued responsibility.

10. The author quoted the Bible in order to make his point regarding:

a. _____ directing.

b. _____ staffing.

c. _____ teaching.

Check your answers with the Answer Key.

8
Data Pattern II: Instructional

INTRODUCTION

As mentioned in chapter 7, when writers use one of the data patterns, their primary purpose is to inform or instruct the reader. You learned that the key to comprehending the informational pattern is to be sensitive to changes in the thinking of the writer or to be able to recognize when the writer completes one subtopic and moves on to a new one.

When you are confronted with an instructional article on a particular subject, the key to comprehending it is to be able to recognize the author's specific instructional steps. Fortunately, most authors

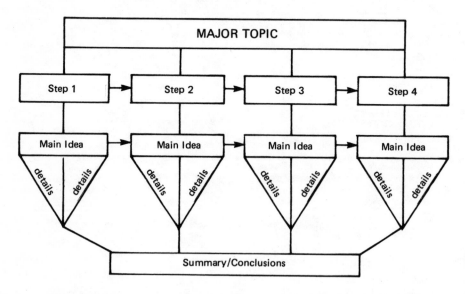

Figure 4 Relationship of Main Ideas to Data: Instructional Pattern

number the steps or highlight them in bold-face headings. The titles of most instructional articles begin with the words "How To."

The diagram shown in Figure 4 illustrates how important main ideas and details are related to the various components (steps) of the instructional type of data pattern.

INSTRUCTIONS FOR ANALYZED READING: "How to Stay Alive During a Holdup"

Even though this instructional article was written for bankers, anyone who is in a bank during a holdup can benefit from the author's advice. Notice how the article is divided into what to do *during* the holdup and *after* the holdup, with special instructions for managers. Read the article and then examine the analysis that follows it.

Analyzed Reading
How to Stay Alive During a Holdup
The Editors, Bank Systems and Equipment

Any bank security program worth its salt has a written teller procedure plan for holdups. Relying on suggestions and regulations from the American Bankers Association, Bank Administration Institute and the Federal Deposit Insurance Corp., it's little wonder that many procedures are strikingly similar.

In answer to our request, several security officers described their teller dos and don'ts to us. Most are tailored to suit each bank's needs. However, we've compiled several lists of procedures to form our own.

DURING

- Do as the robber requests. No staff member should do anything that might jeopardize his or her life or that of another person. Remain calm.
- Activate the surveillance system and alarm as soon and as safely as possible. (Do not trigger the audible alarm when the robbery is in progress, cautions one bank. The audible type should be sounded when the bandits have left the office.)
- Observe the robber's physical features, concentrating on the bandit nearest you if more than one. Notice such things as:
  1. Whether he or she is wearing a mask or disguise.
  2. The kind of weapon he is using—revolver, automatic, pistol, rifle, shotgun.
  3. Names by which the bandits refer to each other.
  4. Age and weight. Compare them to your own.
  5. Oddities in physical appearance, speech, dress or movements.
  6. Use of left or right hand when holding the gun.
- Try to use money from the open cash drawer starting with ones emptying each compartment in sequence, twos, fives, tens, etc. If forced to pay out

packaged bills, have them stored so the same sequence can be followed. Give no more than the amount he demands. Try to include your bait money.

- To prevent harm to customers, do not call or shout aloud, "Stop that man," etc.
- If the robber leaves evidence, such as a note, try to put it aside and out of sight, if it can be done safely. Do not handle it unnecessarily. Give it to the police when they arrive.
- After the robber has left, observe how he makes his getaway, by foot or car. Notice his direction and license number of the car, if any.
- Talk to no one immediately after the holdup. Go to the officer in charge.

AFTER
- Do not discuss the details of the robbery with others. Teller should record observations on suspect identification forms. Relay information to FBI, police and those people authorized by the security officer or auditor.

Managers Have Their Own

Branch managers have their own set of procedures to follow after a robbery. Some follow here:

- Sound the silent alarm if it hasn't been activated.
- Call the local police, if they haven't arrived already, and the nearest FBI office. Notify the president of the bank and the security officer.
- Send someone outside to meet the authorities when they arrive. (One bank reported that the FBI and police have waited outside a bank for the bandits to come out. Meanwhile, the bank officers waited in the bank for the police while the bandits had already left.)
- Lock doors temporarily to control access.
- Protect the teller's cage and other areas where the robber may have left fingerprints or other evidence.
- Find out the names and addresses of other persons who witnessed the crime or escape. Ask them to record their observations.
- Do not mention the amount of loss or names and addresses of witnesses to unauthorized people.

ANALYZED READING ANALYSIS: "How to Stay Alive During a Holdup"

The basic ideas in this article are presented below. Notice how the ideas are associated with the different subtopic components of the instructional data pattern.

	Ideas
Pattern Component	(Instructions)
During Holdup	Do what robber says
	Activate alarm when it is safe
	Observe physical features
	Use money from open cash

	Do not shout
	Save evidence
	Observe getaway
After Holdup	Do not discuss robbery
	Record observations
	Relay information to authorities
Managers (after holdup)	Sound silent alarm
	Notify authorities
	Lock doors
	Protect teller's cage
	Identify witnesses
	Ask witnesses to record observations
	Do not mention loss amount or witnesses' addresses

When several specific ideas are presented in an instructional article, you can sometimes remember them better by using mnemonic devices. For example, you could associate the "During Holdup" instructions with the phrase $U\text{-}SO_2D_2A$, remembering that the letters *o* and *d* each have two instructions.

U — Use money from open cash
S — Save evidence
O — Observe physical features
O — Observe getaway
D — Do what the robber says
D — Don't shout
A — Activate alarm

The "After Holdup" instructions can be associated with *Star War's R2D2* (2 *R's* and 2 *D's*).

R — Record observations
R — Relay information to authorities
D — Don't discuss robbery
D — Directly go to officer in charge (implied)

The manager's instructions can be associated with the phrase *SPIN LAD.*

S — Sound silent alarm
P — Protect teller's cage
I — Identify witnesses
N — Notify authorities
L — Lock doors
A — Ask witnesses to record observations
D — Do not mention loss amount

INSTRUCTIONS FOR UNTIMED READING: "Eight Concise Techniques for More Effective Management"

In this article, the author, in simple language, tells readers how they can become better managers. Read the article and then see if you can jot down the eight techniques without referring to the article.

Untimed Reading

Eight Concise Techniques for More Effective Management

Louis J. Frangipane

They may be such obvious facts that it might seem unnecessary to reiterate basic management principles. But the reality is that the fundamentals do need periodic restatement. Under the short-term and future project pressures of the administrator's job, the executive often doesn't have the luxury of being able to sit back and ask him or herself "What am I really doing?"

Of course, after reflection the administrator knows that his primary responsibility is to get programs, plans, and projects executed through other people. Remember that management is an activity in itself. An administrator doesn't do the work himself or herself.

Don't forget that people are your greatest asset. Your success as an administrator will be measured by your ability to lead, to motivate and to create a stimulating environment for others.

The ability to lead implies establishing an atmosphere in which subordinates will follow willingly and with enthus-iasm. To do this, they must have confidence in your ability, your sincerity of purpose, and your sense of fair play. They must recognize and adopt your goals because they are convinced it is in their best interests to do so.

The techniques outlined below are listed separately, but obviously they overlap. In fact, the "Technique of Management" is an integration of all these fundamentals into an overall philosophy, style or attitude. Every manager should develop his or her own style. After all, each executive is also an individual.

Following are some basic management techniques to remember:

Technique No. 1: Planning

Plan your day—set goals and priorities.

Plan the work of your people. Planning gives direction to the day's activities.

Plan on ways to improve your company's activities; be alert to "the better way."

Technique No. 2: Organizing

Make sure you know your responsibilities and your span of authority.

Let each person working for you know what you expect.

Organize the activities in your department to meet your planned objectives.

Delegate authority to specific people and hold them responsible for their performance.

Technique No. 3: Controlling

Determine what factors indicate good performance and measure these factors regularly.

Take corrective action when planned programs get out of control.

Let your people know that you are aware of their accomplishments or whether they need to improve.

Exercise discipline. Let people know the rules and procedures through training. Be consistent in your application of the rules.

Technique No. 4: Leadership

Develop your leadership qualities— know your own job and the jobs of the people working for you.

Make considered decisions promptly. Develop confidence in yourself and the confidence of others in you.

Show fairness and integrity.

Set the pace, show enthusiasm and perseverance for meeting schedules, budgets and other goals.

Demonstrate, through planning, that you know where you are going and are determined to get there as quickly as possible.

Maintain a pleasant attitude and a sense of humor. Let your people participate in planning and decision making.

Get your people involved.

Share responsibility for mistakes. Defend your people.

Establish a track record of getting results.

Technique No. 5: Understanding People

Recognize the differences in your people. Learn their strong points and work on their weak ones.

Find out what turns them on; recognize their accomplishments publicly, criticize constructively in private.

Show an active interest in them as individuals.

Learn their personal objectives and guide them toward achievement.

Technique No. 6: Be an Effective Communicator

Keep your supervisor advised.

Work effectively with other supervisors, other departments.

Learn to coordinate activities to achieve results.

Let your people know what's going on in the company.

Let individuals know developments or changes that will affect them—before they occur.

Make yourself available for private discussions with your people. Keep their confidence.

Be a good listener; recognize the symptoms of problems, make corrections promptly.

Welcome suggestions for improvements—give an honest evaluation of each suggestion.

Technique No. 7: Handle Complaints Skillfully

Be receptive to employee complaints and handle them in a positive way to improve employee relations. Also determine if the complaint is a symptom of a general condition.

Follow up to make certain the complaint is resolved.

Develop an awareness toward working conditions.

Listen, explain, try not to be offensive.

Technique No. 8: Employee Development

Develop employees to their fullest potential.

Provide employees with challenge when possible.

Delegate tasks to determine capabilities.

Surround yourself with capable people and help them grow. This will help your own advancement.

Recognize that most employees seek the opportunity to improve themselves.

"Show the way" by example. Maintain your own level of competence.

Never stand in the way of an employee's progress for selfish reasons.

UNTIMED READING COMPREHENSION CHECK: "Eight Concise Techniques for More Effective Management"

Directions: List Frangipane's eight techniques for becoming a better manager. Do not refer to the article. When you have finished, go back to the article to check your answers.

1.

2.

3.

4.

5.

6.

7.

8.

How did you do? If you did not recall all eight techniques, you may want to try another mnemonic device. How about HEELP COP? (Remember, 2 *E's.)*

H — Handle complaints skillfully
E — Effective communicator
E — Employee development
L — Leadership
P — Planning

C — Controlling
O — Organizing
P — People (understanding them)

INSTRUCTIONS FOR PACED READING: "How to Negotiate a Computer Contract You Can Live With"

The pacing rate for this article is 600 words per minute. This means that you should finish reading the article in 4 minutes and 10 seconds, or a total of 250 seconds. Ask someone to tell you when the time has expired. The article contains approximately 2,500 words. After reading the article, write down your answers to the test that follows.

Paced Reading

How to Negotiate a Computer Contract You Can Live With

Joan Prevete Hyman

A standard computer contract exists to protect only the vendor. Nevertheless, when negotiation time comes many banks fail to add to the document clauses that would safeguard the users from risks.

Hardware users also are advised to be skeptical when negotiating. Many vendors at times will go into contract talks with a "trust-me" attitude. But let the buyer beware: If it's not in the contract, it's not in the deal.

Industry consultants, independent and bank affiliated attorneys and systems officers offered these warnings to *Bank Systems & Equipment* during exclusive interviews.

TOO LITTLE KNOWLEDGE, TOO MUCH TRUST

Too little awareness and too much trust on the bank's part cause it to waive its own protection in a computer contract. For example, legal eyes don't even get to see many of the computer contracts to which a bank agrees.

"You get a room full of banks," challenged Charles E. Harris, vice president of legal affairs for the $2 billion-asset Sunbanks of Florida, Inc., Orlando, "and about 50 per cent will admit they have their contracts looked at by a lawyer."

More than that, those lawyers that do get a peek probably don't have a computer contract background. "Attorneys that banks use for hardware negotiations are not necessarily up on computer contracts," contends Dick H. Brandon, president of Brandon Consulting Group, New York, which specializes in data processing contracts. Attorneys that a bank employs for acquisition contracts are more than likely the same people that handle real estate contracts, home mortgages and other legal areas, he notes. (Brandon is co-author, with attorney Sidney Segelstein, of a book entitled *Data Processing Contracts.* It is published by Van Nostrand Reinhold, New York.)

If attorneys do sit in on talks, they may have a problem explaining the bank's needs. "Lawyers are intimidated by this technology," says Thomas K. Christo, a Boston attorney specializing in computer-related litigation. Young lawyers coming up through the ranks may be more familiar with computers, he points out. But a vendor "will capitalize on the user's (and the older lawyer's) lack of computer education," Christo adds. "The vendor tries to oversell the technocracy."

PROTECTION IS FORGOTTEN

A bank also puts too much trust in the vendor, to the point where the user's protection is forgotten or considered unnecessary. "A user shouldn't have more confidence in the vendor doing something than the vendor does," warns Ken Brindle, vice president of International Computer Negotiations (ICN). (The Winter Park, FL firm offers information and help on negotiations of this type.)

Often the data processing officer will be on the vendor's side. "He wants his machine," Brandon points out. "He doesn't care what's on the contract. He was sold on the machine."

Trust also stems from the "aura of respectability and infallibility" that the computer industry still works under, Christo adds.

Compound all of this with a constant sales pitch, notes M. Arthur Gillis of M. Arthur Gillis Associates, an independent consultant in Chevy Chase, MD. "Vendors will say they'll help the bank all the way. That's verbage [sic]. But if the banker hears it enough he might say to himself, 'Well, I've heard it so much it must be true.'"

KEY PROMISES GO UNWRITTEN

And that's where a bank will go wrong—failing to document any vendor's key promises. Claims and promises mean little, industry sources say, if they are not in the contract. And if it's not in what is called the "four corners" of the contract, it's not in the deal.

As Brandon explains it, nothing else but the contract is admissable in court—even if it's a paper signed by the vendor at a later time. "So a vendor can promise stuff free—training, software—but if it's not written down on the contract, you can't claim it later. With a standard contract, you only get a box."

Typical of what can happen is the First National Bank of Decatur's experience. The $150 million-deposit Illinois bank got caught on the "trust me" phrase and signed a standard contract. "It's dangerous," admits Steve Mitchell, vice president of operations. The vendor assured the bank that certain problems would not crop up during the period of service—and they did. The company was "unresponsive" in solving the situation, Mitchell relates.

More often than not, Christo concludes, the standard contract "doesn't reflect what was promised."

STANDARD CONTRACT LEAVES MUCH TO BE DESIRED

What's in a standard hardware contract? "It doesn't specify much of anything, except price," Christo states. Brandon gives some examples: A standard IBM contract of a few years ago (it has since been revised, but it is basically the same, Brandon says) under "Installation" says that the user shall "provide a suitable installation environment." This environment, he points out, is never described in the standard form. Under "Service" the contract states that IBM will maintain the machine in "good working order." "No one knows what this is," Brandon asserts. "The maintenance contract should have specifics."

In effect, the standard contract "hedges what the vendor will do—if it says anything about what the vendor will do at all," Harris concludes.

To cover yourself, Brandon advises attaching a statement at the end of the standard form. The statement could say, as an example: "The following letter takes precedence over the standard clauses in the standard contract."

It's only within the last few years that users have had the chance to change the standard agreement. "Buyers haven't had the freedom to negotiate with large vendors," Christo maintains. Most large firms were not willing to put in writing clauses that would protect the user. Now more litigation verdicts are favoring the buyer, he notes (Catamore Jewelry Co. vs IBM; Colorado Blue Cross vs Honeywell). Vendors therefore "are beginning to realize that they should make negotiations possible. If a contract says something, it may protect them as well."

NEGOTIATIONS START WITH REQUEST FOR PROPOSALS

For the bank, negotiations basically begin with request for proposals (RFP). These are very valuable, especially when one vendor is favored at the outset, according to Brandon. "I've never had a case where the deal wasn't better by 10 per cent when other proposals were asked for." Users should ask for responses from at least three manufacturers, say those interviewed.

Here, the bank should specify to each firm what is wanted. "Tell the vendor what you're looking for in terms of price, performance, reliability," Brandon explains. And be specific in asking for speeds, downtime percentages, other features. "A vendor and a bank may have different perceptions of what is wanted. If you want the machine to generate reports, the machine will give you reports. But do you want reports every 30, 60 or 90 days?"

The RFP can also ask leading questions, according to Ken Brindle. "These can set things up for negotiation time." One large New York bank found this to be true during its RFP. According to one of the bank's EDP negotiators, the bank wrote "conditions" into the proposal. Vendor responses didn't answer the conditions specifically, "but they came close. This initiated discussions for clarifications."

Keep competition high on the request for proposals, Brindle recommends. This is true even if the bank is working with an incumbent vendor, he adds. "You're not committed to it."

Pittsburgh's Dollar Savings Bank concurs. The $1 billion-deposit thrift selected another firm for its computers over the bank's incumbent vendor. "We were open-minded in our proposal evaluation," recalls Howard Sleppy, vice president of data processing at the time (now vice president of operations). "We weren't swayed by the vendor we already had. We wanted the best people for the job. We went into it like we never saw a computer before in our lives."

GO IN WITH A TEAM

When talks start, the bank should go in with a specified negotiations team. According to Brindle, the group should consist of the senior DP person, his or her support people (if it's a large contract), a legal representative, a financial man/woman and a professional advisor (accountant or consultant). Consultant Gillis adds that the bank president should be involved if the bank is small, say $100 million. In any event representatives from diverse backgrounds can "educate each other" in the unfamiliar areas, Sunbank's Harris maintains.

A bank and manufacturer get down to the nitty-gritty when they face across the table. What should banks seek during negotiations? Brindle advises looking for "performance with a balancing act on price and protection. A vendor could say, 'We have a computer for a great price, but it's been standing around in the warehouse for years.' Or the vendor could say, 'We have this great performing computer, redundant, everything. But bring your checkbook.'"

Performance should be specified in the request for proposal. But, again, industry officials urge that a user get as specific in the unit's performance features as possible.

COVER YOURSELF

Price negotiations depend on who you deal with. Gillis reports that IBM "doesn't negotiate price." However, Harris maintains that the computer giant does give concessions, such as conversion and system support. But usually no dollar discounts are handed out, he notes. So if you're looking for a low price machine, Gillis adds, you may have to protect yourself in other areas (non-delivery, bankruptcy, etc).

Above all, contract experts warn, protect yourself from risks. Anticipate where the vendor will fall and try to protect yourself through added clauses. (Brandon's book mentions 250 clauses for various DP contracts.) Brandon goes so far as to advise clients to play the "what-if" game. "Try to figure out all the things that can go wrong," he urges. "For example, 'What if my computer salesman is replaced?'; 'What if I'm replaced?'" And talk over penalty clauses if the vendor fails to meet expectations.

Those interviewed suggested several user protection clauses that could be negotiated into the contract:

Acceptance Criteria

Some clause should indicate when the bank will take possession but only if the machine meets "minimum standards," Harris points out. These standards should be spelled out in the "four corners." If you're benchmarking, Brindle cautions, benchmark the equipment that will be installed in your house. "A vendor may not test the equipment you've asked for." Also Gillis insists an acceptance test be made at the vendor's plant. "If the bank tests the machine only at its offices, and the unit fails to meet standards, the vendor might say it was due to bad shipping."

Maintenance Assurance

"It's a given that the machine will break down," one consultant remarks. When dealing with a firm with a poor track record for service, a bank may want to talk over additional protection. One consultant came upon a situation like this. He aided a bank in tacking on these extra service points:

1. That the maintenance person must arrive within a certain timeframe to service the machine.
2. That the bank have the maintenance person's home phone number.
3. That the service person have at least five years of bank computer experience.
4. That no system component substitutions be made.
5. That new, used or reconditioned equipment be specified and sold to the bank.

In addition, a buyer should talk with other users of the same equipment to get their views on operation and service. "Make sure the product exists," Brindle stresses. And "never pioneer anything," warns Brandon. "The earliest Christians got the hungriest lions. Let everyone else get the problems. Never be a first-time user of equipment. You don't know what will go wrong with it."

Contract negotiations time is also strategy time. Using various ploys a vendor can sometimes smooth-talk you out of something you want and into something you don't want. These ploys can be obvious or veiled, depending on the vendor's skill in playing them and the bank's skill in picking them up. Computer contract experts gave *BSE* some samples a vendor will use:

● "Look at the bank down the street. They've installed our system and they're doing great." (Vendors will constantly point to success stories, Gillis warns.)

- "Here's everything you need for one low payment." As ICN's "CNReport" newsletter states, the user may not stop and analyze each package component to determine whether it is really needed.

- "You're getting our best price." Large banks are especially subject to this ploy, says "CNReport." "This is because they are already impressed by their own size and clout with their vendors. Computer vendors play on this corporate ego," the newsletter notes. "They have to do little further convincing that the quoted price is the best price."

The best defense against these is to "take the deal apart," Brindle recommends. "A vendor puts a nice ribbon on the package. But take it apart, and examine each part individually."

TIME AND COMPETITION ARE USER'S ALLIES

A buyer's best allies during negotiations are time and competition. Harris of Sunbanks suggests reserving at least 30 days for the table. "If you don't have this time to kick price around, you can't use price as a negotiating technique. If you have the time, and you are not satisfied (with negotiations), you can go to someone else."

And deadlines can be deadly for the user. "Once you set a deadline for yourself, that's bad," counsels Brindle. "The vendor will beat you over the head with this. You're under pressure" to come through with a machine at a certain time.

Too much time negotiating, however, can work against the bank. Negotiations can go on for months, sometimes years, experts say. "Usually the bank will tire first," Brandon contends. "The bank only negotiates maybe once in five years. The vendor negotiates every day." With a 'let's get it over with' attitude, a bank may give up and give in to the firm's suggestions, he says.

When it's used well, time allows you to seek out the competition. Experts advise talking with two vendors at the same time. "We negotiated with two vendors until the very last day," recalls Howard Sleppy from Dollar Savings. "And both were aware of it. We didn't use any ploys and neither did they. At least I wasn't aware of any."

But if talks are not going your way, "you must be willing to say 'no' and throw the vendor out," stresses Harris. "I've never seen anyone who wasn't willing to come back." As Brindle puts it: "You're a potential buyer; you're not obligated."

BE A SKEPTICAL BUYER

If anything, be a skeptical buyer, the consultants and lawyers told *BSE.* Take a "show-me" attitude to negotiations. "It's the vendor's game we're playing and they do it for a living," Brindle warns. "Under the best of conditions, you'll be outgunned. If you're mentally prepared, it helps. So don't take the first offer out of the box."

Arthur Gillis agrees but "you can't get everything you want. The natural tendency is 'get all you can.' But you can't make the vendor lose money. So be realistic."

"But don't assume anything," he continues. "Be skeptical and downgrade some ridiculous claims. Keep the vendor honest."

PACED READING COMPREHENSION CHECK: "How to Negotiate a Computer Contract You Can Live With"

1. Most bank lawyers:

   a. _____ are specialists in data processing contracts.

   b. _____ are not specialists in data processing contracts.

   c. _____ are disinterested in data processing contracts.

2. According to the author, banks typically have:

   a. _____ put too little trust in the vendor.

   b. _____ carefully negotiated with the vendor.

   c. _____ put too much trust in the vendor.

3. With respect to vendor promises, banks should:

   a. _____ not be too demanding.

   b. _____ trust those given orally.

   c. _____ get them in writing.

4. The most specific item in a standard computer contract is the:

   a. _____ maintenance clause.

   b. _____ delivery clause.

   c. _____ price

5. Maintenance clauses can be made more specific by:

   a. _____ adding a letter to the standard clauses.

   b. _____ using proper terminology.

   c. _____ making them as long as possible.

6. The typical computer negotiation should begin with:

   a. _____ a written introduction.

   b. _____ a request for proposals.

   c. _____ telephone calls to various vendors.

7. When negotiating, banks should be represented by:

   a. _____ an individual bank officer only.

   b. _____ a single lawyer who is an expert in computers.

   c. _____ a team of negotiators.

8. The best place to test the equipment is:

   a. _____ in the vendor's showroom.

   b. _____ in the vendor's plant.

   c. _____ in the bank itself.

9. With respect to new products, it is advisable to:

   a. _____ wait until someone else has tested them.

   b. _____ buy them because they will be cheap.

   c. _____ give them as much of a chance as the "name" vendors.

10. Large banks are often mislead into believing they are getting the best possible:

a. _____ service.

b. _____ product.

c. _____ price.

Check your answers with the Answer Key.

INSTRUCTIONS FOR SKIM READING: "How to Survive an IRS Tax Audit"

Using the skimming techniques you learned in chapter 2, skim the following article in order to answer the five *"W"* questions *(Who, What, Where, When, Why)*. Also identify three ways to survive the audit. Time yourself to find your skimming rate; you should take no longer than 1 minute and 50 seconds to finish the article. Check your answers in the Answer Key. (Remember, a score of 50 percent or higher is acceptable when skimming.) Determine your skimming rate from the Words Per Minute: Skimming Chart, then record your skimming rate and comprehension score on your Skim Reading Progress Chart.

Skim Reading

How to Survive an IRS Tax Audit

Sidney Weinman

Your income tax returns are finally completed, signed, and in the mail. You feel that you can sit back and relax when suddenly the fear sets in. Most of us live in mortal fear of having our tax returns audited by the IRS. But notification that your return has been selected for audit should not shock or frighten you.

The sad truth is that most people who are audited wind up poorer than before the audit. But if you are properly prepared, you will do better on an examination, and in some cases even get the government to send you some additional money.

To begin with, an audit notification does not necessarily mean that there is a suspicion of tax evasion or any other illegal act. More than 80% of the returns

audited are selected by an IRS computer which is programmed to select returns which contain items that look like they can produce additional tax for the government if investigated. The exact criteria used by the computer are a tightly guarded secret, but apparently include such items as:

- Very high itemized deductions,
- Dependency exemptions claimed for parents or other relatives,
- An unusually large refund claimed on the return.

The return least likely to be audited is one on which only salary income is reported and the standard deduction is taken. But even among such returns, the IRS computer selects a small percentage at random. In addition, if you've been audited before and the government came out ahead, you may find your returns being looked at for the next few years.

Some returns are audited on the basis of information obtained from informers. If you have claimed a questionable item on your return, or if you failed to report an item which might be includible in your income, don't brag about it to friends or relatives. There is no way to be certain that someone else hasn't overheard you. And many people have learned to their dismay and sorrow that friends and even members of their family have squealed on them. Not every lead results in an audit, but a good number of them get at least a preliminary investigation.

The purpose of any audit is to verify the accuracy of items reported on a return. The tax laws permit the IRS to make an extensive examination of the financial affairs of any taxpayer. The easiest way to survive an audit is to prepare for one at the time you prepare your tax return. And bear in mind that, even though you may pay someone to prepare your return, its contents and substantiation are your responsibility.

Make sure that you have documentation—cancelled checks, receipts or other proof of payment—for the deductions claimed. Very few people are actually audited, but assume that you will be and prepare yourself accordingly. An audit might not be started until a year or more after you file your return. Don't trust your memory. Your records and worksheets should be complete enough so that you can reconstruct all entries and computations on the return. Unfortunately, deductions claimed on a tax return are often disallowed solely because the taxpayer doesn't have the necessary proof to back up the deductions.

Even if you haven't kept your receipts, etc., all is not lost. Remember that the recipient of your payment should have a record of it. Thus, for example, if you don't have your receipts but can get your church or doctor to give you a statement summarizing your contributions or payments for the year being audited, the IRS will be satisfied.

Audits fall into two categories—*office* and *field*. The field audit is generally employed on more complex returns and, as its name implies, is usually conducted outside the IRS office. The agent would normally complete the audit at the taxpayer's place of business or some other convenient location (for example, the office of the taxpayer's attorney or accountant), so long as the pertinent books and records are available.

The audit will cover all items on the return, but the agent can be expected to concentrate on unusual items. For example, if you claimed only a nominal amount for charitable contributions, the agent might only glance at your checks or receipts without tallying them. The audit may be completed quickly if the agent is satisfied that the return properly reflects income and deductions, or several visits may be needed to complete the audit. You'll speed things up if you have all the necessary records available. Not knowing where things are or hedging on the answers to routine questions waste time, create friction, and can raise suspicions of fraud in the agent's mind.

There are two types of office audits, *interview* and *correspondence*. Unlike the field audit, they are generally limited to specific items on the return. If you're selected for an office audit you will receive a letter from the local IRS office advising you of the items being checked. In a correspondence audit, all that you have to do is send the supporting documentation (checks, receipts, etc.) to IRS.

To protect yourself in case of loss, you should make and retain photocopies of all documents and send the originals by registered or certified mail.

Interview audits take place at the local IRS office at a time and date specified in the initial letter from IRS. Don't ignore the letter and hope that IRS will forget about you. They won't. However, if the date stated in the letter is not convenient, a postponement can easily be arranged by contacting the IRS representative whose name and telephone number appear on the letter. And if you have moved since filing your return so that you can't appear at the IRS office serving your former home, the audit will either be handled by correspondence or transferred to the local office serving your new home.

A state which has an income tax can initiate its own audit. In addition, some states have contracts with IRS to audit returns selected by IRS. Even if the audit isn't done under contract, the results will be reported to IRS. If you have valid grounds for objecting, don't agree to a state adjustment merely because only a small amount of tax is involved. The IRS will use the same adjustment as the basis for what will turn out to be a much larger addition to your federal tax.

In some cases an audit can work to your benefit. Say, that in the course of getting ready for your audit, you find a check for a deductible item which you failed to claim on your original return. If presented with the substantiation, the agent must allow the item even if it results in the government owing you money.

Not surprisingly, in about two out of every three audits the IRS agent recommends that additional tax—a deficiency—be paid. You don't have to accept the agent's findings, and if you feel that they are unfair or unwarranted you should demand a review.

There are several review steps available within the IRS, starting at the local office and extending to the appellate division. After exhausting these remedies, if you're still not satisfied, you must go to court. Here you have a choice.

You can pay the additional tax and bring an action for refund in the U.S. District Court. Here your case can be decided by a jury if you want. Or you can bring the case to the Tax Court and here you don't have to pay the tax in advance. You can't get a jury trial in the Tax Court but small claims procedures are available in cases involving no more than $1,500 of additional tax. This means that the case can be heard informally and without regard to rigid rules of evidence. The average taxpayer can represent himself and save a bundle on legal fees.

No one is overjoyed at the prospect of having his tax return put through the audit wringer. But if you keep your head, are organized, and have the documentation to back up your figures, you will come out of it in much better shape than if you merely resign yourself to it in terror.

Finishing time:_____

SKIM READING COMPREHENSION CHECK: "How to Survive an IRS Tax Audit"

1. *What* is the article about?

2. *Who* gets audited?

3. *Where* does the audit take place? (2 places)

4. *When* does the audit take place?

5. *Why* does the audit take place? (Give three reasons.)

6. List three ways to survive an audit.

Check your answers with the Answer Key.

INSTRUCTIONS FOR SKIM READING: "How to Get a Loan From The SBA"

Using the skimming techniques you learned in chapter 2, skim the following article in order to answer the five *"W"* questions *(Who, What, Where, When, Why)*. Time yourself to find your skimming rate; you should take no longer than 1 minute to finish the article. Check your answers in the Answer Key. (Remember, a score of 50 percent or higher is acceptable when skimming.) Determine your skimming rate from the Words Per Minute: Skimming Chart, then record your skimming rate and comprehension score on your Skim Reading Progress Chart.

Skim Reading

How to Get a Loan From The SBA

The Office of Public Affairs of the U.S. Small Business Administration

Recently, after a national survey, the U.S. Chamber of Commerce listed 12 top complaints of small business owners. Compliance with government regulations headed the list. In its constant quest for solutions to small business owners' problems, the U.S. Small Business Administration (SBA) explores all avenues, and this "top of the list complaint" is no exception.

When the government seeks to improve the health or safety of the small business community through inspections that could result in required changes in equipment, facilities, or methods of operation in order to comply with federal standards, the SBA can offer assistance through its Occupational Safety and Health Loan Program.

Any small business judged likely to suffer economic injury as a result of upgrading its plant or equipment to comply with federal standards may be eligible for financial aid. Loan proceeds may be used for new construction, remodeling or renovation, or to meet starting costs and continuing fixed costs should operations be discontinued because of construction or other changes.

There is no dollar limit on these loans.

However, direct loans and the SBA share of a bank participation loan are limited to $500,000 (except in cases of extreme hardship). Loan maturity is based on the applicant's need and earnings, but repayment must be at the earliest possible date. The maximum term is 30 years.

OVER $40 MILLION IN LOANS APPROVED

Between the beginning of this type of assistance in September 1971 and the end of December 1976, SBA approved $40.9 million in loans to help small firms comply with government regulations under the Occupational Safety and Health Act of 1970.

In this effort, SBA has joined hands with OSHA to ease compliance with federal standards. Together the two agencies try to insure a fair, impartial review of safety and health matters affecting small businesses and to educate employers in the benefits of good work safety and health programs. By mutual agreement of the agencies, chambers of commerce, trade organizations, insurance groups, and bankers are drawn into consideration of the business owners' problems.

This alliance is due in part to regional SBA-OSHA hearings to determine how to fulfill the needs of small concerns. At one such hearing in Illinois, a representative of the Illinois State Chamber of Commerce urged that employers be taught "to effectively use their accident records, run safety programs, and change work habits and attitudes to encompass the safety factor." The chamber of commerce spokesperson also suggested more simplified procedures for applying for a variance to an OSHA standard.

To learn what other specialized forms of relief might be developed, the SBA did an in-depth study on the effects of government regulations on small business. The study, a first on this subject, was released last year. It addresses the problem of regulatory overkill, principally as it affects small manufacturing concerns. Entitled, "The Impact on Small Business Concerns of Government Regulations that Force Technological Change," the study points out, among other things, that although the major source of impact is the federal government, in certain instances the states have imposed stricter standards, further compounding the problems of small firms.

TRAINING AND COUNSELING AVAILABLE

A deeper knowledge of overall SBA assistance programs can help owners with any type of problem. Even prospective small business owners can benefit from the advice and counseling available free of charge at local SBA field offices. SBA-sponsored workshops, seminars, and training courses are available to guide small operators through the difficulties of planning and managing a business. Publications on all aspects of starting and operating a business are available—most of them free, some at a nominal charge.

Financing through many lending programs tailored to meet the specific needs of the prospective or established owner is offered through loans participated in or guaranteed by SBA.

Personnel at local SBA field offices also can demonstrate methods of obtaining federal contracts and bid or performance bonding, to those needing such assistance.

During the past fiscal year alone, SBA financial assistance (business loans, disaster loans, surety bond guarantees,

Small Business Investment Company funding, etc.) amounted to approximately $3.2 billion.

General requirements for loan eligibility are that applicants be small business owners, be of good character, and show that the proposed loan is for sound value or so secured as reasonably to assure repayment.

The agency cannot make a loan if the firm can obtain funds from a bank or other private sources.

Supplemental information on avail-able help from the Small Business Administration can be found in the following publications:

- Occupational Safety and Health Loan Program (SBA Fact Sheet-3)
- SBA – What It Does (OPI-6)
- SBA Business Loans (OPI-18)

For details on SBA programs and services, business owners should contact the nearest SBA office, listed in telephone directories under "U.S. Government."

Finishing time:_____

SKIM READING COMPREHENSION CHECK: "How to Get a Loan From The SBA"

1. *What* is the article about?

2. *Who* can get a loan?

3. *Where* can a loan be secured?

4. *When* can a loan be secured?

5. *Why* would a loan be sought?

Check your answers with the Answer Key.

INSTRUCTIONS FOR RAPID READING: "How to Get a Good Consultant"

Read this article as fast as possible while trying to maintain a comprehension score of 70 percent. Time yourself. When you finish the article, write down your reading time in the space provided at the end of the article. Answer the comprehension questions following the article, then check your answers with the Answer Key. Determine your reading rate from the Words Per Minute: Rapid Reading Chart, then record your reading rate and comprehension score on your Rapid Reading Progress Chart.

Rapid Reading

How to Get a Good Consultant
Jean Pierre Frankenhuis

Management consultants are generally hired for the wrong reasons. Once hired, they are generally poorly employed and loosely supervised. The result is, more often than not, a final report that decorates an executive's bookshelf with as much usefulness as *The Life and Mores of the Pluvius Aegiptius* would decorate his coffee table—and at considerably more expense.

By no means, of course, do all consulting engagements lead to unsatisfactory results. Satisfactory results are usually due to management's intuitive respect for common sense in making decisions about when to hire consultants, whom to hire, what they are to do, and how they are to do it. The last two decisions can be viewed in the light of objective, logical procedures; it is the subjective aspects of the first two and their importance as a decision-making guide that bear consideration here.

Private and public organizations seek the help of consultants for three reasons: for savings, for an independent view, and for expertise. No one can quarrel with these aims, but their interpretation and use are often debatable.

The assumption that the one-time expenditure for a consultant will be smaller than the salaries and benefits paid to newly hired personnel may be justified for small projects. Obviously, you would not employ a specialist in administrative procedures when you could get a consultant to do the job for $5,000.

Once you reach a certain size, you must weigh the economics of the situation and the side benefits of in-house development against a possible dependency on a consultant. It is well to keep in mind that, unless there is a strong possibility of follow-up work, consultants are masters of the art of vanishing as soon as their fee has been paid.

The second often-used reason for hiring a consultant is to obtain an independent view as a means of settling a dispute at the top level about the solution to a problem. There are, however, three more fundamental reasons for seeking an outsider's viewpoint than executives' indecision: poorly pesented solutions; lack of credibility of the persons in charge of recommending the "best" option; and personal issues such as antagonism, political pressure, and jockeying for position in the hierarchy.

Whatever the reasons, the consultant's survival instinct will cause him to side with the seat of power in the organization. Much to his relief, he will find that a number of proposed options can be discarded without endangering his "professional integrity." As for the remainder, they are reasonably sound so that at little risk, for the company or for him, he can choose or reject any of the options.

It becomes a simple matter of redoing the analysis before picking the answer that most closely approaches the opinions of the influential members of management—and incorporating minor variances for good measure that reflect other opinions. So much for independence.

The most common reason for hiring a consultant is to supplement limited in-house capabilities or to handle a project that company personnel lack the time to deal with. If it is understood that a consultant's services are being used on a temporary basis, one cannot argue with this reason. Of course, before the hiring, someone within the company must define the job to be performed and designate a person to supervise the work continually.

While this approach evokes a "mother's helper" image, it is advantageous to both parties, provided that the fee is fair. The client gets the job done, and the consulting firm may have the opportunity of giving staff members on-the-job training at little risk and for an acceptable profit.

The three common reasons that I have considered do not meet the most basic criterion: a management consultant must be a last-resort solution for any project in which he is not merely to assume the passive role of executor. Journeymen consultants are quick to seize on the opportunity for chargeable time, and to them any reason is acceptable. In the context of the three reasons described, however, consulting is hardly descriptive of the work.

WHEN TO HIRE

It is wise to treat your problem as a difficult sickness: the symptoms are clearly identifiable, the causes are not, and the standard remedies do not work. In short, you should hire a consultant when your organization finds itself beyond the stage of two aspirins and rest for a headache that refuses to go away.

The consultant's usefulness is determined by the results of implementing his recommendations, not by the recommendations themselves. Consequently, if you doubt the quality of the managers and subordinates who must live, day in and day out, with solutions prescribed by nonoperational outsiders, or if you doubt the ability of top and middle management to react to future environmental changes affecting the original recommendations—then you are not ready for a consultant.

Before going on, I should make a distinction between private industry and government entities. Federal, state, and local governments are often obliged to balance necessary projects against restrictive budgets and uncontrolled staff increases. An attempt to hire experts on a permanent basis may run afoul of civil service regulations on salary levels and qualifications, legislative opposition, and public displeasure at the size of the government bureaucracy. It is much simpler to make use of a hidden fund for temporary consulting help, which is seldom contested. Taking this step may be unreasonable, but it is a fact of life.

In private industry, consultants provide two distinct services: specialized advice for the future and imaginative solutions for the present.

Specialized Advice

Most advice provided by consultants relates to future investments or approaches to new developments such as designing a five-year plan for new EDP applications and hardware, defining the needs of a distribution system, establishing the desired characteristics of a new product in a developing market, selecting the site for an overseas production facility, or locating an acquisition candidate. In undertaking such a project, the consultant should possess an extensive background coupled with advanced techniques that the company is unlikely to have now or to want to acquire.

A consultant's effectiveness in such tasks is closely related to the client's ability to express his needs, understand the results, and implement the recommendations. This scope excludes esoteric activities such as long-range planning or long-term economic forecasting.

In the case of long-range planning, it is difficult to comprehend how the same management team that cannot outline its objectives and strategy could implement someone else's plans—not to mention evaluate his worth or reaction to unexpected variances. A new management team, not a surrogate, is needed.

Similarly, a sweeping economic forecast that predicts a glowing future for any country willing to pay for the work or a gloomy forecast for the world to satisfy the latest ecological trend have two traits in common: actual data can be conveniently readjusted in the face of unexpected but frequent incidents such as oil crises, and 20 years from now such forecasts will be as academic as last year's astrology charts.

Imaginative Solutions

The greatest contribution a consultant can make is his experience. He has seen your problem, or a variant thereof, in other situations; he has devised solutions to it or has absorbed solutions implemented by previous clients. He should be a living compendium of case studies.

Thus the imagination a consultant brings to your problems is not necessarily superior to yours; you are simply taking a shortcut. While the top executives of your company, given a little time, could reinvent the wheel, the use of outside expertise allows you to examine, at a reasonable cost, all the wheels that have been invented.

Of course, you think your wheel has some unique features. Demystification is needed on the subject: with the exception of technical aspects such as manufacturing processes, the same managerial problems repeatedly crop up. In data processing, for instance, the great new theory is "distributed processing." It is no more than a return to the decentralized approach of 15 years ago, with the differences that minicomputers have become extremely powerful and some centralization is now possible through the accessibility of telecommunications.

A consultant who knew in 1961 how to design interactive production, marketing, and financial systems should do as good a job for you in 1977. All he needs is a computer expert to introduce to the design some technical innovations, if necessary, such as data-base management and teleprocessing.

WHOM TO HIRE

Consultants and consulting organizations can be arbitrarily separated into three categories: individual specialists, small firms with staffs of specialists, and large, multidisciplinary companies. Each presents advantages and drawbacks that you should consider carefully in addition to needs and expectations of your own.

Quality of the Resource

As a rule, in dealing with an individual consultant, you can get a clear picture of his experience, personality, and performance because the person whom you interview is the one who will do the job. You can easily check the references and verify the extent of his or her involvement in previous projects. It is very likely, at any rate, that you singled him out through the recommendation of a business contact, so the references are usually personal.

Much the same is true of a small firm with, say, a half dozen members; almost certainly you will work with the same people who are selling the job. Generally, such firms are formed to pool resources in order to provide each individual with a steadier, if sometimes lower, income.

Large- and medium-size companies are altogether a different breed. Their duties are often split between the "sellers" and the "doers," between the "managers" and the "operators." Those persons with technical expertise and the ability to sell handle the preliminary talks, define the approach, set the extent of the job, and, most important, establish the size and qualifications of the team that will work on the project. Quite often also, they supervise the work, their involvement depending on the experience of the team.

In regard to that experience, the client must take a stand. In their proposals, management consultants often include a reference list of clients who are either in your industry or whose problems appear to be similar to yours as well as the names and backgrounds of some of the staff. Such references, intended to influence your choice, may be full of distortions. Here are some of them:

- You have no assurance that the consultants listed will actually form part of the team. Invariably the list includes top officers who are now dedicated to the administration of the company. Precisely because of their technical qualifications, experience, and reputation, they have climbed the hierarchical ladder to a level where they have ceased to be consultants.

- The written backgrounds of staff members often highlight those areas of competence that best suit the needs of the project. This emphasis may not be commensurate with an individual's actual ability or experience.

- The description of a person's work pinpoints neither his other real role nor the extent of his involvement. Words such as "participated in" or "assisted" may conceal his minor role in the project.

- For reasons of confidentiality, clients are described in elliptical terms such as "a major this" or "a leading that." In a brochure there is reason for confidentiality, but you are entitled to a verbal identification of these clients. If your prospective consultant does not trust your discretion, why trust his?

- Work performed for previous clients is often described in as little detail or with as many generalities as the background of the consultants. Consulting firms seldom, if ever, describe the *practical* results of their involvement. Rarely will they commit to paper a bold assertion such as "through this project the client achieved X dollars in savings" or "gained Y% of the market." (Obviously, you will also never read, "The client decided the

recommendations were inapplicable and did not implement them.")

- Successful jobs may have been performed by another office of the firm in another part of the world; and, if so, that is where the know-how for your project will remain.

You should evaluate the firm as you would an individual, regardless of any objections it may raise, on the basis that it will be fully responsible for reaching the established objectives. Moreover, if you are planning to sign the consultant to a fixed-price or fixed-ceiling contract, you should stipulate that the firm will absorb any cost overruns. You should also insist on the inclusion of a penalty for overruns that is severe enough to motivate the consultant to meet the deadlines. There would be little consolation for you in knowing that the financial burden of an overrun or of redoing parts of a poorly executed project lay on the consulting firm; the fact is that other deadlines important to you may have been missed and related scheduled action may have to be delayed.

Apart from the questions of payment and inconvenience to you, you must consider the quality of the work done in the overrun period. It is reasonable to assume that if the consulting firm must work overtime to correct its mistakes at its own expense, the firm's greatest concern will be for speed. The objective is no longer to do the best job but to finish it quickly.

As a prospective client, you are of course entitled to meet the participants scheduled for the assignment—though you may have to overcome objections based on "the firm's policy." Treat these participants as individual parts of a whole, try to evaluate their actual involvement in previous projects, and explore their background and experience—just as you would for an independent consultant.

Obtain the hourly or daily rate and establish whether it is commensurate with the experience and technical know-how of each participant and the amount of responsibility each will have in the team. If the work to be done lies in a specialized area of your company for which you are not directly responsible and in which the performance of its manager is not in question, include him or her in these discussions.

All this is time-consuming and may seem unjustified, particularly if you are considering one of the well-known management consulting firms. But you do not select a consultant on the basis of a name brand or a fancy brochure. By making the effort now, you can assure yourself that the price you pay for the services will be reflected in the quality of the work done.

Does Size Matter?

Some large consulting firms claim that they offer greater expertise in more fields than their small competitors. When, however, a client holding this expectation contracts with one of the major firms, he often just gets more fields. The successful, respected large firms limit the number of fields in which they seek business and on which they stake their reputations. For the client, it is not a question of putting all his eggs in the same basket but of putting the proper egg in a well-selected basket.

One category of management consultants I have not considered is the "Big Eight" and other large audit firms. Their consulting departments fall in the "supermarket" classification: "you need it, we've got it." Actually, however, they have four undisputed areas of expertise, at least as far as private industry is concerned: finance, EDP, executive

search, and employee benefits. These strong points derive from their early role of providing supplementary services to audit clients.

A majority of audit partners in these firms still treat their consulting activities as the frosting on the auditing cake. One can understand that an audit represents repeated income, year after year, and clients seldom switch; that an audit is mandatory for a publicly owned company; and that responsibility, until the recent past at least, is limited.

Consulting projects, on the other hand, are usually one-time affairs; expertise must be sold amid fierce competition; recommendations fully engage those who make them; and mistakes are factual rather than subject to interpretation of accounting standards. In providing consulting services, the auditors are merely cleaning your windshield while continuing to perform their main task of pumping gas.

The question of independence is important. Would the outside auditors criticize weaknesses in your internal controls when the system has been designed by their own consulting department? Can they be truly objective when they highlight the need for new administrative procedures or an inventory control system?

Until this recurring controversy is settled, there is one simple approach to take: never use the same firm for both auditing and management consulting at the same time. You will find that the competitive instincts of accounting firms create a better product in both fields if you keep them separate.

HOW MUCH TO PAY

Consultants generally calculate and quote their professional fees on an hourly or a daily basis, on the amount of time estimated to be necessary to do the job, and, for their assignment teams, on the number and category of each consultant. Category rates for members of a consulting team are as much a function of their experience as of their salary ranges.

There are two special cases: the "on-call" consultant, whose services are sought on a regular basis but for short periods of time and who charges only for the time spent; and the consultant "on retainer," whom you pay a minimum fee for a certain period whether or not you make use of his services. In both cases, the consultant normally acts more as an adviser on particular matters, such as taxes, than as a problem solver with wider scope.

Rates are usually competitive and depend heavily on reputation, years of experience, and specialization. An individual consultant's fee may strike you as very high, since you know he will be the sole beneficiary of the income and that multiplication of his daily rate by the number of working days in the year probably shows him to be earning far more than you do. The catch, though, is that he will be lucky to work six to eight months of the year; the rest of the time he is prospecting for new jobs.

In the case of a consulting firm, its rate must cover overhead, salaries, benefits, management, and complimentary services, whether or not you are being charged directly for professional staff services.

Factor of Expenses

Traveling expenses are easily identified, estimated, and budgeted. Such is not the case, however, with nontraveling expenses—that is, secretarial help, typing, editing, printing, copying, telephone, and other ancillary services. Their impact should not be ignored, since they are either included in the daily rate structure or billed in addition to the professional fee at an average ceiling of 10% to 15% of the fee.

In its proposal to the prospective client, the consultant should clearly state his policy on nontraveling expenses. If they are included in the rate schedule, you are then in the same situation as a consumer in a store that accepts certain credit cards; the store's prices take into account the commission to be paid to the credit-card issuer, whether or not you use the card. If nontraveling expenses are included in the rate structure, you can do little about it, though you can make it a point of negotiation. But such added costs hardly constitute a prime criterion in selecting a consultant.

Individual consultants must usually pay extra for services such as typing and preparation of audio-visual presentations. Here you have two options: request itemized copies of bills paid by the consultant for services directly related to the job or make as many of these services available to him as your resources permit.

If the cost of nontraveling expenses concerns you when negotiating with a large consulting firm, you have a right to request the rates it applies to administrative services. Don't be surprised to find that they are higher than those of companies whose main business it is to provide these services. While the added cost may not be significant, it says much about the philosophy and efficiency of the consulting firm.

Finishing time:_____

RAPID READING COMPREHENSION CHECK: "How to Get a Good Consultant"

1. Small companies are apt to use the services of a consultant because:

   a. ＿＿＿ they have much money in their consultant account.

   b. ＿＿＿ there are fewer specialists in the company.

   c. ＿＿＿ their problems are greater than those of large companies.

2. According to the author, consultants usually:

   a. ＿＿＿ side with those in the top level of the organization.

   b. ＿＿＿ disagree with those in the top level of the organization.

   c. ＿＿＿ are completely independent.

3. According to the author, an organization should hire a consultant:

   a. ＿＿＿ only when one is definitely needed.

   b. ＿＿＿ often as a means of revitalizing the organization.

   c. ＿＿＿ only when imaginative solutions are needed.

4. If you doubt that members of the organization can implement recommendations, then:

   a. ＿＿＿ hire a consultant immediately.

   b. ＿＿＿ retrain your top and middle managers.

   c. ＿＿＿ do not hire a consultant.

5. Consultants provide most of their advice on:

   a. ＿＿＿ improving the interpersonal relations of the staff.

   b. ＿＿＿ future investments and new developments.

   c. ＿＿＿ specialized in-service skills training.

6. A consultant's greatest contribution is his:

   a. ＿＿＿ personality.

   b. ＿＿＿ academic training.

   c. ＿＿＿ experience.

7. When dealing with an individual consultant, you will find it easy to:

   a. ＿＿＿ determine his weaknesses.

   b. ＿＿＿ negotiate for a lower consultant fee.

   c. ＿＿＿ check his references.

8. A weakness of the large consulting companies is that:

   a. ＿＿＿ they are too busy to do an adequate job.

   b. ＿＿＿ their references may be distorted.

c. _____ their fees are much higher.

9. When signing a consultant to a fixed-price contract, be sure that it stipulates:

a. _____ when your payment is due.

b. _____ the number of consultants on the job.

c. _____ a penalty for overruns.

10. The consultant's recommendation should be:

a. _____ usable.

b. _____ clearly written.

c. _____ esoteric.

Check your answers with the Answer Key.

9
Reading Rate and Comprehension: Posttests

INTRODUCTION

The point was made in chapter 1 that the one question you would want answered after completing the exercises in this book is, "How much did I improve?" The purpose of this chapter is to answer that question.

You will take two posttests to determine your reading performance. By comparing the results of these tests with your pretests, you will be able to compute the improvement in your reading efficiency rate. Directions for scoring the tests and for determining your reading efficiency improvement rate are on pages 231–233.

INSTRUCTIONS FOR POSTTEST 1: "Inside the Country, Outside the Law"

The purpose of this posttest and the one that follows is to determine your present reading efficiency. Time yourself as you read the following selection. When you finish reading the selection, write down your reading time in the space provided at the end of the selection. Then answer the comprehension questions in Posttest 1 based on the selection. Directions for scoring your posttests and determining how much your reading has improved follow Posttest 2.

Posttest 1

Inside the Country, Outside the Law
Ray Marshall

Recently, a comic strip appeared in *The Washington Post* which sheds some light on the grave problem of illegal aliens, or as I prefer to call them, "undocumented workers."

The comic strip featured the owner of a Chinese restaurant, but it could have as easily been a Mexican restaurant or a greasy-spoon diner. The restaurant owner is saying, "Some of my chefs do get temperamental, but I know how to keep them in line." At this point, the straight man says, "How's that, Lee?" And the owner answers, "I just pick up the kitchen phone and say, 'Operator, give me the Immigration Service.'"

It's one of those moments where humor cuts a little too close to reality for comfort. For, in a few words, this comic strip has accurately portrayed the working conditions that many undocumented workers face in this country.

It is a classic carrot-and-stick situation. The carrots are jobs in America that pay better wages than are available in the worker's native land. The stick is that the undocumented worker is subject to blackmail every day of the year.

What few have realized is the degree to which the problem of undocumented workers is one of the most serious civil liberties problems that we face. For the undocumented workers represent an underclass who live among us but are outside of the protections of all of our basic labor laws.

There have been studies which have found that as many as 40 percent of all Mexicans working in this country illegally are being paid less than the minimum wage. Other undocumented workers find that they have been hired at one wage and paid—when they are paid at all—at another. Often, undocumented workers are forced to endure unsafe working conditions or brutal treatment by their employers and other unscrupulous people who always seem to be standing by to exploit the defenseless.

When an American citizen or a resident alien is faced with these problems, there are many effective remedies available under the law. When an undocumented worker is deprived of his rights, he has no one to call. He does not dare complain to the Government for fear that he will be deported. And he knows that any complaint to his employer will only lead to a call to the Immigration Service.

The result is that the undocumented worker labors "scared and hard." He is in a country that prides itself on its political freedoms, but he lives outside the protection of the law. He works in a country that prides itself on the "safety nets" that it has created for the American worker, yet he is totally at the mercy of his employer. In a very real sense, the undocumented worker is a man—or woman—without a country.

Unlike unemployment, or energy, or welfare reform, the problem of undocumented aliens has not received longstanding public discussion. Too many people have clung to the mistaken notion that the problem was both temporary and reversible. Although the flow of undocumented workers may vary from year to year, the basic pattern is clear. As long as there are vast discrepancies between the opportunities in this country and those in the underdeveloped world, the United States will continue to be a beacon to the unemployed around the world.

Estimates suggest that Mexico is the country which is the largest source of undocumented workers. This is understandable since there is no border in the world with more extreme economic differences than the border between us and Mexico. As long as Mexico has one of the world's highest birth rates, as long as Mexico cannot create enough jobs, then the temptation to sneak across the border will be irresistible.

The Immigration and Naturalization Service has never been one of the more popular Government agencies. This is inevitable since the task of deporting individuals is one of the saddest jobs that any government has to do. It is rarely the affluent who are deported. Those who fear the Immigration Service are almost always the destitute and the friendless.

None of us want to return to the days of mass roundups of aliens. None of us want the border between us and Mexico to look like the Berlin Wall. None of us are insensitive to the terrible human tragedies that can accompany immigration policy. Yet continued inaction on the issue of illegal aliens would bring grave consequences, since the existence of an underclass of undocumented workers represents a serious civil liberties problem.

No democracy can flourish with an underclass outside the protections of its basic law. If history is any guide, perhaps the first generation of undocumented workers will endure their privations in relative silence. But the children of these undocumented workers will doubtless be the focus of the civil rights movement of the 1980's.

Another problem with undocumented workers is their effect on the American labor market. The use of substandard labor becomes a self-fulfilling prophecy. Employers lack an economic incentive to modernize labor-intensive methods that feed on cheap labor. These employers structure jobs that are so demeaning that only the frightened and desperately poor undocumented workers will take them. And then they claim that they can't get anyone but the undocumented workers to take these jobs.

In understanding this problem, it is important to recognize the ways in which today's illegal immigrants are different from the immigrant streams who entered this country in the 19th and 20th centuries.

The European immigrants came to this country legally and never had to hide from the Immigration and Naturalization Service. The European immigrants came in an era when there were no basic protections for American workers. There were no minimum wage laws, no full employment policy, and no occupational safety and health acts. Today's undocumented workers repre-

sent a subclass that allows employers to undercut these standards that we have fought for so long to enact into law.

There are many demographic factors that point up the differences, as well. Most of the 19th century immigrants were from countries with low birth rates and declining opportunities. Today's undocumented workers come from countries with birth rates that are soaring out of control and eroding what jobs do exist in their economics. Lastly, the 19th century immigrants came at a time when this country was not conscious of long-term unemployment. Today's workers, of course, come at a time when we are all seriously worried about job opportunities for American citizens.

Any actions taken to address the problem of undocumented workers must be based on the circumstances surrounding today's illegal influx. The first point is an awareness that the problem of undocumented workers illustrates the degree to which the United States is affected by the problems of the underdeveloped world. We can no longer turn a deaf ear to the problems of world poverty. The millions of undocumented workers who live among us illustrate that world poverty is not just their problem; it's our problem, as well.

Ultimately, the only total solution to the problem of undocumented workers is the creation of jobs in the countries from which these workers flee. There is, of course, a very real limit on how much we can do by ourselves, and we cannot wait for these other countries to solve their problems before we tackle ours. But I think that it is important to target some of the money which we spend on bilateral and multilateral foreign aid on the real problem of creating jobs in the source countries of the stream of undocumented workers.

A second consideration is a recognition that it is important to eliminate the incentives for undocumented workers to enter this country. That means a focus on the employers who hire these workers and subject them to substandard pay and working conditions. Ultimately, illegal immigration must be seen as a labor market problem. And the only way to alleviate it is to develop some system of civil penalties for those employers who hire undocumented workers.

Another important component of any comprehensive policy on undocumented workers is some form of amnesty. Most of the undocumented workers are hard-working, law-abiding men and women who came to this country in quest of greater opportunity. Many of them have developed family and community ties. It would represent a personal tragedy—and a loss of many productive individuals—if they were to spend the rest of their lives in terror of the Immigration Service.

Amnesty is the most compassionate thing that this country can do. It is also the only practical approach to a problem that for too long has been ignored. The days of the mass roundup of suspect aliens is over. That's why amnesty must be an ingredient in any humane policy for dealing with the problem of undocumented workers.

A final point is that the problem of undocumented workers cannot be considered apart from the country's immigration policies. Immigration is a complex issue raising many questions and historically arousing many fears. Yet immigration policy must be a key consideration in efforts to address the problem of undocumented workers equitably and well.

Finishing time:_____

POSTTEST 1: "Inside the Country, Outside the Law"

1. The situation depicted in the cartoon strip illustrates:

   a. _____ the dilemma facing many undocumented workers.

   b. _____ a typical restaurant owner.

   c. _____ a gross exaggeration of the truth.

2. The "carrot" in the "carrot-and-stick" situation described in the article is:

   a. _____ the workers.

   b. _____ the fringe benefits.

   c. _____ the jobs.

3. Most undocumented workers receive:

   a. _____ the minimum wage.

   b. _____ food and shelter, but no salary.

   c. _____ less than the minimum wage.

4. When undocumented workers have work-related problems, they can:

   a. _____ complain to the Government.

   b. _____ do little or nothing about it.

   c. _____ usually solve them by conferring with their employers.

5. Compared to the energy problem, the undocumented alien problem has received:

a. _____ less public attention.

b. _____ more public attention.

c. _____ about the same amount of public attention.

6. The largest source of undocumented workers comes from:

a. _____ Canada.

b. _____ Mexico.

c. _____ England.

7. Employers rationalize hiring undocumented workers by claiming that they are:

a. _____ better workers.

b. _____ the only ones who will take the jobs.

c. _____ less likely to leave the job.

8. Undocumented workers have:

a. _____ helped to improve the economy of the United States.

b. _____ generally returned to their homeland.

c. _____ increased the problem of job opportunities for Americans.

9. One solution to the problem is to:

a. _____ help to create jobs in poor foreign countries.

b. _____ severely punish undocumented workers.

c. _____ force employers to treat undocumented workers more humanely.

10. The author's attitude towards undocumented workers is:

a. _____ negative.

b. _____ condescending.

c. _____ sympathetic.

Check your answers with the Answer Key.

INSTRUCTIONS FOR POSTTEST 2: "Dealing With Slow Payers"
Time yourself as you read the following article. When you finish reading the selection, write down your reading time in the space provided at the end of the selection. Then answer the comprehension questions in Posttest 2 based on the selection. Directions for scoring your posttests and determining how much your reading has improved follow Posttest 2.

Posttest 2

Dealing With Slow Payers
Rick Stephan Hayes

Most people when they borrow money (or get supplies on credit) have every intention of paying the debt back. It is extremely rare that a businessperson will borrow money or take supplies on credit with the intention of never repaying. Usually something happens in the interim time between getting the supplies and paying for them that forces the businessperson, against his better judgment, to become slow in his payments.

Generally, the reasons for becoming slow are business financial problems. If you (the credit manager) have done your job well, that is, you did a full analysis on the customer's financial condition before you extended credit, your chances of encountering this problem will be rare. But unfortunately no matter how careful you are, problems will arise. Besides business financial problems there are several other reasons for a customer becoming a slow payer including oversight; bad paying habits; laziness; personal misfortune or disaster; or dissatisfaction with you, the supplier. Problems of customer oversight or dissatisfaction with orders can be easily solved and do not present a permanent problem for collections. Laziness may be turned into action by a phone call or personal visit. Financial overextension and business and personal disasters are the problems that will cause you the most difficulties.

Collections from slow payers is a most delicate process. If collections are done right they should create goodwill, retain business already on the books, and promote repeat business. Collections done poorly can cause loss of temper, animosity, and loss of business. The procedures required to maintain good collections are simple but sometimes go against human nature. Remember collectors are salespeople (aggressive, patient, and optimistic) who are selling a very difficult product: *present* payment for *past* benefits.

In the past few years, accounts receivable and collection periods have been growing at unprecedented rates. Recently, especially in the poor economic years of 1974 and 1975, business started developing an automatic tendency to let suppliers become bankers by slowing or withholding payments. If you realize that this is happening and develop techniques for combating the problems (such as staying on top of collections and billing sooner) you will be able to do well.

I do not need to tell you that collections are important to profits. But did you know that if you have bad-debt losses of only $50, and your company's net profit percentage is 5 percent, $1,000 in sales would be required to cover the losses?

The first step to good collection is a well-planned collection policy. Collection policy should establish the time allowed to pass before the first collection step is taken and the intervals between each stage of the collection process. Collection policy should include guidelines for when to use collection agencies. When, if ever, attorneys should be used for suits, should also be made clear by the collection policy. The amount of bad-debt losses allowable and at what stage debt should be considered "bad" and written off should be understood.

The major aspects of a collection procedure are classification of the debtor; determination of collection tools to be used; and improvement of collection efforts.

In classifying customers and getting results from collections, it is best to do the following. First, you should research the customer's file, then classify the customer by past performance or by an educated guess. Next you should use your collection tools, such as letters and telephones, in the order of reminders, appeals, and compulsion. If these tools are not successful, then the credit manager must use outside collection agencies or the courts. During the entire procedure, feedback from the courts or agents should be sought.

CLASSIFICATION OF ACCOUNTS

Earlier, we discussed the general classification of accounts into automatic (orders processed without checking for almost every amount); semiautomatic (orders up to a certain amount processed without checking); nonautomatic (average); and marginal categories. When accounts become past due (which could happen to any of these classifications) they fall into new categories related to the cause of their delinquency. The categories of delinquent payers are: confused, negligent, not-at-fault delinquent, seasonally delinquent, chronically slow, and cannot pay. Each of these categories must be dealt with differently just as each type of account (automatic, semiautomatic, and so on) must be dealt with differently.

Confused accounts are accounts which are either unclear about what the terms are, have lost their invoices, or who do not want to pay the account "because the balance is too small to be bothered with." These types of slow payers will pay you once they understand the terms, are sent duplicate invoices, or when they are billed for a larger amount that they can tack onto the "small balance." All these accounts are basically honest, and, with the exception of the "small balance" folks, will cause little difficulty to your collection efforts. You can understand that certain accounts would rather wait until they have larger balances before they pay, but all these small balances add up.

Negligent accounts are those where the debtor has the money and the intention to pay, but needs reminding that the bill is past due. Sometimes company employees are instructed not to pay until they get a past due notice. One way to solve this problem, if you notice that a customer is doing this constantly, is to send out the past due notice early.

Not-at-fault delinquent accounts are those that have had some disaster strike. This would include natural disasters such as fire, flood, earthquake, or blizzard, as well as difficulties such as material shortages or labor troubles. If any of these disasters occur, you should do what you can to get your customer back on his feet. These are usually short-term problems and do not affect your long-term collection efforts. Instead of pressing the customer in times like these, it might be a good idea to explain that you understand the difficulties and that your company will voluntarily suspend the debt repayment required for a few months. Your customer will remember you when the troubles are over, and the future benefit to your company far outweighs the temporary loss of income.

Seasonally delinquent accounts are those who fall behind in payments when their slow season comes. When production is slow, but a company must maintain its fixed overhead costs, they may experience temporary monetary problems. If the company is well-managed, they would have made allowances for this during the fast periods, but unfortunately there is little you can do about this except wait. Just make sure if you have to carry this customer that you are not the only one not being paid.

Chronically slow accounts fall into two types: (1) the customer who has the money but makes creditors wait as a matter of policy and (2) the customer who is undercapitalized and depends on trade credit to finance operations. Customers who have the money but make you wait are a tough case because they figure that they can go to a competitor if you do not like waiting. The best way to deal with this type of customer is personally and/or speed up your past due notices. If you find that the account is undercapitalized and is using your money to keep afloat, it might be wise to review your terms or even drop the account. The type of customer who falls into this category is the chronic slow payer who promises payment, but does not keep the promise or even answer your inquiries. The marginal account that is new or on your "watch list" might also fall into this category. The other two types of customers whom most credit persons have run across in this category are the complainer who refuses to pay for any plausible reason and the dissembler who insists that the check has already been mailed when in fact it is still sitting on his desk.

Cannot pay accounts may admit that they are temporarily short of capital pending a loan or some capital injection. In fact, they may be seriously close to insolvency. These are the accounts that give the credit person the biggest headaches and may end up as bad debts. The best thing to do is to press for immediate and full or partial payment. If your efforts prove unsuccessful, consider the possibility that aid from your company and other suppliers might rescue the debtor company. Attempts should be made to bring the creditors together to work out a solution. If the company is virtually bankrupt, it is time to investigate legal action. Remember, it is always better to catch this type of situation early and do something about it, than to wait and let it sink under its own weight.

Overall, with all the different categories and types of delinquency, your collection program must be flexible. It must be designed to cover all your past dues, while at the same time conforming to your company policy. First, does your organization expect that your customers will be reasonably prompt or is a certain leniency extended? When is the proper time for you to begin pressing for payment? One day after the invoice becomes past due or a week? two weeks? a month? Usually the longer the paying period terms, the longer you will delay your dunning process. If your company requires payment in 10 days after shipment, you may want to send the first reminder more quickly than a company with 60-day terms.

Finishing time:_____

POSTTEST 2: "Dealing With Slow Payers"

1. The major reason for slow payment is:

   a. _____ bad paying habits.

   b. _____ financial.

   c. _____ laziness.

2. It is most important to be patient with:

   a. _____ not-at-fault delinquents.

   b. _____ confused accounts.

   c. _____ cannot pay accounts.

3. In recent years, collection periods have:

   a. _____ increased.

   b. _____ decreased.

   c. _____ maintained the status quo.

4. The first step in a good collection procedure is to:

   a. _____ send a past-due notice immediately.

   b. _____ contact the customer personally.

   c. _____ establish a policy.

5. After you research the delin-

quent customer's file, you should:

a. _____ use your collection tools.

b. _____ classify the customer.

c. _____ contact an outside collection agency.

6. The customer who loses his invoice is usually classified as a:

a. _____ negligent account.

b. _____ chronically slow account

c. _____ confused account.

7. The best way to approach the chronically slow account who has the money is:

a. _____ personally.

b. _____ with a collection agency.

c. _____ patiently.

8. It is a good practice to send past-due notices early to:

a. _____ confused accounts.

b. _____ negligent accounts.

c. _____ seasonally delinquent accounts.

9. Prompt action is most important when dealing with:

a. _____ confused accounts.

b. _____ cannot pay accounts.

c. _____ negligent accounts.

10. With respect to *all* types of account categories, the collector should be:

a. _____ flexible.

b. _____ aggressive.

c. _____ patient.

Check your answers with the Answer Key.

HOW TO SCORE YOUR POSTTESTS

Reading Rate

Refer to the Words Per Minute: Rapid Reading Chart to determine your reading rate for each posttest. On page 251, you will find the Posttest Reading Efficiency Chart. In the blank located between the words *Posttest 1* and *WPM* (words per minute), write in your reading rate score. Do the same for Posttest 2.

Comprehension

The answers to the comprehension questions for the two posttests appear at the end of the Answer Key. Credit yourself with ten points for each question you answered correctly. When you have determined your posttest scores, enter them on your Posttest Reading Efficiency Chart.

Place your comprehension scores in the blanks between *WPM* and *%* *comprehension.*

Averages

To determine your average reading rate score, add your reading rate scores for the two posttests and divide by two. Determine your average comprehension score by adding your comprehension scores for the two posttests and dividing by two. Enter these average scores on the posttest chart.

Reading Efficiency

You can now compute your current Reading Efficiency by taking your average rate (WPM) and multiplying it by your average percent of comprehension.

$$\underline{\hspace{3cm}} \times \underline{\hspace{4cm}} = \underline{\hspace{4cm}}$$
Average Rate   Average % Comprehension   Reading Efficiency

Enter this score on your chart.

Rate Flexibility Score

You can determine your rate flexibility score by subtracting your Posttest 2 Reading Rate score (line 2) from your Posttest 1 Reading Rate score (line 1). Write this number in the space next to *Rate Flexibility Score* located on your Posttest Reading Efficiency Chart. If your reading rate for Posttest 2 was higher than it was for Posttest 1, then write a zero next to the flexibility score.

HOW MUCH DID YOU IMPROVE?

Follow the steps below to determine your reading efficiency percentage improvement.

1. Subtract your Pretest Reading Efficiency score from your Posttest Reading Efficiency score. This gives you your *gain score.*
2. Divide your Pretest Reading Efficiency score into your *gain score.* This will give your percentage improvement. An example follows.

Posttest Reading Efficiency: 420
Pretest Reading Efficiency: − 205
                                    ─────
                                    215 Gain score

$$
\begin{array}{r}
1.04 \\
205 \overline{)215.00} \\
\underline{205} \\
1000 \\
\underline{820} \\
180
\end{array}
$$ = 104, or 104%

Percentage improvement 104%.

Space is provided on page 251 to calculate your percentage of improvement.

Most business people who have completed materials similar to the ones contained in this book have made gains between 40 percent and 200 percent. The author sincerely hopes you did as well or better!

Answer Key: Comprehension Checks

Note: Your comprehension scores for the pre- and posttests, the rapid reading exercises, and the skim reading exercises should be recorded on the appropriate progress charts. The untimed readings are not placed on a chart. Most of the exercises contain ten multiple choice questions; therefore, you should credit yourself ten points for each correct answer. There are special scoring instructions for exercises that contain fewer than ten questions.

Chapter 1: Reading Rate and Comprehension: Pretests

Pretest 1: "The Theme of the Park is Safety"

1. b
2. a
3. c
4. a
5. b
6. c
7. a
8. a
9. c
10. c

Pretest 2: "To Whom Should You Extend Credit—Nonfinancial Analysis"

1. c
2. a
3. a
4. c
5. b
6. b
7. c
8. a
9. c
10. b

Chapter 2: Skimming

Purposeful Skimming: " 'Sexism' and Modern Business Communications"

Any five of these nine statements:

1. Use a subject line instead of a salutation.
2. Use *Ms.* exclusively for women.
3. Use a signature that reveals gender.
4. Use the plural pronoun form or mix *he* and *she.*
5. Refer to women as *women* rather than *girls.*
6. Use parallel expressions.

234

7. Avoid insinuations that women are less capable than men.

8. Avoid using the occupational ending man, as in chair*man*.

9. Avoid using gender modifiers such as *male* nurse.

Purposeful Skimming: "Secretarial Survival Skills"

Any six of these nine statements:

1. Ask questions.

2. Listen.

3. Record information.

4. Locate information.

5. Develop chronological files.

6. Follow directions.

7. Track the executive.

8. Make decisions.

9. Work under pressure.

Purposeful Skimming: "Real Estate"

Any three of these four statements:

1. By claiming that land value will double every five years.

2. By giving the impression that land is being sold very quickly.

3. By claiming that valuable resources go with the land senior citizens will buy.

4. By offering 'free land' for the price of a deed transfer.

Purposeful Skimming: "The Office of the Future and Its Impact on Employees"

Any five of the following eight statements.

1. It will use a total systems approach.

2. Heavy dependence on electronic devices.

3. Less use of paper.

4. Concern for energy conservation.

5. Open office, moveable partitions, and modular furniture.

6. Secretaries will be administrative assistants.

7. Employees will need to be more adaptable, flexible, and creative.

8. Employees will need to make important decisions and to have a technological orientation.

Purposeful Skimming: "Essentials For Becoming a Top-Level Secretary"

The correct answer is italicized:

The characteristic that separates the top-level secretary from the average secretary is that the top-level secretary can *make decisions*.

Purposeful Skimming: "The Moral and Ethical Climate in Today's Business World"

1. b

2. Any three of the following statements.

   a. Bendix has a clear policy of having an uncompromising standard of honesty.

   b. Audits are organized.

   c. Definitions were redefined.

   d. New guidelines and instructions were communicated throughout the company.

   e. Bendix conforms to the guidelines of the organization for Economic Cooperation and Development.

Chapter 3: Main Idea

Selected Passages

1. Topic: You (the manager)

   Main Idea: You should encourage your workers
                             to make decisions with the recogni-
                             tion that mistakes will be made.

   Check Out: *Why:*If workers just try to avoid
                             making mistakes, work will not
                             improve.

                             *How:*Let workers know you want
                             them to make decisions and
                             you expect mistakes to be
                             made; do not expect workers to
                             be up to your standards of
                             being correct about 58 percent
                             of the time; admit your own
                             mistakes.

2. Topic: You (the manager)

   Main Idea: You have a weakness in your organi-
                             zation if you have positions that
                             require people to have unique com-
                             binations of abilities.

   Check Out: *Examples:*Salesmen who must have
                             the ability to both open
                             and service accounts;
                             managers who must have
                             the ability to both start and
                             manage new facilities;
                             clergymen who must func-
                             tion both as ministers and
                             administrators; professors
                             who are expected to per-
                             form well both as teachers
                             and as researchers.

3. Topic: Assistants

   Main Idea: Assistants often do not know what
                             their responsibilities are.

   Check Out: *Examples:*He may substitute for his
                             boss; do detail work; carry
                             out special projects; have

clear-cut responsibilities; function at the pleasure of his boss; may train to replace his boss; may do boss's paper work.

4. Topic:

Images

Main Idea:

A good image is necessary if you expect to be a quick success.

Check Out:

Why: You are competing with established businesses while you are unknown.
How: Plan carefully and conscientiously.

5. Topic:

Promiscuity

Main Idea:

Promiscuity in business can create a damaging image.

Check Out:

Why: It will label you as an individual of poor character; your career can be hindered or ruined.

6. Topic:

McDonald's new headquarters.

Main Idea:

McDonald's new open-planning headquarters was well received by the critics.

Check Out:

Examples: Building Design and Construction praised it, as did *Interiors.*

7. Topic:

Companies

Main Idea:

Companies are telling little about their innovations.

Check Out:

Why: They do not want the world to know about their failures; but more importantly, successful innovations are seen as highly valued discoveries and often result in companies going into the business of job consulting. Such companies include Travelers, American Airlines, Lockheed, and Ralston Purina.

8. Topic: Zero-base budgeting

    Main Idea: Zero-base budgeting will have significant impact in middle and lower levels of management.

    Check Out: *Where* and *How:* In industry, where profits should improve; in government, where the taxpayer services will improve with new programs replacing obsolete ones.

9. Topic: Suggestions

    Main Idea: The nature of suggestions rather than the source should be considered.

    Check Out: *Example:* Some of the most unlikely sources can render invaluable service.

10. Topic: Foreign businessmen

    Main Idea: Foreign businessmen, as opposed to American businessmen, dislike organizational charts.

    Check Out: *Example:* The French businessmen, as explained in Granick's book.

11. Topic: Creative groups

    Main Idea: Small, creative groups surrounding a creative leader can bring about change.

    Check Out: *Examples:* The small, central nucleus of groups led by Charlemagne, Henry II, Lenin, and Kennedy. They also can be found in art, science, military, social reform, and industrial groups.

12. Topic:	Changing times
Main Idea:	Changing times call for organizations that are concerned with both human behavior and production.
Check Out:	*Why:* Because without this dual concern, organizations will not function effectively and attain their objectives.
13. Topic:	Leaders
Main Idea:	Leaders who lead from a distance lose credibility.
Check Out:	*Why:* They are perceived as impotent and lose their influence.

Chapter 5: Problem-Solution Pattern

Untimed Reading: "How to Stop Time-Waste on the Job"

Score *20 points* for each correct answer:

Problem:	The management of work force is poor.
Effects:	Businesses waste as much as $300 billion each year.
Cause:	Front-line managers do not know how to use human resources; they are untrained. They are poor at scheduling, give inprecise directions, fail to staff correctly for high and low work loads, fail to coordinate resources, and lack work discipline.
Solution:	Follow the seven steps of work force management.

Paced Reading: "The Trouble With Drugs"

1. c
2. b
3. a
4. a, c
5. b, c, d, g, h

Paced Reading: "No Vacancy"

1. c
2. b, c
3. a, c, e
4. c
5. b
6. b, e

Skim Reading: "All Deposits, No Returns—The Story of Suzie's Bank"

Score *25 points* for each correct answer:

1. b
2. a
3. c
4. c

Skim Reading: "Investigators Tackle Computer Crime"

Score *20 points* for each correct answer:

1. a
2. c
3. b, e
4. a

Rapid Reading: "The Trouble With Open Offices"

1. c
2. b, d, e, h
3. d
4. c, a, e, f

Rapid Reading: "Dermatitis: Causes and Cures"

1. a
2. a, e
3. b
4. a
5. a, c, d, g
6. g

Chapter 6: Persuasive Pattern

Untimed Reading: "What Does Your Briefcase Tell About You?"

Score *33 points* for each correct answer:

1. a
2. b
3. b

Untimed Reading: The Business of Business Schools; Part I: The Attack

Score *25 points* for each correct answer:

1. Grayson's theory is that business schools do not adequately train students in the "practice" of business.

2. He cites his own survey, which indicated certain shortcomings of business school graduates; he also documents Professor Ward's study and Marshall and Harrell's findings showing little correlation between academic success and business achievement as well as the poor correlation between the ATGSB test and business achievement.

3. Business schools created an unnecessary dichotomy between theory and practice or "education" and "training," a dichotomy that business faculty perpetuates. Faculty members have had little or no practical business experience, and their teaching techniques lend themselves to theoretical topics rather than practical topics. This practice is endorsed by deans and

department chairmen. "Real World" managers do not interact with business schools. Students themselves prefer the "passive," theoretical orientation. Deans and department heads set up a reward system that favors those professors with "theoretical" leanings. The AACSB denies diversity.

4. There would be an emphasis on "learning by doing." More colleges would hire faculty members with practical experience, regardless of degrees attained. More faculty members would be involved in practical research and teaching. There would be increased student-faculty-business interaction. There would be a change in business school admission standards.

Paced Reading: "Workweeks and Leisure: An Analysis of Trends, 1948-75

1. a
2. c
3. b
4. b
5. c
6. a
7. c
8. b
9. a
10. a

Paced Reading: "NFL Coaches and Motivation Theory"

1. c
2. a

3. b
4. a
5. b
6. a
7. c
8. c
9. c
10. a

Skim Reading: "The Business of Business Schools; Part II: The Defense"

Score *25 points* for each correct answer:

1. d
2. a, e
3. b

Skim Reading: "American Workers Evaluate the Quality of Their Jobs"

1. c
2. a
3. b
4. c
5. a
6. b
7. b
8. c
9. a
10. b

Rapid Reading: "Women In Management: An Endangered Species?"

1. c
2. c
3. a
4. b

5. c	2. a
6. b	3. b
7. a	4. a
8. b	5. c
9. a	6. b
10. c	7. a

Rapid Reading: "The Frightened Consumer?"

	8. c
	9. a
1. c	10. c

Chapter 7: Data Pattern I: Informational

Untimed Reading: "The Trauma of Systems Change"

Score *20 points* for each correct answer:

Subtopic *(Stage)*	Idea *(Characteristic of Stage)*
1. Denial	The drastic, threatening change is denied by manager. MBO will not work, "objectives can't be applied to my job."
2. Anger	Manager belittles organization, lashes out at boss.
3. Bargaining stage	Manager thinks of ways of evading the MBO approach; manager tries to get boss to change his mind or get additional resources.
4. Depression	Manager thinks of leaving company or may not perform at all on the job.
5. Acceptance	Manager leads his staff and himself to learn more about MBO.

Paced Reading: "Improving Employee Motivation in Today's Business Environment"

1. b	6. b
2. a	7. a
3. a	8. c
4. c	9. b
5. c	10. a

Paced Reading: "Dads on Duty"

1. b
2. c
3. a
4. a
5. b
6. c
7. a
8. c
9. a
10. c

Skim Reading: "Taking the Profit out of Arson"

Score *20 points* for each correct answer:

1. a, c, d, g, j

Skim Reading: "Solar Energy: A $10 Billion Industry By the Year 2000?"

Score *25 points* for each correct answer:

1. Seattle
2. Answers vary according to where you live. Refer back to the article for the correct answer.
3. Answers vary according to where you live. Refer back to the article for the correct answer.
4. It is inexhaustible and free.

Rapid Reading: "TM"

1. a
2. c
3. b
4. a
5. c
6. c
7. c
8. b
9. c
10. b

Rapid Reading: "The Unreasonable Manager"

1. b
2. a
3. a
4. b
5. c
6. c
7. a
8. c
9. a
10. b

Chapter 8: Data Pattern II: Instructional

Paced Reading: "How to Negotiate a Computer Contract You Can Live With"

1. b
2. c
3. c
4. c
5. a
6. b
7. c
8. b
9. a
10. c

Skim Reading: "How to Survive an IRS Tax Audit"

1. *What:*	Tax audits.
2. *Who:*	Those people selected by the computer (80 percent).
3. *Where:*	Place of business or at the local IRS office.
4. *When:*	Often a year or more after you have filed.

5. *Why:*	Because you have:
	  a. high itemized deductions or high dependency exemptions
	  b. a large refund claim
	  c. an informer has identified you.

6. Three survival techniques:	1. Document and have proof for all deductions. 2. Always have necessary records available and organized. 3. Demand a review if dissatisfied and go to court if necessary.

Skim Reading: "How to Get a Loan From the SBA"

Score *20 points* for each correct answer:

1. *What:*	Loans
2. *Who:*	Small business owners of good character who show that the loan is for sound value.
3. *Where:*	From the Occupational Safety and Health Loan Program.
4. *When:*	Loans have been available since 1971 and can be applied for at any time.
5. *Why:*	To pay for required facilities, equipment, and procedures to improve the health and safety factors of the business.

Rapid Reading: "How to Get a Good Consultant"

1. b	6. c
2. a	7. c
3. a	8. b
4. c	9. c
5. b	10. a

Chapter 9: Reading Rate and Comprehension: Posttests

Posttest 1: "Inside the Country, Outside the Law"

1. a
2. c
3. c
4. b
5. a
6. b
7. b
8. c
9. a
10. c

Posttest 2: "Dealing With Slow Payers"

1. c
2. a
3. a
4. c
5. b
6. c
7. a
8. b
9. b
10. a

WORDS PER MINUTE: SKIMMING CHART

MINUTES AND SECONDS	DEPOSITS (975 Words)	CRIME (541 Words)	SCHOOLS (1,600 Words)	WORKERS (5,000 Words)	ARSON (1,750 Words)	SOLAR (2,000 Words)	TAX AUDIT (1,450 Words)	SBA LOAN (800 Words)	SECONDS
:30	1,950	1,082	3,200	10,000	3,500	4,000	2,900	1,600	30
:40	1,462	811	2,400	7,500	2,625	3,000	2,175	1,200	40
:50	1,170	649	1,920	6,000	2,100	2,400	1,740	960	50
1:00	975	541	1,600	5,000	1,750	2,000	1,450	800	60
1:10	836	464	1,371	4,286	1,500	1,714	1,243	685	70
1:20	731	406	1,200	3,750	1,313	1,500	1,088	600	80
1:30	650	361	1,066	3,332	1,166	1,333	967	533	90
1:40	585	325	960	3,000	1,050	1,200	870	480	100
1:50	532	295	872	2,726	955	1,091	791	436	110
2:00	488	271	800	2,500	875	1,000	725	400	120
2:10	450	250	738	2,308	808	923	669	369	130
2:20	418	232	685	2,143	750	857	621	343	140
2:30	390	216	640	2,000	700	800	580	320	150
2:40	366	203	600	1,874	657	750	543	300	160
2:50	344	191	564	1,764	618	705	511	282	170
3:00	325	180	533	1,666	583	666	483	267	180
3:10	308	171	505	1,578	553	631	458	253	190
3:20	293	162	480	1,500	525	600	435	240	200
3:30	278	155	457	1,428	500	571	413	229	210
3:40	266	148	436	1,363	477	545	394	218	220
3:50	254	141	417	1,304	456	522	378	208	230
4:00	244	135	400	1,249	438	500	363	200	240
4:10	234	130	384	1,200	420	480	347	192	250
4:20	225	125	369	1,153	404	462	335	185	260
4:30	217	120	356	1,111	389	444	321	178	270
4:40	208	116	343	1,071	375	429	311	171	280
4:50	201	112	331	1,034	362	414	299	166	290
5:00	195	108	320	1,000	350	400	289	160	300
5:10	189	105	310	967	339	387	280	155	310
5:20	183	101	300	937	328	375	272	150	320
5:30	177	98	291	909	318	363	263	145	330
5:40	172	95	282	882	309	353	255	141	340
5:50	167	93	274	857	300	343	249	137	350
6:00	162	90	266	833	292	333	241	133	360
6:10	158	87	259	810	283	324	235	130	370
6:20	153	85	253	789	276	316	228	126	380
6:30	150	83	246	769	269	307	223	123	390
6:40	146	81	240	750	262	300	217	120	400
6:50	143	79	234	731	256	292	212	117	410
7:00	139	77	229	714	250	285	207	114	420

DIRECTIONS: USE either the **Seconds** column or the **Minutes and Seconds** column to find your skimming rate. In the columns under the selection title, find the words-per-minute rate that corresponds to each skimming time.

WORDS PER MINUTE: RAPID READING CHART

MINUTES AND SECONDS	PRETEST 1 (1,900 Words)	PRETEST 2 (1,600 Words)	OPEN OFFICES (2,200 Words)	DERMATITIS (2,200 Words)	WOMEN (2,500 Words)	CONSUMER (1,350 Words)	TM (2,550 Words)	MANAGER (1,684 Words)	CONSULTANT (3,350 Words)	POSTTEST 1 (1,530 Words)	POSTTEST 2 (1,530 Words)	SECONDS
:30	3,800	3,200	4,400	4,400	5,000	2,700	5,100	3,368	6,700	3,060	3,060	30
:40	2,850	2,400	3,300	3,300	3,750	2,225	3,825	2,526	5,025	2,295	2,295	40
:50	2,280	1,920	2,640	2,640	3,000	1,620	3,060	2,020	4,020	1,836	1,836	50
1:00	1,900	1,600	2,200	2,200	2,500	1,350	2,550	1,684	3,350	1,530	1,530	60
1:10	1,629	1,371	1,886	1,886	2,142	1,157	2,185	1,443	2,871	1,311	1,311	70
1:20	1,425	1,200	1,650	1,650	1,875	1,012	1,912	1,263	2,512	1,147	1,147	80
1:30	1,267	1,066	1,467	1,467	1,666	900	1,700	1,122	2,233	1,020	1,020	90
1:40	1,140	960	1,320	1,320	1,500	810	1,530	1,010	2,010	918	918	100
1:50	1,036	872	1,200	1,200	1,363	736	1,390	918	1,827	834	834	110
2:00	950	800	1,100	1,100	1,250	675	1,275	842	1,675	765	765	120
2:10	876	738	1,015	1,015	1,153	623	1,177	777	1,546	706	706	130
2:20	814	685	942	942	1,071	578	1,093	722	1,436	655	655	140
2:30	760	640	880	880	1,000	540	1,020	674	1,340	612	612	150
2:40	712	600	825	825	937	506	956	632	1,256	574	574	160
2:50	670	564	776	776	882	476	900	594	1,182	540	540	170
3:00	633	533	733	733	833	450	850	561	1,117	510	510	180
3:10	600	505	694	694	789	426	805	532	1,058	483	483	190
3:20	570	480	660	660	750	405	765	505	1,005	459	459	200
3:30	542	457	628	628	714	385	729	481	952	437	437	210
3:40	518	436	600	600	682	368	695	459	914	417	417	220
3:50	495	417	574	574	652	352	665	439	874	399	399	230
4:00	475	400	550	550	625	337	637	421	838	382	382	240
4:10	456	384	528	528	600	324	612	404	804	367	367	250
4:20	439	369	508	508	577	311	589	389	773	353	353	260
4:30	422	355	488	488	555	300	567	374	744	340	340	270
4:40	407	343	471	471	536	289	546	361	718	327	327	280
4:50	393	331	455	455	517	279	528	348	693	316	316	290
5:00	380	320	440	440	500	270	510	337	670	306	306	300
5:10	368	310	426	426	484	261	494	326	649	296	296	310
5:20	356	300	413	413	469	253	478	316	629	287	287	320
5:30	345	291	400	400	454	245	464	306	609	278	278	330
5:40	335	282	388	388	441	238	450	297	591	270	270	340
5:50	326	274	377	377	429	231	437	289	574	262	262	350
6:00	316	267	366	366	416	225	425	281	558	255	255	360
6:10	308	259	357	357	405	219	414	273	543	248	248	370
6:20	300	253	347	347	395	213	403	266	529	242	242	380
6:30	292	246	338	338	384	207	392	259	515	235	235	390
6:40	285	240	330	330	375	202	382	253	503	230	230	400
6:50	278	234	322	322	366	198	373	246	490	224	224	410

cont.

DIRECTIONS: Use the **Seconds** column or the **Minutes and Seconds** column to find your reading rate. In the column under the selection title, find the words-per-minute that corresponds to your reading time.

WORDS PER MINUTE: RAPID READING CHART (cont.)

MINUTES AND SECONDS	PRETEST 1 (1,900 Words)	PRETEST 2 (1,600 Words)	OPEN OFFICES (2,200 Words)	DERMATITIS (2,200 Words)	WOMEN (2,500 Words)	CONSUMER (1,350 Words)	TM (2,550 Words)	MANAGER (1,664 Words)	CONSULTANT (3,350 Words)	POSTTEST 1 (1,530 Words)	POSTTEST 2 (1,530 Words)	SECONDS
7:00	271	229	314	314	357	192	364	241	479	218	218	420
7:10	265	223	307	307	349	188	356	235	467	213	213	430
7:20	259	218	300	300	341	184	348	230	457	208	208	440
7:30	253	213	293	293	333	180	340	226	447	204	204	450
7:40	248	209	287	287	326	176	333	220	437	200	200	460
7:50	242	204	281	281	319	172	326	215	428	195	195	470
8:00	237	200	275	275	312	168	319	212	419	191	191	480
8:10	233	195	269	269	306	165	312	206	410	187	187	490
8:20	228	192	264	264	300	162	306	202	402	184	184	500
8:30	223	188	259	259	294	158	300	198	394	180	180	510
8:40	219	184	254	254	288	155	294	194	386	177	177	520
8:50	215	181	249	249	283	152	288	191	379	173	173	530
9:00	211	178	244	244	277	150	283	187	372	170	170	540
9:10	207	174	240	240	272	147	278	183	365	166	166	550
9:20	203	171	235	235	267	144	273	180	358	163	163	560
9:30	200	168	231	231	263	142	269	177	352	161	161	570
9:40	196	165	227	227	258	139	264	174	346	158	158	580
9:50	193	162	223	223	254	137	259	171	340	155	155	590
10:00	190	160	220	220	250	135	255	168	335	153	153	600

DIRECTIONS: Use the **Seconds** column or the **Minutes and Seconds** column to find your reading rate. In the column under the selection title, find the words-per-minute that corresponds to your reading time.

SKIM READING PROGRESS CHART

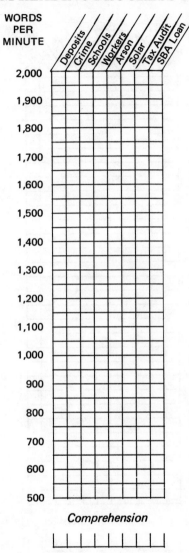

Directions: Put an *x* along the line under each skim reading exercise to show your words-per-minute rate for that selection. Write your comprehension score in the comprehension box below the reading rate chart.

RAPID READING PROGRESS CHART

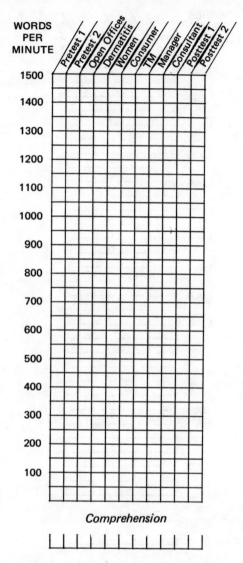

WORDS PER MINUTE

Pretest 1 / Pretest 2 / Open Offices / Dermatitis / Women / Consumer / TM / Manager / Consultant / Posttest 1 / Posttest 2

1500
1400
1300
1200
1100
1000
900
800
700
600
500
400
300
200
100

Comprehension

Directions: Put an *x* along the line under each test and rapid reading exercise to show your words-per-minute rate for that selection. Write your comprehension score in the comprehension box below the reading rate chart.

PRE-/POSTTEST RESULTS

Pretest Reading Efficiency

Pretest Rate 1	____	WPM	____	% Comprehension
Pretest Rate 2	____	WPM	____	% Comprehension
Rate Flexibility Score	____			
Average Reading Efficiency	____	WPM ____	____	% Comprehension

Posttest Reading Efficiency

Posttest Rate 1	____	WPM	____	% Comprehension
Posttest Rate 2	____	WPM	____	% Comprehension
Rate Flexibility Score	____			
Average Reading Efficiency	____	WPM ____	____	% Comprehension

HOW MUCH DID I IMPROVE?

Posttest Reading Efficiency Score   _____

Pretest Reading Efficiency Score   _____

Gain Score   _____

$$\text{Reading Efficiency} \overline{)\frac{\text{Percentage of Improvement}}{\text{Gain Score}}}$$

Pretest

Complete your percentage of improvement here.